Challenging the Men

Greta Waitz winning the 1980 New York City Marathon in the world best time of 2 hours 25 minutes 42 seconds. Of the 12,000 or so starts she finished 74th! Greta Waitz has returned the best times for women for the last 2 or 3 years at events from 3,000m to 42,000m. She is also world champion cross country runner. In 1984 there will be, at last, an event on the Olympic programme suitable for her supert talents.

Credit Steven E. Sutton. All sport.

Challenging the Men

The Social Biology of Female Sporting Achievement

K.F. Dyer

University of Queensland Press
St Lucia • New York

© University of Queensland Press, St Lucia, Queensland 1982

Typeset by University of Queensland Press
Printed and bound by Silex Enterprise & Printing Co, Hong Kong

National Library of Australia
Cataloguing-in-Publication data

Dyer, K. F. (Kenneth Frank), 1939–.
    Challenging the men: women in sport.

    ISBN 0 7022 1652 6.
    ISBN 0 7022 1921 5 (pbk.)

    1. Sports for women. I. Title.

796.'01'94

Library of Congress Cataloging in Publication Data

Dyer, K. F. (Kenneth F.), 1939–
    Challenging the men.

    Bibliography: p.
    1. Sports for women. 2. Women athletes. 3. Sports–
Physiological aspects. I. Title.
GV709.D9   796'.01'94   81-21846
ISBN 0-7022-1652-6   AACR2
ISBN 0-7022-1921-5 (pbk.)

For Maureen, who helped me more than she knows in understanding the issues with which this book is concerned. And for Lesley, Geraldine and Joanne, whose present and future happiness and fulfilment mean so much to me.

Contents

Illustrations

Tables

Figures

Introduction

In the later years of the nineteenth century a certain Henglo's circus toured around Ireland. When visiting Dublin it normally organized a sports meeting and in 1891 it added a women's 100 yard race to the regular programme of events. This race, run on Saturday 8 August 1891, was won in a time of 13 seconds by Miss Eva Francisco. This athletic performance was not only the first in Ireland by a woman, but is now accepted as the earliest fully attested woman's athletic performance in the whole of Europe.

In succeeding years, on other visits of the circus to Dublin, further 100 yard races were held and on 25 June 1898 the Misses Guinness and Nolan dead-heated in the amazing time of 12.0 seconds. Although equalled in the USA in 1910 and again in 1912 this time remained unbeaten by women until 1921.

After this astonishing achievement women's athletics disappeared from Ireland for fifty years. It was stamped out by the combined effects of religious conservatism, male chauvinism and political division. In Southern Ireland the church authorities effectively kept it out until the 1960s, but in Northern Ireland women's athletics was re-established somewhat tenuously after the second world war. In April 1947 the Queen's University Belfast athletic championships were held and a six event programme for women was included. The 100 yards was won by Pat Laverty in a time of . . . 12.2 seconds!

The modern Olympic Games began in 1896 in Athens and except for the war years have been held every four years since. Most sports in the Olympics were men-only affairs in the early years. In 1928 in Amsterdam, after several years of agitation and pleading, women were finally admitted as track and field competitors. The women's programme was a tiny one of five events, the longest track event being the 800 metres. In this event the winner, L. Radke of Germany, broke the then women's world record. Her exertions and those of some of her fellow competitors were such that they collapsed on the track at the finish, much as many men have done before and since at the end of hard fought races. So horrified were the male administrators at this sight that the 800 metres was immediately removed from the women's Olympic programme, leaving a 100 metres as their only individual track event. A 200 metre event was added in 1948, an 800 metres reappeared in 1960 and 400 metres and 1500 metres were added in 1964 and 1972 respectively. There matters stuck until 1984 when, in Los Angeles, a 3000 metres and a marathon will be added to the women's Olympic programme. Photograph 7 shows the finish of the fateful 800 metre race with Radke of Germany just beating Hitomi of Japan.

Is there any evidence in this picture to warrant the removal of the 800 metres from the Olympic programme for thirty-two years?

The 3000 metres is now on the programme of the Commonwealth Games, the European Championships and many national championships. Women are now running 5000 metre races as fast as the men medal winners in the 1912 Olympics; they are running 10,000 metre races as fast as the medal winners in the 1924 Olympics; and they are running marathons, which are more than 42,000 metres, faster than the 1948 medal winners. Persistent requests to have an event longer than 1500 metres included on the Olympic programme still met with blank refusals by the male members of the International Olympic Committee until the 1984 Games.

In 1967 American athlete Kathy Switzer wanted to run in the famous Boston Marathon in the USA. She duly entered as student K. Switzer and not until she stripped off her track suit at the start did the organizers realize she was a woman. She was then dragged, protesting, from the lineup by race officials who explained that not only was it illegal for her to run but that she had to be protected from her own folly in thinking she could actually complete a marathon. Vigorous intervention by a friend allowed her to run and she success-fully finished the course. In the years succeeding women were specifically banned from competing in marathon races anywhere in the USA, a restriction which was only lifted in 1972. In the 1979 Boston marathon there were a total of 7,877 competitors, among whom were 520 women. Bill Rodgers won the men's race in 2 hours 9 minutes and 27 seconds, the leading women's time was 2 hours 35 minutes and 15 seconds by Joan Benoit, which placed her 477th overall. In all 20 women beat 2 hours 55 minutes in this race. The then world record for women's marathon of 2:32.30 set by Greta Waitz in the New York City Marathon in 1978 would have been good enough to win a gold medal in the marathon at the London Olympics in 1948. In recent years women have successfully run in fifty and even one hundred mile events and have finished in front of many men. Indeed they have often finished the course when no man has done so.

These stories illustrate the highly conservative social and religious pressures, the irrationality and the sheer ignorance that have in the past hindered the development of women's athletics and deterred women who wished to participate in the sport. They also hint at the tremendous improvements which have occurred in women's performances when they have been given the opportunity to compete.

In the pages that follow are many similar stories of pettiness of mind, of lack of vision, of meanness and stupidity in the history of sport. Unfortunately these attitudes still exist, at local and club level as well as in international competition. Many sportswomen today can recount stories from their own experiences of being discouraged or ridiculed when attempting new sports or new events; of being warned against or positively forbidden to compete or participate for health or safety reasons; of battling against lack of facilities, lack of money, lack of recognition and lack of opportunities. And it is often clear enough that behind each of the reasons or excuses given for not allowing women to compete, there have been hidden assumptions by those making them that women's performances are and will always be much lower than men's and that women's sport does not matter much anyway.

These stories contain the underlying messages of this book: namely that women's sporting performances are improving rapidly; that but for the lack of opportunities they might be considerable better than they currently are; and that women are likely to continue improving rapidly in the foreseeable future.

The structure of the book is as follows: the general biological requirements for high sporting achievement — strength, endurance, skill and so on — are identified and discussed, and it is concluded that a wide variety of biological attributes can contribute to sporting success provided they are practised in the right sport. Some of the social and cultural requirements for high sporting achievement are then examined: opportunity, coaching, encouragement, sharp competition, incentives, social attitudes and so on. These are of profound importance, at least as important as the biological factors, but are also widely variable: depending very much on the particular social structure of the country under examination and the sport concerned.

The phenomenon of sex is then considered, what it is and what the differences between the sexes are, real and imagined, in some of those areas previously identified as biologically and socially important in sporting performance.

The knowledge gained is then applied to some of the principal sports which women are now taking by storm: notably athletics, but also some of the other speed sports, swimming, skating, cycling and so forth. Some other sports, including those which have hitherto been exclusively men only, are also considered. Throughout the book the position of sport in general and women's sport in particular in various countries is examined in order to investigate the relationships between opportunity, incentive and performance in them.

Finally I turn to those hazardous pastimes of explaining the past and predicting the future. The massive improvement of women's performances in the last twenty years or so can largely be explained in terms of improved opportunities, training, encouragement and incentives. Evidence is marshalled to explain women's generally inferior performances in the past and to suggest that they will either equal or nearly equal the performances of men in many events in many sports before the end of the century.

It seems quite clear that there are few if any sports practised safely and successfully by men in which women cannot also participate with equal safety and with almost equal success. Biological differences between the sexes probably mean that some women's performances will always be inferior to those of men; but conversely they also suggest that some men's performances will be inferior to women's. Just which are which and the magnitude of the ultimate differences cannot be known for certain, however, until sporting opportunities are more nearly equal.

CHAPTER ONE

Women in Society: Women in Sport

In modern western societies (and probably most other societies in the world) women have different roles, different expectations, carry out different tasks, have a different range of recreational interests, have different abilities and are rewarded differently to men. Women are also, of course, biologically different to men, and many see the biological differences as just about the only cause of these social differences between the sexes.

But others are not so sure. They argue that many sex differences are the consequences of entrenched expectations of society, of different upbringing, and are a legacy from the past when biological and medical knowledge was quite rudimentary and often wildly inaccurate. They see biological differences as neither an explanation for social differences nor a reason for social discrimination or exploitation. Indeed, some go so far as to say that some of the biological differences are largely a consequence of social differences.

For example, women, on average, are not so strong as men. But the differences are usually not very great; they are rarely of any real importance in most occupations and are certainly not such as to prevent women doing any particular job. In many non-western societies women typically do most of the hard work of agriculture, food preparation and fetching and carrying. In the industrialized countries during wartime women showed that they could successfully take over in traditionally male dominated occupations. They showed then and often have continued to show that they can, given practice, become as adept and efficient as moving and lifting weighty objects, at managing heavy machinery, at working accurately, rapidly and efficiently under conditions of noise and stress, and generally becoming as used to hard physical labour as men. But most jobs in which strength or obvious physical efforts is required continue to be denied to women. They therefore have little opportunity to either acquire or demonstrate these skills and are thus in a classic catch 22 situation.

Why is this? A number of reasons are commonly put forward to support such job discrimination. The unions in many industries are determined to protect the jobs of their male members, and they also wish to prevent women entering new industries because of the fear that employers will pay (and women will accept) lower rates for the job: a fear for which there is much historical justification. There is the belief that many jobs are unladylike, and will destroy femininity, perhaps through the development of heavily muscled bodies, or the ravages to hands and skin which industrial occupations cause, or perhaps through the heavy drinking and smoking traditionally associated with and almost needed in some heavy industrial occupations. There is also a strain of social conservatism, often associated with religious attitudes, which has emphasized the place of women in the family as child-bearers, mothers and homemakers to the exclusion of all else.

In the Soviet Union and other Eastern European countries, great strides have been taken removing official discrimination against women. The Soviet constitution, indeed, states: "Women in the USSR are accorded equal rights with men, in all spheres of economic, state, cultural, social and political life." But this does not in fact mean that all jobs are open to Russian women. The Russians see nothing incompatible between the doctrine of equality of the sexes and shielding women from influences that would impair their ability to bear healthy children. Women in the Soviet Union are not considered fitted for the heaviest type of physical labour, for example. It is also still largely taken for granted that women are better able to rear the children and carry out domestic chores while men carry out the affairs of business and state.

But even if it is the case that some differentiation of tasks among people in society results from biological differences among them, there is no necessary relationship between this and the value judgments made about the tasks involved. If a variety of tasks are required for the successful functioning of society, the reasons why some are rewarded more than others must be largely arbitrary and result from sociological pressures, not biological differences. This applies particularly with respect to the differential status and material rewards so commonly given to one sex relative to the other. Obviously, it is mainly prejudice and social inertia which bring about women's different and largely inferior position in society today.

These conclusions are as relevant to the sports field as to the work place. Women have less opportunity to play most sports than men, they are given less encouragement and less financial or other inducements to do so, and in many sports the attributes required are in direct contrast to those which men currently expect and value in women. The facilities for and status of women's sports are almost always inferior to those of men and their performances are almost always inferior. Nevertheless, the inferior performances of women have usually been attributed to biological reasons which, in turn, have been used to justify the financial and other discrimination. But the simple and apparently obvious biological reasons for differential treatment and performance of the sexes are now being questioned on the sports field just as they are being questioned in the work place.

The investigation of biological differences between the sexes and their effects is not easy. Many of the obvious anatomical and functional differences are genetically determined, but other differences such as height, weight, intelligence and personality are the product, in varying degrees, of both genetic and environmental factors. Still others, including most of the behavioural differences between the sexes, are largely the result of the social environment and social expectations of the time.

Biological differences cannot be investigated in a social vacuum, nor can social change be stopped while the investigation is carried out. Their effects on social performance are also almost impossible to measure. How are we to assess the achievements and performances of, for example, Marie Curie, Agatha Christie, Indira Gandhi, Billie Jean King, Olga Korbut, Alicia Markova or Ella Fitzgerald against their male or female predecessors? Many of their abilities and their achievements are just immeasurable and lie entirely within the realm of value judgements.

But in many sports objective comparisons between the achievements of men and women are possible, and at least some of the social and biological factors contributing to these achievements can be isolated. These include speed sports and the jumping and throwing events which are carried out under identical or closely similar conditions. In these, each contest is essentially a biological experiment and the results are good scientific data. It is these sports with which this book is primarily concerned.

This book is therefore concerned with phenomena which are biological: the innate ability of men and women to run, swim, jump and throw; psychological: why they do these things and the effort they put in; and social: the opportunity, training and encouragement to do them. To understand sex differences in achievement, the reasons for them and the possibilities for reducing them, we must take into account biology, psychology and sociology.

At present everything seems clearcut and unambiguous. In almost all sports in which both men and women participate, women perform at a level significantly inferior to that of men. They always have performed at an inferior level and it is almost universally believed that they always will. But women have in the past been subject to strong social pressures almost from birth, designed to deter them from striving for maximal success and high achievement in most sports. The roles of woman and successful athlete are almost incompatible in most western countries. Women who wish to participate in sport and remain feminine have faced great stress: high achievement in a sporting context has tended to detract from, rather than enhance, their feminine image in the eyes of men, and by choosing sport in the first place, they have tended to place themselves outside the social mainstream.

For a girl to be labelled as a tomboy, for example, is to be labelled as a female having trouble reaching womanhood. An ardent adult sportswoman is often thought of as not completely feminine. The sex role stereotype of men is active, aggressive, competitive, whereas that of women is passive, non-aggressive and largely non-competitive. The male role encompasses the strong and successful athlete; the female role encompasses the weak and retiring non-athlete. There is, or has been, a view of women athletes that they are not only socially deviant but flying in the face of biological reality and predestination as well. Most people believe that women are not meant to compete with men, and that those who try are not only doomed to failure, but are demonstrating, somehow, something imperfect in their makeup as women.

But the position and performance of women in sport today is very different from that portrayed by these common beliefs and attitudes. In many sports women's performances are improving much faster than men's. Statistical analyses suggest that women's performances will equal or even exceed those of men in some events in the not too distant future. Furthermore, women are now participating in many events that hitherto were closed to them. They are, for example, running, swimming and cycling in long-distance events with marked success; they are becoming jockeys, racing car drivers, footballers and even weight lifters. As well as competing in a much wider variety of sports in ever-increasing numbers, women are undertaking training and competition schedules as gruelling and time consuming as most men; they are organizing themselves on professional circuits, and they are combining sports careers with marriage and the bearing of children. Perhaps most important, the financial support for, and the financial incentives in, different women's sports are slowly and erratically, but quite noticeably, increasing.

A wide variety of reasons have been and still are advanced by male-dominated sporting hierarchies to explain their reluctance to open up all sports and all events to women participants. There are alleged physical, physiological and psychological shortcomings of women compared to men, leading to the belief, still far from dead, that women will positively harm themselves by competing in some events. There are assertions that to train for and compete in many events is unfeminine, will result in musclebound bodies devoid of sexual attractiveness and give rise to permanent sexual damage. As famous Australian athletics coach, Percy Cerutty, once put it: "Who wants straight-legged, narrow-hipped, big-shouldered, powerful women, aggressive and ferocious in physique and attitude?"[1] There are quasi-religious objections concerning the display of the female body in sporting situations. And there are economic arguments concerning the lack of attraction to the public and hence to entrepreneurs, TV stations, Olympic committees and the like, of sporting events involving women.

At present, then, there is a pronounced paradox in the sporting world. On the one hand we are told that women cannot, should not and will not compete against men with any expectations of success in most sports. On the other hand, women have their own competitions in many of these sports and statistical analysis, where appropriate, suggests that their performance will approach, equal, or exceed men in most of them within the lifetime of the present participants. This book explores this paradox, its validity, origins and likely resolution.

CHAPTER TWO

Sport and its Requirements

1. WHAT IS SPORT?

The definition of sport is a complex and controversial matter. Everyone has their own ideas as to what constitutes sport and what does not. The activities which one race, culture or class calls sport are often enough regarded with amusement, disdain or incomprehension by others; some people's sports are other people's pastimes and are yet other people's hard work. Sport can be a leisure or play activity. It can be a recreation, a pastime, a full time activity or a multi-million dollar industry. The boundaries between these are by no means clearcut, but if women's abilities on the one hand, and their opportunities on the other, are to be examined, a fairly rigorous definition is needed. The whole area of ludic activity, play, recreation, games and sport has been much investigated in recent years by sociologists. An extended discussion of the issues involved and a sample of recent definitions can be found in chapter 10 of *Surfing Subcultures,* an examination by sociologist Kent Pearson of one sporting activity. His attempts to decide whether surfboard riding and/or surf life saving are true sports forces him to consider carefully possible definitions of sport.

There seem to be three common features in most of those activities classified as sports in different countries and cultures of the world. First there has to be a defined objective which has to be attained in a mutually agreed manner; there has also to be formal organization or very strong historical social tradition which defines the objectives, sets and supervises the rules and oversees local, national and, if appropriate, international competitions. The passage from marbles through to lawn bowls, or from rounders to softball to baseball, shows how rather similar activities grade from play to sport; from informal recreations to highly institutionalized, ritualized and bureaucratized athletic activities.

Secondly, there has to be the utilization of some particular abilities or skills to achieve this defined outcome. These abilities are usually physical but, as in the case of shooting or darts, for example, may be primarily perceptual. It is not so much the nature of the activity or the level of skill displayed which is important so much as the value attached to it in terms of the physical outcomes. On this basis chess would not be considered a sport, because the outcome is based on the conceptualization of particular moves rather than their sheer physical execution.

The third requirement is that of competition. This is usually in the form of competition for supremacy between two or more individuals or teams. Sometimes the competition is indirect, as in the case of competition against the recorded performance of another individual or side, measured against various established standards. In some of the so-called "conquest" sports, mountaineering, hang gliding, surfing, bullfighting and so on, the direct competition is against some inanimate or animate object. But as the comparative aspects become more important, so these activities become sports rather than recreational or other activities.

Each of these three requirements can be considered as a continuous variable and their contribution in any particular activity can be high or low. Play activities have a low content of them all. Recreational activities may have high components of skill — hunting, shooting, fishing, surfing, gliding and so on — but lack the competitive element which makes them truly sports. Their transposition into target shooting, equestrian events and the like, with their attendant competition and formal rules and international controlling bodies, does convert them into true sports.

Using arguments similar to these, Pearson in *Surfing Subcultures* accepts a definition of sport originally due to American Harry Edwards as follows:

> Activities having formally recorded histories and traditions, stressing physical prowess through competition, within limits set in explicit and formal rules governing role and position relationships, and carried out by actors who represent or who are part of formally organized associations having the goal of achieving valued tangibles or intangibles through defeating opposition groups.[1]

He goes on to represent these three dimensions of sport diagrammatically in a form similar to that shown here as figure 1. Those activities which do not score highly on all three dimensions are not conventionally considered sports. Thus chess or bridge have very high competitive content but almost no physical activity. Those activities which do score highly on all three dimensions are sometimes referred to as athletics. This book is certainly concerned primarily with sports defined in this sense, that is those which do score highly on all three dimensions. In analyzing women's improving performances and opportunities we must remember these three dimensions. The biological and social contributions to success along each one are likely to be very different, although often complementary and always equally important in facilitating and promoting participation and success in any sport.

While sport, as distinct from play, can be defined in terms of a high component of physical prowess, social competition and complexity of organization, it cannot be understood solely in these terms.

All sports involve social interaction, and group behaviour may be as important as individual physiology or psychology. Team sports are necessary social activities, but even the most individualistic sports have national or international associations, rule books and traditions of conduct or achievement and therefore

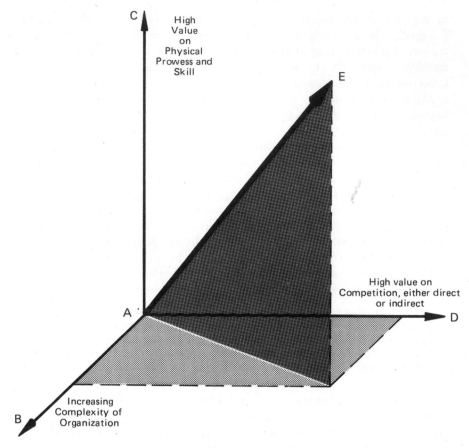

Fig. 1. A three dimensional conceptualization of ludic activity – play, recreation and sport. All those activities close to A would be regarded as play. Activities scoring highly in the plane BAD only include bridge, chess; those scoring highly on plane BAC include boxing, wrestling; those scoring highly on plane DAC include the conquest sports. True sports are those scoring highly on all three counts, that is, towards point E.

have some social dimension. In other words, sports and sporting performances have to be studied as a part of human social behaviour.

But sports must also be considered from the point of view of society as a whole and as various subcultures which have their own integral structures and value systems. Sports have become social systems, sometimes characteristic of the society in which they are practised, sometimes not; they have teachers and trainers, spectators, commentators, analysts, awards, rewards and social status; many of the participants have roles as entertainers, folk heroes and community leaders. Sports become institutionalized and ever more firmly embedded in the social system in which they arise. Some sports become widely accepted, others do not. Some become largely professional, others do not. Some sports become associated with particular regions and classes, others do not. National bodies are created, commercial bodies and governments become involved in support and sponsorship, the whole thing is continuously chronicled in books, newspapers and specialist magazines, and becomes virtually part of the folklore of the community involved. The place of women in any particular sport therefore depends on the norms and values of that particular sport *and* on the overall acceptance of that sport in a wider socio-cultural context.

Sport has become an integral part of school curricula at primary and secondary levels. Indeed in some East European schools and American universities it virtually *is* the curriculum. It has become enmeshed in ritual and display, for example in the modern Olympic Games with their elaborate opening and closing sessions, their salutes and medals to the winners, and the national feting of the winners (or disgrace of losers) in so many countries. In many sports the ritual, the spectacle, the local or national identification with individual or team, is as important as or more important than the game itself.

Finally it is clear that sport has become an integral part of social and political policy in many countries. Particular sports are encouraged or discouraged by medical authorities, government and religious leaders on the basis of the supposed benefits or disbenefits to the nation as a whole or to particular groups within it. Sport and politics are inextricably linked, indeed sport is a political weapon today. But it is also big business which no social or economic planners can ignore.

In summary, then, a sport is an individual activity in which an individual satisfies his or her physical, psychological and social needs, and also a social activity moulded by all the pressures which affect other social activities such as education, religion or work. Sports also have to be regarded as social systems. A particular game, tournament or competition is a social activity. The sport itself is a social system with status, hierarchies, cohesion, recruitment into and out and its own place in the fabric of society. Sport overall is a major socio-political and economic activity and is an essential attribute of modern societies which impinges on the lives of all who live in them.

2. CONTRIBUTING FACTORS TO SUCCESSFUL SPORTING PERFORMANCE

It has been shown that sport is a broad based cultural activity, organized in a complex manner which involves a high degree of competition and physical prowess in its execution. Corresponding to these four essential components to sport in general, the factors which contribute to successful performance in any particular sport can be grouped into four main areas: variables in physique and physiology; different skills and abilities; the psychological makeup of the individual concerned and the social psychological influences which affect him or her. Finally there are the broad sociological and cultural factors characteristic of the whole society, which affect all of its members from birth. Some of these factors are listed in figure 2. There are certain minimum conditions specified by each of these which have to be met before any sporting activity can be undertaken. But these conditions are often less restrictive than supposed. The 'Wheelchair' Olympics, for example, shows that even those severely physically handicapped can participate in serious international sport, providing the sporting activity is carefully defined with the needs and abilities of the participants borne carefully in mind. It should be remembered in this context that almost all national and international sport is defined and controlled by men largely to suit men.

Physical Components		Skill Components	
Physical Endowments	*Physical Fitness*	*Neurological*	*Cognitive*
Physique	Available energy	Gross motor skills	Memory
Height		Fine motor skills	Intelligence
Weight	Circulatory capacity	Kinesthesis	
	Endurance	Reaction time	
	Strength	*Perceptual*	
	Flexibility	Acuity of the senses	Spatial ability
	Trainability		

Psychological Components		Cultural Components
Individual	*Social*	Socialisation through family, class, race and sex
Competitiveness	Peer group pressures	Educational provision and encouragement
Achievement	Sex, class and ethnic role awareness	Religious, political and social pressures
Motivation		Facilities provided
Stability		Social and financial rewards
Sociability		
Aggression		

Fig. 2. Some of the contributing factors in human sporting performance.

It is a mistake to regard any one of these groups of contributing factors as more important than any other in facilitating outstanding performances. It has in the past been assumed, in the speed and endurance events with which this book is primarily concerned, that physical attributes have been most important, that skills are somewhat less important and that the psychological and cultural factors are of relatively little importance altogether provided that they allow certain minimum levels of participation.

This book puts a great deal more emphasis on social and cultural factors than has hitherto been the case. It has been neglect of the importance of these in explaining differences between men's and women's performances which is responsible for the general air of surprise which permeates society (male society at least) when women produce sustained levels of performance which show that they really are catching up.

In one sense, the very fact that the requirements of successful sporting performance are divided up in this way itself causes further misconceptions. The real world cannot be divided up so simply; biological, psychological and social phenomena like this are inextricably linked. For example, the physical endowments of height, weight, strength, endurance and so on are a function of innate genetic potential, but they have to be developed in the right environment, which in this context means such things as an optimum diet, and freedom from disease, injury, the need to overwork and so on. But in a social environment, which puts emphasis on physique and physical accomplishments, individuals may take a greater pride in development of their physique, training harder and competing more fiercely than they otherwise would. This is particularly the case in the differentiation between men's and women's physique which western societies have hitherto valued. Men are characteristically portrayed as muscular, active, hard, strong and agile; women are usually seen as just the opposite in every respect. Neither the sex object projection nor the maternal projection of women has been thought of as compatible with an athletically competent physique. The desire to change their weak helpless image is leading many women to train harder, compete more vigorously and more successfully. This in turn is leading to a total re-evaluation by both men and women of a desirable physique.

An adequate social environment is essential in other ways. We all need love, protection, security and education if we are successfully to grow and mature. Each human genotype is unique but so, too, is each environment in which the genotypes develop. Indeed each genotype, to some extent, creates its own environment. The distinction between genotype and environment is really quite artificial, whatever human characteristic is being considered.

In the succeeding chapters, the biological, the psychological and then the socio-cultural requirements of sporting performance are examined separately. But this is merely an organizational device, not one which either reflects or recommends any fundamental or clearcut distinction between them.

CHAPTER THREE

The Biological Requirements of Successful Sporting Performance

1. PHYSICAL ENDOWMENTS

Men and women come in all shapes and sizes. *The Guinness Book of Records* informs us that the tallest recorded man was one Robert Wadlow who at his death, when aged twenty-two, was 2.72 metres tall and weighed 199 kilograms. The tallest woman was Ginny Bunford who was 2.31 metres tall when she died aged twenty-six. The shortest recorded adult male was 67 centimetres tall and weighed 5.4 kilograms when aged nineteen. The shortest woman was 59 centimetres at age nineteen when she weighed a little less than 4 kilograms.

All these, of course, were genetically or physiologically abnormal and could never have been proficient sportsmen or women. But there are enormous variations amongst normal men and women. The tallest people in the world are the Tutsi, Nilotic herdsmen of East Africa. The men's average height is 1.85 metres and may be as much as 2.29 metres. At the other extreme are the African pygmies, whose men average only 1.32 metres, and women only 1.24 metres. Variation among members of the same race is not normally as great, but is still substantial. Figure 3 shows that American men average 1.74 metres, ranging from less than 1.50 to more than 2.00 metres. American women average 1.62 metres, ranging from 1.40 to 1.90 metres. There is obviously considerable overlap between the sexes.

Now differences in height and weight may obviously confer considerable advantages in various sports. In some sports such as boxing, wrestling, weight-lifting and judo, individuals compete against only those in their own weight group. A flyweight champion is as much a champion as a heavyweight champion and is recognized as such. Curiously enough, no sports are segregated into height groups, although height is an obvious advantage in some sports. Most sports are segregated by sex, as if sex itself were more important than other physical differences.

This book is concerned mainly with the speed sports, running, swimming and so on, and with field athletics. These are all sex segregated. But in none are the participants divided into weight (or height) groups, although there are arguments that such divisions should be effected, particularly in the field events, many of which, inevitably, are dominated by the tall and the heavy.

Maximum running speed is not influenced very much by height itself. Taller people have longer legs and can therefore take longer strides, which helps them

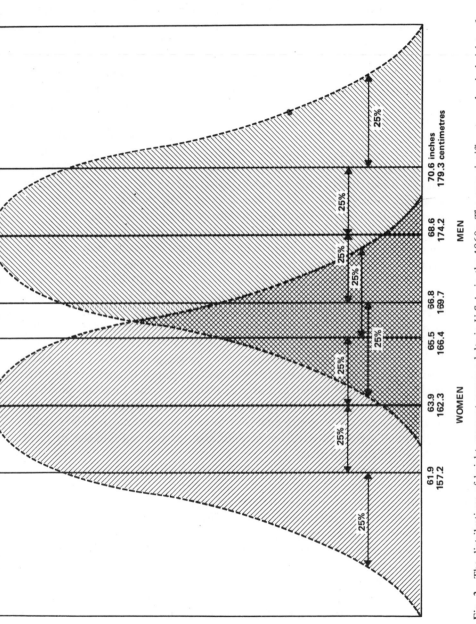

Fig. 3. The distributions of height amongst young adults in U.S.A. in the 1960s. The very significant overlap in heights of the sexes is obvious. The data come from H. W. Stoudt et al, *Weight, Height and Selected Body Dimensions of Adults*, US Public Health Service Publication No. 1,000, Series 11, No. 8.

run faster. But they can't move their legs so fast and this slows them down. In any case, the result of most running races does not depend much on the contestant's maximum speed. In the sprints it depends mainly on acceleration and in the longer events it depends on muscular endurance, oxygen transport and so on.

Acceleration is produced by large muscles, but not very effectively if they have a large body to move. Tall people are therefore handicapped over the sprints. Their length of leg and generally greater muscular power do give them an advantage in the 400 and 800 metres, but at longer distances muscular endurance and oxygen usage are more important. Taller people can take in and use more oxygen but they must work harder to move their bodies. Air resistance increases with the surface area of the body which, of course, is greater in tall athletes. Tall runners are therefore also handicapped in the long distance events.

Similar disadvantages apply to taller cyclists and skaters. Long-legged cyclists can develop greater force and greater leverage than their short-legged rivals, but it is doubtful if this outweighs the disadvantages of being tall.

In swimming the disadvantages of height are much less. The body is supported by the water and those with light bones and some body fat are at an advantage. There is no air resistance and technique is so important in keeping the body horizontal and high in the water and in actually executing the arm strokes and kicks, that physique is less important. Tall swimmers are more successful, mainly because of the greater amount of muscle they have.

One speed sport in which tall people are at a marked advantage is rowing. A long trunk and arms confer an advantage in applying leverage to the oars and developing a long stroke. Since the body weight is supported by the boat, successful rowers can be quite heavy with well developed leg and arm muscles. Canoeists tend to be lighter and shorter than rowers but long and powerful arms are still required. With this exception, the balance of advantages and disadvantages in the speed sports tends not to be large and over the whole range of sports and events individuals of very different heights can find one or more which particularly suits them.

In the jumping events taller people have inevitably an intrinsic advantage. Greater height increases both muscular force and the distance through which the muscles can shorten before leaving the ground. Taller people usually have a higher centre of gravity and can therefore clear a greater height without lifting their centre of gravity any more than a shorter competitor. Leanness is an obvious advantage, keeping the weight to be lifted to a minimum, although considerable muscular energy is required and therefore jumpers are usually quite well built.

Taller people are also systematically favoured in the throws. An increase of ten per cent in height, for example, increases the available muscular force by about twenty-one per cent. But it is also a very great advantage to release the missile, be it javelin, shot or discus, as high as possible above the ground.

In the shot put it is calculated from angles and speed of release that for every centimetre higher that the shot is released a centimetre of distance is gained. The strength requirement in the throws is obvious, but the need for considerable body acceleration to achieve maximum speed of projectile at the moment of delivery puts a limit on body size.

To summarize, taller people can take in more oxygen, have more muscle, have longer limbs and greater height above the ground. In the track sprints, long distance running events, gymnastics, skating and cycling the weight of the body and its size (increasing wind resistance mainly) outweigh these advantages. In jumping and throwing events tallness is a systematic advantage, especially when coupled with moderate but not overdeveloped musculature.

How does this affect the sexes? Women's performances will be inferior to men's in many sports simply because of their lower average height and lesser amount of muscle. But their closeness to men's performances in swimming (see chapter nine), in which tall men seem to be favoured, suggests that either this has been much over-emphasized in the past or that women have some compensating advantages. In some events, notably longer distance running, cycling and skating, women's physique undoubtedly confers some advantages. In others, mainly the athletic field events and rowing, women are at a systematic and largely inescapable disadvantage to men.

In the last few years many studies of the physique of successful athletes at the Olympics and elsewhere have shown that particular sports and events are indeed dominated by competitors of particular physical types, but they have demonstrated the variability in body types in each event and shown that theoretical optimal sizes can never be taken as more than a guide. The pages of sports history are full of exceptions to any rules on this (see pages 93-95); there are many highly successful tall sprinters, short jumpers and so on. All of this argues for some modest differentiation of competitors into classes by height and/or weight in those events or groups of events where there are inbuilt advantages for taller competitors. If this were done, the differentiation by sex might come to be seen as unnecessary.

2. PHYSICAL FITNESS

All sports, indoor or outdoor, of speed, stamina, strength, skill, mental ability or whatever, require for their successful prosecution that physical fitness is attained and maintained. Physical fitness has five basic components:
(a) The amount of energy available in the muscles;
(b) The efficiency and capacity of the heart, lungs and blood circulation;
(c) muscular endurance;
(d) muscular strength; and
(e) general body flexibility.

Each of these can be improved by training. Although distinct, they are inter-dependent and it is impossible significantly to improve one without also improving the others. Consequently the amount of training and the capacity to benefit from it is of crucial importance for the level of physical fitness ultimately obtained. The components of physical fitness are illustrated in their sporting context in figure 4.

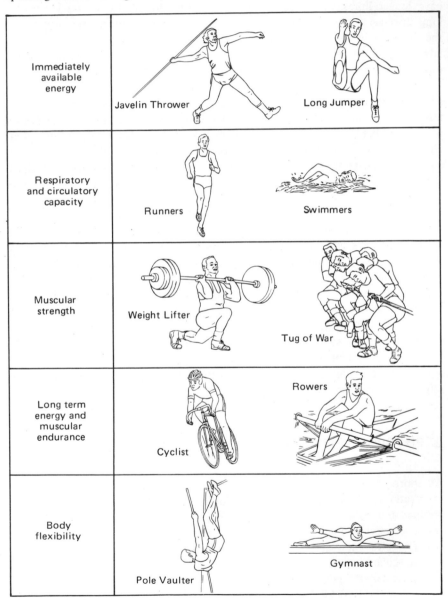

Fig. 4. The components of physical fitness shown in their sporting context.

(a) The Energy Available in the Muscles

The ultimate source of energy for the human body is the food we eat. But not much of the energy liberated by the breakdown of food is directly used to do work, least of all in a sporting situation. Most of the food products are stored in various parts of the body as different types of proteins, sugars and fats. All of the energy used by muscles is provided by the breakdown of a chemical compound called adenosine triphosphate or ATP and it is therefore the amount of this in the muscles and its rate of manufacture from the stored products which are the limiting factors on the amount of available energy. ATP is a complex molecule but it consists essentially of three phosphate groups joined to a central structure. It is the breaking of the bonds between the phosphate groups and the central structure which release energy.

There are three mechanisms by which ATP is made available in muscles, corresponding to short, medium and long term energy requirements. The short term energy requirements are provided by having the ATP, which is broken down during muscular contraction, continuously reformed by the energy liberated during the breakdown of another phosphate-rich compound, phosphocreatine (PC), which is also present in the muscles. This ATP–PC system is an oxygen free or anaerobic system and is the source of energy used in the explosive events such as the sprints, throws and jumps. Under maximum usage all of the phosphate stores are used up in about ten seconds and alternative energy sources must then be utilized.

The second mechanism for producing ATP involves an incomplete breakdown of stored food products to lactic acid also in the absence of oxygen. The glucose which is produced by the digestion of food is stored in the muscle and liver as glycogen, but can be reconverted to glucose when required. It is then broken down in the absence of oxygen to form lactic acid and ATP, a process known as glycolysis. It is the accumulation of lactic acid which causes the pain of continued exertion and which ultimately stops further muscular contraction. There are thus two limitations on using energy from this system: the amount of glycogen/glucose available and the level of lactic acid that the muscles can tolerate and at which they can still function.

This lactic acid system provides a very rapid supply of ATP for activities performed at maximum rate for about two or three minutes, such as track events up to 800 or 1000 metres and swimming events up to 200 metres. Using up all of the immediately available ATP by these two mechanisms creates what is called the oxygen debt (see figure 7). Oxygen will ultimately be required but its need can be postponed during the first period of maximal exercise.

The third source of ATP, the oxygen system, is directly dependent on the air breathed in during exercise. In the presence of oxygen a glucose molecule is completely broken down to carbon dioxide (CO_2) and water (H_2O) and a great deal more ATP is produced than in the lactic acid system. Lactic acid does not accumulate and hence muscular fatigue does not occur so soon. This oxygen system is important during lengthy exercise performed at a submaximal rate. During such activities there is ample time for the blood to supply muscle cells with enough oxygen, which in turn can supply most of the ATP demanded by exercise performed at this rate.

The general characteristics of these three energy systems are set out in table 1 and the energy reserves they contain in table 2. To put these figures into perspective, an average sedentary man requires about 8500 kilojoules in a twenty-four hour period. Marathon runners may use more than 14,500 kilojoules during a race; long distance cyclists may use more than 42,000 kilojoules during an event and channel swimmers may require even greater energy expenditures.

Table 1. General characteristics of the three mechanisms by which ATP is formed.

Mechanism	Source	O_2 Required	Relative ATP production	Consequences
Anaerobic				
ATP-PC system	Phosphocreatine	No	Few; limited	Oxygen debt
Lactic acid system	Glycogen (glucose)	No	Few; limited	Oxygen debt Lactic acid accumulation Muscular fatigue
Aerobic				
Oxygen system	Glycogen, fats, glucose	Yes	Many; unlimited	Gradual exhaustion

Table 2. Energy sources in the human body.

Source	Site	Quantity of energy in kilojoules	Minimum time to exhaustion*
Phosphocreatine	Muscle	30-42	8-10 seconds
Glycogen	Muscle	6,750	1-2 hours
	Liver	1,680	
Fat	Fat Deposits	210-280,000	20-40 days
Protein	Mainly Muscle	42,000	40 days

* Under conditions of maximum sustainable usage. It should be emphasized that body protein and fat cannot be completely used – death would intervene. The figures quoted are the maximum utilizable reserves.

There are not precise boundaries between the usages of these three energy systems and in middle distance track events all three are used. After Juantorena's win in the 800 metres at the Montreal Olympics, commentators remarked that he had converted it into a sprint event. From the point of view of energy systems used this is probably true, as can be deduced from figure 5. At the 1968 Mexico Olympics held at an altitude of 2240 metres, performances in the

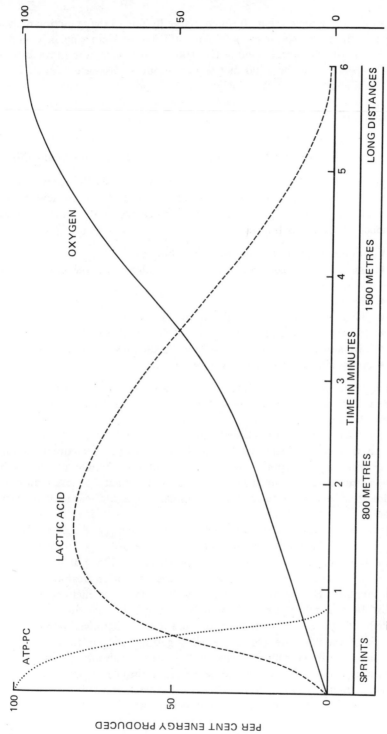

Fig. 5. The relationship between energy sources used and the duration of exercise and the distance of track events.

long distance aerobic events suffered markedly due to the reduction of available oxygen; the men's sprint events up to 400 metres were won in world record times, all of which still stand.[1] The 800 metres event was run a little faster than expected and the 1500 metres just about as fast as expected. The 1500 metres therefore marks the changeover from primarily non-aerobic to aerobic energy sources. It is at the moment the longest event for women in the Olympic programme!

(b)   The Efficiency and Capacity of the Heart, Lungs and Blood Circulation

In any sporting event lasting more than a few seconds the supply of oxygen and nutrients to the cells is of crucial importance. There are several variables involved in determining the levels and efficiency with which they can be supplied. They are as follows:

- movement of air into and out of the lungs;
- transfer of oxygen from lung air sacs (alveoli) to the blood in the lung capillaries;
- the output of the heart;
- the amount of blood available to the muscle tissue;
- transfer of oxygen from the blood in the muscle capillaries;
- diffusion from the muscle capillaries to the muscle fibres;
- metabolic events in the muscle fibres.

Changes in the value of some of these variables under maximal exercise are shown in figure 6. A number of anatomical and physiological features determine these changes.

First there is the vital capacity of the lungs; this is the maximum volume of gas that can be exhaled from the lungs following a maximum inspiration. It depends on the volume of the lungs and the strength of the respiratory musculature. An untrained person has a vital capacity of less than five litres whereas an average trained distance runner has a vital capacity of nearly six litres.

Secondly, there is the maximum breathing capacity, the maximum amount of air that can be moved in and out of the lungs over a period of time. Average men have maximum breathing capacities between 125–170 litres per minute, whereas trained distance runners may have capacities greater than 210 litres per minute. This maximum breathing capacity, or a high percentage of it, must be maintained for long periods of time. Trained distance runners are able to breathe over 120 litres per minute for more than twenty minutes.

These variables are concerned with getting oxygen to the lungs, where exchange with the blood occurs in tiny sacs, or alveoli, surrounded by tiny blood capillaries. The red blood cells passing through these capillaries bring in carbon dioxide attached to the chemical haemoglobin which is then exchanged for oxygen for transport to the working tissues. The number of red cells and

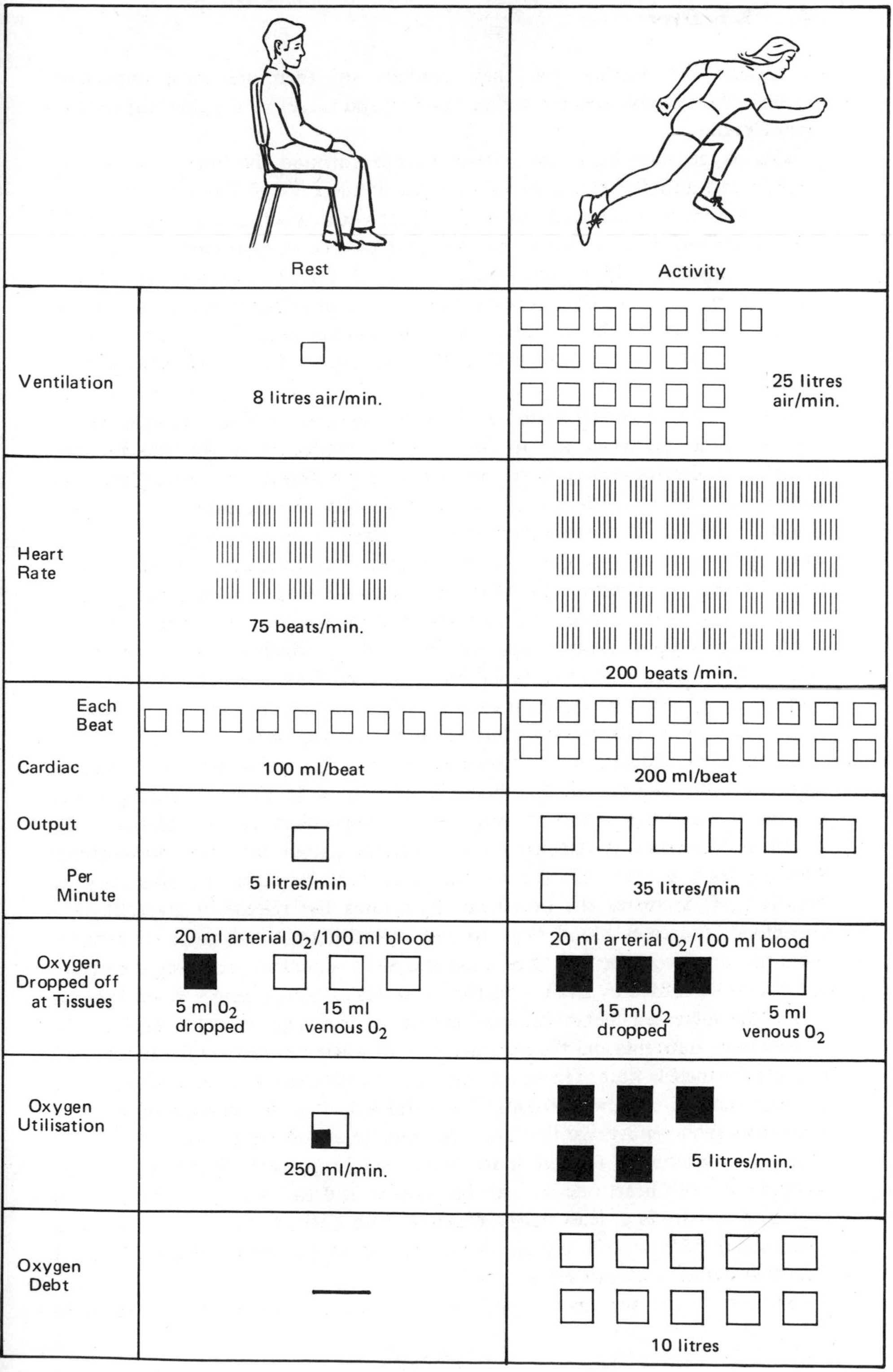

	Rest	Activity
	Rest	Activity
Ventilation	8 litres air/min.	25 litres air/min.
Heart Rate	75 beats/min.	200 beats /min.
Cardiac Output Per Minute	Each Beat 100 ml/beat — 5 litres/min	200 ml/beat — 35 litres/min
Oxygen Dropped off at Tissues	20 ml arterial O_2/100 ml blood — 5 ml O_2 dropped — 15 ml venous O_2	20 ml arterial O_2/100 ml blood — 15 ml O_2 dropped — 5 ml venous O_2
Oxygen Utilisation	250 ml/min.	5 litres/min.
Oxygen Debt	—	10 litres

Fig. 6. Changes in some physiological measurements during maximum exercise.

the amount of haemoglobin they contain are therefore most important. Trained athletes have a much higher number and therefore a greater capacity to carry oxygen.

This oxygen-carrying blood is then pumped around the body. The volume of the heart and the efficiency of its musculature control this. The volume of blood which can be pumped out of the heart with each beat is about 200 milli-litres in trained persons, nearly double that of sedentary persons of the same age and physique. When performing maximal exercise the trained runner's heart can pump thirty-five to forty litres per minute compared to twenty to twenty-five litres for the untrained heart. And trained individuals can maintain these maximal values, or something close to them, for considerable periods of time.

Having pumped greater volumes of higher oxygenated blood into circulation per unit time, provision has to be made for getting it to the muscles. The numbers of arteries leading to the muscles and the density of the capillary beds within the muscles are increased by training, with the increases being proportional to the role that the muscle involved plays in the task being trained for. The capillary density in the calf muscles, for example, can double during a long training programme. The blood is thus delivered to the muscles more rapidly, in greater volume and carrying greater amounts of oxygen. Muscles contain an oxygen binding pigment, myoglobin, which has six times more affinity for oxygen than does blood haemoglobin. This, coupled with increased acidity, temperature and carbon dioxide (CO_2) concentration in the muscles, promotes oxygen exchange from haemoglobin to myoglobin.

When an individual starts or expects to start hard physical activity, hormonal and metabolic changes in the body initiate a wide range of physical and emotional responses which directly affect respiration and circulation. The hormone adrenaline is released by the adrenal glands into the blood-stream which relaxes the bronchioles of the lungs and increases the efficiency of breathing. It increases the heartbeat, stimulates the release of glycogen into the blood, decreases blood flow to the digestive tract and stops its muscles from moving food. The feeling of tenseness and excitement preceding important effort is both caused by and is a further stimulus of these changes. Once exercise starts, the increased metabolic requirements of the major muscles result in the depletion of nutrients and the accumulation of waste products in the tissue fluid bathing the muscle fibre. The blood supply is then increased to remove the waste products and bring new nutrients. The total output of the heart needed to do this varies from an average five litres per minute at rest up to about thirty-five litres per minute in trained individuals exercising hard. This results from increases in both heart rate and stroke volume, and the potential for major and sustained activity is at least partly dependent on both. The heart rate increases from about 75 beats per minute (bpm) at rest to between 180 and 220 bpm during sustained maximal effort.

Because of the increased blood flow and constriction of blood vessels in parts of the body, blood pressure rises. The spleen contributes some of its reserve red blood cells to the circulation in order to increase the oxygen and carbon-dioxide carrying capacity of the blood. All of these factors increase the flow of blood to the working muscles during exercise.

During even mild exertion there is an increased demand for oxygen by the cells. Therefore, both the depth and rate of breathing increase. The volume of air exhaled with each breath rises from five hundred to twenty-five hundred millilitres and the breathing rate increases from fifteen to fifty breaths per minute. The result is that the amount of air used may increase from a resting level of six to ten litres per minute up to the maximum breathing capacity of two hundred litres per minute in trained men. At the same time, decreased concentrations of oxygen and increased concentrations of carbon dioxide in blood coming from the muscles improves the exchange of these gases at the lungs because of the greater concentration differences across the gas-exchange membrane.

As a result of these changes the amount of oxygen actually used by the tissues in a trained person may increase from between 200 to 350 millilitres per minute at rest to between four and six litres per minute when exercising. This latter figure is referred to as maximum aerobic power or max VO_2. Maximum aerobic power is important to athletes but is not an infallible guide to ability; some of the variations among top runners is shown in table 3 and for other sports in table 9.

Table 3. Variation in maximum aerobic power among different athletes.

Runner (s)	Max VO_2 (l/min)	Max VO_2[a] (ml/kg/min)
Peter Snell[b]	5.50	73.3
5 US world class distance runners	5.05	77.5
9 US nationally ranked long distance runners	4.69	71.8
6 South Australian distance runners	4.50	67.7
6 South African distance runners	3.95	62.4
Derek Clayton[c]	3.78	64.4

a. Figures for both men and women in other sports are shown in table 9.

b. 800 metres world record holder 1964-65.
   800 and 1500 metres gold medallist at Tokyo Olympics.

c. Marathon unofficial world record holder 1969.

If the oxygen requirement exceeds oxygen available to the tissues, a person can still continue activity until their particular maximum oxygen debt tolerance is reached. This oxygen debt, the concept of which is illustrated in figure 7, can be between six and ten litres and can be fully contracted in twenty seconds. The panting and very heavy breathing which continues for some time after exertion is the evidence for this paying back of the oxygen debt. Lactic acid

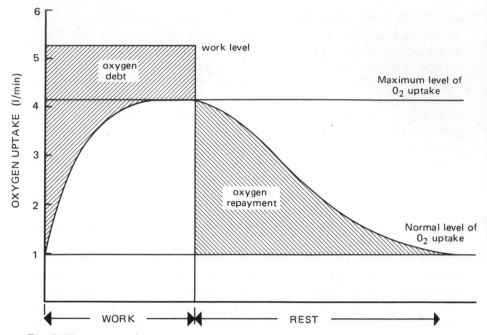

Fig. 7. The concept of oxygen debt. Oxygen uptake may be slow in reaching its maximum level and even when it reaches it the work level may be such that more oxygen is required. This extra oxygen demand can be carried for a while but eventually has to be met when work ceases. In some cases work will have to stop if the oxygen debt capacity is exceeded or if the debt is carried too long.

is converted back to glucose, other depleted substances in the muscles are restored and oxygen in the tissue fluids is replaced. Among the important variables in athletic performance is the size of the oxygen debt which can be contracted and the length of time for which it can be carried before being repaid.

When the respiratory and circulatory systems are able to keep up with the oxygen requirement, oxygen uptake and heart rate level off, and this level of effort can be maintained for a long period. Some highly trained individuals can maintain a steady state as high as eighty-five per cent of maximal oxygen uptake, which explains the success of many long distance runners who do not have exceptionally high levels of maximal oxygen uptake. American runner Ron Daws, for example, could sustain a heart rate of 177–80 beats per minute for the duration of the marathon. This was no less than ninety-five per cent of his maximum heart rate of 187.

During prolonged exercise glucose levels in the blood are maintained initially by the liver's release of stored glycogen and its breakdown to glucose. But by the end of about an hour, as glycogen stores are depleted, fats become the most important glucose source. Women may have here a potential energy source not so readily available to men or so efficiently usable by them.

(c)   The Endurance of the Muscles

If a person can lift a weight of one hundred kilograms from floor to chest level once only, that person's maximum strength is one hundred kilograms. If another person can do it more than once their maximum strength must be greater. The lower the proportion of maximum strength used in any exercise the greater can be the muscular endurance.

As muscles work they restore their own oxygen and fuel supplies, and dispose of lactic acid and other metabolic waste products. As long as these two processes operate at basically the same rate, muscles can continue to work with efficiency. However, when an imbalance is reached in which the rate of waste product (mainly lactic acid) accumulation is cumulatively greater than the oxygen and fuel intake, physiological equilibrium is upset and fatigue sets in. Reaction time slows down and the muscles stiffen. Improvement in endurance comes from an increased ability to endure the pain and discomfort of fatigue and the body's ability to increase energy production to as high a level as possible above the resting level. These adjustments are brought about by involving more muscles, by increasing the activity of enzyme systems in the aerobic and anaerobic pathways and by the development of more blood capillaries, thus providing the working muscles with more oxygen and fuel and facilitating the removal of waste products.

(d)   The Strength of the Muscles

Strength is the capacity to exert force or the ability to do work against resistance. Muscles increase in strength, but not necessarily in size, when a workload over and above any previous demands is placed upon them. Muscles of the same size may vary in the amount of fatty tissue they contain and fat inhibits muscle efficiency, because it lacks contractile power and limits the speed and amount of contraction by acting as a friction brake. Conversely muscular strength can increase two or three times or more without a proportional increase in muscle bulk necessarily occurring. A gain in strength is accompanied by a significant increase in both the size of the fibres and the number of blood capillaries in the muscle and by a resultant gain not only in power but also in speed and endurance. There is also an increase in the development of connective tissue within the muscle bundles which adds to the general toughness of the muscles and enables them better to withstand the stresses and strains imposed by vigorous sporting activity.

(e)   Flexibility of the Limbs and the Body

The flexibility of a given joint depends upon the various physiological characteristics of the muscle and collagenous tissues surrounding that joint and is measured in degrees through which it can move. Minimal trunk flexion and hamstring flexibility, for example, is measured by the simple test of touching the toes with the tops of the fingers while the knees are kept straight.

All forms of physical sporting performance will be improved by increased flexibility, and increase in flexibility must accompany an increase in strength of a muscle or the range of motion of muscle or limb may be much reduced. Regular appropriate exercise will increase both the strength and the flexibility of muscles, tendons and ligaments. Strong muscles are not necessarily large, unwieldy ones; conversely, very flexible muscles can also be very strong.

(f)   The Capacity for Improvement

Sportsmen and women will never succeed without hard and rigorous training. But this training will only be really effective in individuals with a capacity for improvement, an attribute sometimes referred to as trainability. Trainability is the ability of the body processes to be changed in significant and useful ways by means of systematic practice and exercise. Individuals vary, not only in their physique and physiology, but also in the extent to which these attributes may be changed and the changes thus effected then maintained. Changes induced by training can occur in all of the systems important in conferring physical fitness.

The amount of myoglobin, the oxygen binding pigment in the muscles, can be almost doubled. This allows greater oxygen storage and greater capacity to use oxygen during exercise. This is particularly useful to middle distance runners and their equivalents in other sports, since it delays the build-up of fatigue-producing lactic acid and increases the muscle's capacity to extract oxygen from the blood and pass it to the cells where it is required. The amount of ATP and PC stored in muscles also increases so that immediately available energy is increased. The level of glycogen in the muscles of trained individuals is up to two and a half times higher than in untrained, and the rate at which it can be oxidized also increases so that endurance is improved.

The muscles themselves increase in size, strength and efficiency, not only in the arms and legs but also in the chest. This in turn leads to increases in lung volume and the pumping action of the chest. A trained runner can process over twenty per cent more air than an untrained person and can maintain maximum or near maximum breathing capacities for much longer. The amount of oxygen actually used up in doing this is also less. The contraction of trained muscle fibres becomes faster and stronger and they have greater endurance.

The size of the heart increases and the arteries serving the heart musculature increase in number and up to three times in size. The volume of blood which can be pumped out of the heart with each beat is almost doubled as is the amount which can be pumped per minute. The stroke rate which a trained person can maintain is also much enhanced. Within the blood of the trained athlete there are more red blood cells and within each of these red blood cells there is more haemoglobin. The diameter of blood vessels increases, as does the number of small arteries leading to muscles and the density of capillary beds within them.

The consequences of all these changes are twofold: the capacity to take in oxygen and then to transport it around the body is markedly improved, as is the ability to extract and use the oxygen thus transported. Training may improve oxygen transport power by between five and fifty per cent and increase oxygen utilization from a normal seventy per cent up to an athlete's eighty-five per cent. The uptake of oxygen for any given workload therefore declines in trained men and women by significant and approximately equal amounts.

There are a number of other changes induced by training complementary to these. The bicarbonate content of the tissues rises, providing a chemical buffer to neutralize lactic acid as it is formed, thereby reducing unpleasant sensations and delaying the onset of muscular fatigue. Blood levels of cholesterol and certain fats are lowered, blood pressure is lowered and heat dissipation is improved during exercise through early and more vigorous sweating. The amount of fat in the body is reduced. An average young male usually carries about twenty per cent body fat; good distance runners usually have between six and nine per cent body fat.

The net results of training are greater strength and endurance, greater mechanical efficiency, improved neuromuscular co-ordination, improved anaerobic and aerobic performance and more rapid recovery after effort. The precise changes which occur depend on the amount and type of training done: that is, whether it is for speed, strength, endurance or flexibility. Generally speaking the greater the intensity, frequency and duration of training the greater will be the improvement in most functions. The amount of improvement is a function of genetic potential, although the precise importance of genetic factors is unknown.

3. SKILL

The word "skill" has three different meanings in sport. It means efficiency, in particular the efficiency with which chemical energy is converted into human movement in such sports as swimming, running, cycling and so on. It means the precise way various movements and reactions are strung together to achieve some overall optimum in, for example, jumping and throwing events, gymnastics, motor racing, judo, boxing and most ball games. And it means the ability to plan tactics or strategy. Some of the components of skill are shown in their sporting context in figure 8.

When a car is being driven, by no means all the chemical energy of the petrol is used in the act of propulsion. A good deal is converted into heat and noise and much is eliminated as unburnt exhaust gas. Similarly, when the body moves, wastage occurs during muscular contraction as the phosphate energy stores

1. Motor Skills	Footballer	Skier
2. Reaction Time	Sprinter	Fencer
3. Kinesthetic Sense	Diver	Gymnast
4. Mental Abilities	Archers	Chess players

Fig. 8. The components of skill shown in their sporting context.

are broken down. The first meaning of skill is therefore the reduction of this wastage.

The various speed sports differ markedly in their energy-conversion efficiency. Cyclists can convert about twenty-three per cent of their energy intake into mechanical power and the scope for them to improve their technique is limited. Hence there is considerable emphasis on the technical qualities and specifications of the machines they ride, gears, weight, size and so on. In contrast, the overall efficiency of swimming is only about five per cent and there is therefore great potential for improvement. Such things as arm stroke, leg kicks, position of the body in the water and other components of skill are of immense importance and considerable emphasis is placed on them in training.

Skill in running is assessed in terms of biomechanical variables: runners should not overstride, have an excessively oscillating centre of gravity, or have asymmetrical arm movements. Most marathoners seem to be more efficient than middle distance runners and most runners improve over the years, despite no detectable improvements in bodily functions. Presumably the efficiency of leg movements and arm movements is gradually improved and techniques of running into the wind, behind other runners and so on are also improved.

The second usage of skill builds on the first. If and only if skill in terms of efficiency exists can skill in terms of complex sequences of movement be highly developed. Much of the activity becomes an automatic response needing no conscious thought. The more that is automatic the greater can be the concentration on the third area of skill — tactical skill, judgment, strategy and so forth. Some of these may become subconscious — the recognition that an opponent is under stress and ripe for a burst of speed or a two-handed attack and so on — but usually this is a conscious process using intelligence, memory and experience in the sport concerned, grafted on to the first two types of skill which will allow the desired manoeuvre to be executed.

There are three prime contributors to skill defined in terms of efficiency: motor skills; a sense of posture and position in space or kinesthetic sense; and reaction time. Other abilities such as visual acuity are not of major importance unless they fall below normal levels.

There are at least ten separate kinds of ability which contribute to motor skills, separable by complex statistical analysis. But the extent to which these are independent and can be considered independent of flexibility, reaction time, and general kinesthetic sense is not agreed on by experts in this field. There is undoubtedly considerable variability in motor skills among human beings and the correlations between them are often rather low. In other words the possession of one fine or gross motor skill in high degree does not necessarily mean the possession of all or indeed any of the others to the same extent. Furthermore, simple motor skills, either alone or in combination, do not of themselves contribute much to predictions of final athletic performance. The motor skills that are important in sporting achievement are those which are developed and perfected through training and practice. These include the co-ordination, agility and anticipation necessary to play ball games and the various specialized skills necessary for other sports using particular equipment. In other words, division of human motor skills into very detailed abilities is of more use to the academic psychologist than the practising sportsman or woman or their trainers. A number of the differences which have been found between men and women in these skills in laboratory tests therefore do not have much to do with sex differences in performance.

Reaction time is a most important component of skill in a wide variety of sports. It involves three separate steps: the time involved in receiving the stimulus and sending it to the appropriate part of the nervous system; a decision time; and a movement time involving transmission down the motor fibres and the initiation of motor response. The simplest laboratory measured reaction times are probably not much use in predicting response in real life situations, particularly in complex sporting situations, although in the very special situation of reaction to the starting gun in sprint races they may be. Other laboratory research suggests, however, that individual differences in ability to react quickly and move quickly are unrelated.

The capacity for improvement in nervous control is as important as in those processes contributing to physical fitness. The nerves themselves become more efficient at transmitting electrochemical impulses and they activate more muscle fibres, thereby increasing strength. Systematic training and practice ensure that reflex actions, that is, automatic unthinking ones, gradually replace voluntary thinking ones. Movement thereby becomes more efficient. Wasteful muscular contractions become fewer, unneeded muscles relax more fully and movement is simplified. The final result, it has been estimated, is that for a given performance the amount of energy expended after training is only about three quarters of the total energy needed before training. The same sort of process is involved in stringing together particular skills to generate the sequences required in complex sporting activities, a gradual shift from conscious to unconscious activities.

Various mental abilities are required for the third type of skill, including choice of tactical or strategic alternatives, learning ability, memory and so on. There is no firm agreement on how many components of human mental ability there are, nor how clearly they might be separated from one another. Nor is there any agreement on whether mental abilities are determined primarily by inheritance or environment. The fact that in some sports the participants are above average intelligence is more a reflection of the class association of the sports than anything else. A lack of opportunity and facilities in early years is a crippling handicap in very many sports. Lower class boys from urban schools have less opportunity to take up cricket or rugby or even soccer than their middle or upper class counterparts; and the middle and upper class associations of tennis, golf, ice skating and many other sports is well known. Even track and field athletics was, until ten or fifteen years ago, largely an upper class activity (among men) in European countries and dominated by the universities.

Average IQ increases with social class and parental affluence and the increase of IQ with sporting prowess may result from this. It is therefore difficult to tell whether, and if so to what extent, high mental ability itself is important for success in many sports.

The conclusion from all this is that although individuals may differ somewhat in mental abilities such as spatial, verbal, mechanical, analytic, concentrating, synthetic and so on, we do not know why. Nor do we know by how much the pattern of differences may be changed by different rearing procedures, education and/or training. In sport, as in so many human activities, initial small differences and social advantages become magnified and reinforced to preserve the pronounced systems of social stratification characteristic of modern industrialized societies. This is as true for sporting ability and opportunity as for educational opportunity and economic success; those having initial advantages of money, opportunity and perhaps a little extra innate ability are able to capitalize on them, magnify them and in turn ensure that their advantages are passed on to their own children. The interplay of biological and social factors in sport, as in many other fields of human endeavour, is subtle, complex and very profound.

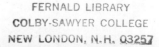

Top left. Chinese women athletes training at the Peking Stadium. Although the Chinese withdrew from the Moscow Olympics, it will surely not be long before the Chinese make a significant contribution to women's athletics and other speed sports. As the most populous nation on earth and one dedicated to equalizing women's opportunities we can anticipate impressive achievements from Chinese women. (Credit: Keystone Press Agency.) **Top right.** The second Tokyo International women's marathon in November 1980. A field this size would have been a large one in most men's marathons until about 1970. The race here is led by Britain's Joyce Smith who went on to win. As a forty-three year old mother of two Joyce Smith won the inaugural 1981 London marathon in the third best ever time by a woman of 2 hours 29 minutes 29 seconds. Although there will be a 1984 Olympic women's marathon there will be no 5000 or 10,000 metres. Why not? (Credit: Keystone Press Agency.) **Bottom left.** Emma Gaptschenko, the Russian world champion and world record holder of 1975. Shooting is an "open" sport in the Olympics (and elsewhere, a woman won the Kings Prize at Bisley in 1932), but archery is not, despite there being a very small difference in best performances between men and women at all distances (see pages 206–7). (Credit: Keystone Press Agency). **Bottom right.** The Cambridge University Women's rowing eight of 1968. A women's varsity race has been rowed since 1965, but the first the general public heard of women's rowing was when a woman was selected to cox the men's Oxford eight in 1981. (Credit: Keystone Press Agency.)

CHAPTER FOUR

The Psychological Requirements of Successful Sporting Performance

While psychological factors influencing participation and performance in sport are just as important as the strictly biological, they are usually more subtle in effect, they are almost always more difficult to measure and are even more imbued with cultural bias. The distinction, between individual attributes on the one hand and the extent to which individuals are aware of and respond to society's evaluation of these attributes on the other, has also to be made.

1. COMPETITIVE ABILITY

Competition is a word used for a variety of social processes. A recent definition given at a conference on women in sport is: "a social process which occurs when the person's activities are directed more or less consistently towards meeting a standard or achieving a goal in which performance, either by the individual or the group, is compared and evaluated relative to that of selected other persons or groups".[1] Psychologists commonly recognize two major types of competition in sport: indirect competition, in which an individual aims at standards such as their own previous achievements and records or best achievements by other individuals; and direct competition in which individuals attempt to maximize their own performance while minimizing those of their opponents, such as in tennis, boxing, and so on, and most team sports.

At the highest levels of sport, competition of either kind dominates everything. Australian miler, Herb Elliott, once said in an interview that: "Races were my proving ground and because athletics was the all-important thing in my life, the races became so that each one overran all my thoughts. For days before a race there was one consuming thought — I must win and no one is going to stop me . . . " Chris Brasher, the 1956 Olympic steeplechase winner, is also reported as saying that: "Early in 1958 I broke the four-minute mile for the first time. My attitude to athletics had now formed and hardened so that before a race I could never shake hands with a rival. The winning of the race was too vital and my feelings too intense, for me to be able to touch the skin of the man I wanted to beat."[2]

Competition has biological, psychological and social components, but the presence of two or more individuals and the presence of an audience conditioning and encouraging the performers, emphasizes the importance of social factors. All human societies seem to manifest three types of behaviour, competitive, co-operative and individualistic, although of course to very different extents. The competitive behaviour of any individual is therefore partly determined by innate personality factors, but mainly reflects the importance of competition in the society in which he or she lives. Differences in competitive behaviour between men and women are, in other words, due mainly to social pressures and can be changed as social attitudes change.

2. AGGRESSION

This too is a word used in a variety of ways. We speak of an aggressive personality, or an aggressive salesman, as well as an aggressive (violent) act. And aggression is a term widely used in a sporting context, as in aggressive running, aggressive play at tennis, chess and so on.

Instrumental aggression is an attempt to achieve some goal and in which harm to another person occurs only because it is the most efficient way of achieving the desired goal. Reactive or goal aggression, on the other hand, attempts to cause injury or harm to another person with both perception of the other person as a threat and the emotion of anger being necessary conditions for it to be shown.

Instrumental aggression is clearly important for sporting success. But there is probably an optimum level, which may vary with different sports, above which aggression probably interferes with the attainment of the overall objectives of the sport. Reactive aggression has a place in a few sports, including boxing and wrestling, but many deny that these are really sports at all for this reason and they have little place in this book. As with competition there are innate and learned aspects of aggression, but the nature of society is of immense importance in its expression. Furthermore, the specific manifestation of aggression depends on the particular situation.

3. MOTIVATION

The will and determination to succeed is important in two principal ways to sporting achievement: it affects the amount and the quality of practice and training which the sportsperson is willing to undertake, and it affects the effort and sacrifice which is put in during actual competition.

Complex skills can only be mastered through intense effort and attention on the part of the learner. It has been said that the most important factor in skill acquisition is that of motivation. This means that the activity should be enjoyable, and it will usually be enjoyable when success is expected and when encouragement and praise is given during learning. Motivation is important in developing a wide range of abilities including motor skills, memory, mental arithmetic and others. Successful motivation can overcome many physical handicaps or shortcomings in skill and ability (see for example pp. 93-98) and can prevent fatigue, for instance, from affecting performance as soon as it normally would. The financial rewards, prestige, status, fame, a place in history and so on which are so much a part of today's sport are important, as is the simple desire to win, to be the best – a commonly manifested motivation. But inner motivation may be a very personal thing. Mountains are climbed "because they are there"; sports are competed in for the satisfaction they give in the manifestation of strength and skill to the individual involved. Herb Elliott commented that: "If I had my chance I would run my races and win gold medals without being in the public eye. You've got to pay the price for these things and the price is being in the public eye." A prominent British soccer player, Brian Walker, spoke for many when he said: "I played football because I had an inner compulsion to do so. Nothing else mattered. Fame, fortune – I never considered these. It was the game that mattered and for it I was prepared from the earliest days to risk my health, my schooling, my hopes of marriage and, eventually, a considerable business career."

On the other hand the particular occasion of crowd, competition and event may be motivating in itself. Mary Peters describes her feelings during the closing stages of the 1972 Olympic Pentathlon high jump competition when a stadium full of spectators was urging her on. "Some day, when science knows even more about adrenalin, it may all be explained. For me, at the end of a day of enormous tension and physical strain, an overwhelming desire to give more and more for my coach and my team manager and those marvellous supporters who had come half way across Europe was pushing me onwards and upwards."[3]

4. PERSONALITY

Personality traits are of immense importance for all sportsmen and women, but because of the many and varied activities which can be called sport, very different personalities can achieve success in different sports. The intense pressure under which modern sport stars operate, however, soon uncovers personality flaws. Only strong well-integrated personalities will avoid depression, over-anxiety, exaggerated sensitivity to failure or criticism and, paradoxically, unconscious fear of success because of the further pressures it will bring to repeat or improve on it.

Research from the Institute for the Study of Athletic Motivation in the USA involving more than fifteen thousand athletes found that those who survive the high drop-out rate from competition are characterized by all or most of the following traits. They have a great need for achievement and tend to set high but realistic goals for themselves and others; they are highly organized, orderly, respectful of authority and dominant; they have large capacity for trust, great psychological endurance, self control, low resting levels of anxiety and slightly greater ability to express aggression; most have a low interest in receiving support and concern from others, a low need to take care of others and low need for affiliation. In general, sportsmen have high levels of dominance, social aggression, leadership, toughmindedness, stability and confidence. Women have rather lower emotional stability and control.

One behaviour trait almost always present amongst sportsmen and women is anxiety before a contest and increased neuroticism and compensation when competitive stress is at its height. A competitor is tested more severely in a few seconds, hours or days of a sporting contest than most others are in years. The ability to accept defeat without loss of motivation for continued training and participation, and without demoralization which might affect later performances is immensely important.

Most successful competitors possess strong personalities that complement natural physical gifts and motor skills. Some have sufficiently strong personality traits to overcome important biological shortcomings. But there are others who possess very few strong character traits, only magnificent physical gifts enabling them to overcome constant tension, anxiety and self doubt. Indeed, it may be the seeking to compensate for their real or imagined deficits which drives them to supreme physical achievement.

It is well known from sporting history that some individuals produced supreme performances at the appropriate times, often well in excess of what they were normally capable. Others failed to win big-time and important events despite being hot favourites and having strings of world record performances behind them. The great Australian runner Ron Clarke, world record holder at one time or another of all events from two miles to ten miles, never won an Olympic nor a Commonwealth Games gold medal in a career of more than fourteen years. On the other hand athletes such as Chris Brasher, the 1956 steeplechase winner; Bob Beaman, the 1968 long jump winner; Billy Mills, the 1964 10,000 metres winner, and others, started their events as relative unknowns, certainly outsiders, and yet achieved supreme personal best performances to win. Lasse Viren's performance in winning both 5000 and 10,000 metres at Munich and Montreal was an astonishing one. He won the 10,000 metres at Munich despite being sent sprawling on to the track more than halfway through the race. But he produced relatively few great performances outside the Olympics. When Mary Peters won the pentathlon at Munich in 1972 she established personal bests in four of the five events to set a new world record of 4801 points, just 10 points (or one tenth of a second in the 200 metres) in front of the silver medallist.

The ability to rise to the occasion, to produce an optimum performance when it is most wanted and when the pressure is on, is one which can surely be identified, if not so easily quantified. It requires tremendous determination, confidence in one's own abilities, tactical wisdom, the ability to deceive one's opponents, to recognize their weaknesses and capitalize on them, all capped with this intangible, personality strength. It is clearly an important component of sporting ability at a wide range of ability levels in probably all sporting contests.

What all this tells us is that psychological variables such as competitive ability, levels of aggression, motivation, personality strength, and others, can often supplement relatively moderate physical and physiological endowments, so that some can win races and turn in performances of which they would not normally be thought capable.

Lucky are they who have developed their physical potential hand in hand with their personality and who can take part for the sheer physical and psychological pleasure it brings. No doubt many more, both men and women, would be in that happy position if some of society's present misconceptions and outdated attitudes could be changed.

5.   ROLE COMPATIBILITY

The concept of role is a technical one in social psychology and sociology. Nevertheless, the general idea is a reasonably familiar one. It refers to the whole collection of attributes associated with a particular position in society as distinct from the personal characteristics of the individual who occupies that position. Roles such as those of parent, teacher, doctor, and so forth, are recognized and obviously every individual fulfils several roles in society. In general, we all seek to minimize role incompatibilities and choose our occupations and recreational pursuits accordingly. But some roles we cannot choose and some are so rigidly defined by society as to make changing them or moving from one to another very difficult.

Amongst the most incompatible roles at present are those of the female in society and the sportsperson. In Muslim countries they may be made legislatively incompatible. In Western societies, the role for girls and women is a feminine one – gentle, unassuming, passive and inactive. But, in order to participate successfully in sport, females must possess a high degree of competitiveness, aggressiveness and achievement motivation. They must demonstrate endurance and be able to take risks. But these are very largely the traits which define the male role. Many adolescent girls find the conflict between the feminine and the sporting roles too difficult to handle and drop out of competitive sport.

It is therefore necessary to recognize that in addition to all the physical and psychological attributes required, women athletes at least require the ability to reconcile or ignore a major role incompatibility.

In some societies, the roles attached to particular classes or ethnic groups are almost as sharply defined and many contribute to similar incompatibilities in at least some sports. The relative absence of American blacks or Australian migrants from some sports, the very few working class equestrians, yachtsmen, rally drivers, and so forth, are examples. The encouragement and great success of blacks in many areas of British sport is an example of a slightly different sort. Many claim that the role of academic success in school excludes black youth and hence they are being encouraged into activities which, for the majority, are of low social status and will bring fewer material rewards than more academic pursuits.

These examples, some of which are examined in other contexts in later pages, underline the significance of role compatibility for men and women in their various sporting activities. The subject is considered in more detail in chapter seven in the section on patterns of socialization.

Top left. The final of the 200 metres at the 1948 London Olympics. The great Fanny Blankers-Koehn is seen leading the field part way through the race. This event gave her one of her four gold medals from these games. The rather poor state of the cinder track in these wet conditions is apparent. The shorts and singlets then deemed acceptable also leave something to be desired for sprinters. The provision of all-weather tracks and general improvement of clothes and equipment are among the many factors which have contributed to improvement of times in the last thirty years. (Credit: Allsport Photographic.) **Bottom left.** The United States women's 4 x 100 metres relay team at the 1968 Mexico Olympics, Wyomia Tyus, Edith Maguire, Iris Davis and Martha Watson. From the time of Wilma Rudolph at the 1960 Olympics, most of the American sprinters have been black and members of the Tennessee Tiger Belles. Tennessee University was for a long time the only institution to offer athletics scholarships. Sport was (and is) one of the few avenues of advancement open to blacks in the USA. Might there also be genetic reasons for the prominence of blacks in sprint events? (Credit: Allsport Photographic.) **Top right.** L. Radke of Germany winning the 800 metres from K. Hitomi of Japan in the 1928 Olympics, the first year in which there was a women's track and field programme (see pages 123–24). Just after this photograph was taken, some of the women collapsed on the track, after they finished. Because of this the event was removed from the women's programme until 1960. (Credit: Central Press Agency.) *Bottom right.* Although the 1500 metres remained until 1980 the longest women's Olympic event, the 3000 metres is well established elsewhere. Ulmasova of the Soviet Union is here seen leading Greta Waitz of Norway and Maracescu of Romania in the 1978 European Games 3000 metres. Waitz as well as being the top 3000 metres runner in recent years, was also world champion crosscountry runner 1980–81 and has been the fastest woman marathoner since 1978. Eastern European women, so successful in nearly every other branch of sport, have hitherto been almost totally absent from events longer than 3000 metres. (Credit: Allsport/Tony Duffy.)

The Social, Material and Cultural Requirements of Successful Sporting Performance

To achieve success in any sport individuals must have the right biological endowments and the mental and personality attributes to utilize them. But they must also have equipment and facilities with which to train and develop their skills. Swimmers must have pools in which to train all year; skaters must have rinks; rowers must have boats and suitable stretches of water; skiers must have snow, and so on.

They all need coaches who can unite ability and training with the very best facilities, to produce optimum performances. These coaches must understand physiology, psychology and the mechanical demands of their sport. They must train their charges hard, but not too hard or too often. They must arrange competition to stretch them, but not demoralize them. In general they must be both demanding and supportive without being either dictatorial or paternal — a major task indeed.

But before champions and top performers can use these coaches and facilities, they must make a start in sport. There must be opportunities and graded series of standards and competitions at school and in the community for youngsters to begin and have their potential recognized. All this requires planning and the provision of large amounts of money and resources by government and/or non-government organizations.

But even all this is not enough. Sport, more than every today, must have its place in national identity and its heroes for the young to model themselves on. One superstar can be the inspiration for a generation of competitors to follow. Rugby players are idolized in Wales and New Zealand; chess players are feted and hero-worshipped in Russia; soccer players in Brazil, cyclists in France, swimmers in Australia, boxers in Cuba and so on. Sportsmen (and to a lesser extent sportswomen) can win awards, privileges and enormous financial rewards through prizes and advertising endorsements. A rowing, rugby or cricket blue from Oxford or Cambridge universities was, and maybe still is in some areas, better for employment prospects in the United Kingdom than a first class honours degree from those universities. In the USA success in sport has been one reasonably sure way that blacks could increase both their social status and their earning potential. In Eastern European countries sporting prowess is one of the best ways to receive an education, priority for housing and the opportunity to travel. The influence of all this on the impressionable young is undoubtedly profound.

The financial returns possible from some sports are now so great that in many countries there have been enormous private investments in tracks, stadia, and pools, and individuals and teams to play in them. These investments bring profits from entrance fees, television rights, sponsorship, advertising franchises and the buying and selling of the players themselves.

In other countries similar investments have been made, but by governments for basically political reasons. The political gains have been both international — victories, medals and so forth, translating into national prestige — and domestic, the deflection or stifling altogether of criticism, complaints and political opposition.

In yet other countries there has been relatively little investment in sport by either government or commercial entrepreneurs. Sportsmen and women of these countries, true amateurs with amateur facilities, have to compete against state or privately financed professionals in international competition.

Sport has increased enormously in importance since the end of World War II in many countries. As affluence spreads and people come to enjoy higher standards of living and shorter working hours, the numbers involved with sport, either as spectators or participants, rise. There is often a belief by those in power that sport is a good thing for their peoples, for their international image and, if successful, likely to aid in keeping them in power. Whatever the reason, the importance of sport in the fabric of most modern societies is increasing.

To repeat: the vast increase in both watching and participating in sport in recent decades has led inevitably to a preoccupation with money. Promoters and advertisers have seen an opportunity to reach an enormous mass audience at relatively very little cost. Participants have seen a way to make very large sums of money, either above board or under the counter. And governments, enthusiastically or otherwise, have felt the need to support sport financially.

The first social and community requirement for successful sport is therefore money and everything it can buy.

1. FINANCIAL PROVISION AND FINANCIAL INCENTIVES

In almost all the developed and many of the developing countries of the world, governments provide money and a greater or lesser degree of administrative regulation for sport. Directly or indirectly, money is provided to schools for sports fields, gymnasia and swimming pools, there are national and local subsidies for sporting complexes, grants to individual sports associations for equipment, travel, coaching and so forth. The actual sums involved, however, vary enormously from country to country.

At the time of the Montreal Olympics, Canada gave over $30 million a year to sports organizations, which represented about $1.50 per head of population. The UK gave $25 million or so, a little less than fifty cents a head. One of the highest levels of financial support for sport in western countries is that of Austria. It has a population of about eight million and in 1978 passed legislation permitting $60 million a year to be spent on sports. It will be interesting to follow the progress of Austrian men and women in world sports in the near future. The government of one of the erstwhile strongest sporting nations of the world, Australia, gave about $1.3 million to sport, or about nine cents a head, in 1976. There has been bitter debate over this in Australia and much comparison between Canadian and Australian performances at recent Olympic and Commonwealth Games.

In 1956 Australia won thirty-six Olympic medals including thirteen golds and was third in the unofficial national points championship behind USA and USSR. In 1976 Australia won only five medals, none of which was gold, and was thirty-second on the national ranking list. In 1956 Canada won three golds and seven medals overall to finish seventeenth on the list of nations. In 1976 Canada won eleven medals maintaining its position of seventeenth overall, despite much increased opposition from Eastern Europe and African nations. In the 1978 Commonwealth Games Canada headed the list of medal winning countries for the first time, winning a record number of gold medals. England was second and Australia a surprising third. Much has been made of these changes of fortune and their relationship to government financial support. Some at least must be due to these different levels of funding.

In many countries including Canada, Britain, Denmark, West Germany, the Netherlands and Russia, national sports lotteries are run to provide some of the money for sport. In what is still the most affluent country of all, however, and arguably still the world's most successful sporting nation, the USA, money still comes largely from private enterprise channelled through universities and colleges and the major football and baseball leagues. Some of the major stadia in the USA are publicly financed by city authorities, but the relucance of the Los Angeles City Council to underwrite the costs of the 1984 Olympics emphasizes the limited influence of government funding. Some state and federal money is used to finance state university facilities, which does give these governments some limited say in policy making. But considerable controversies have arisen when government has attempted to intervene and influence the way its money is spent. For example, the United States Congress passed an Education Amendment Act in 1972, one of the provisions of which sought to prohibit sex discrimination under any educational programme receiving any federal money. Six years later that was still being fought through the courts as male dominated sports organizations protested at what they claimed were its likely catastrophic effects on American sports funding.

Many commercially sponsored sports such as baseball, cricket, football (in its numerous codes), cycling, motor racing and basketball are virtually restricted to one or a few countries, are largely male dominated or both. But golf and tennis, primarily because of their televisual qualities, have become enormously popular with spectators and hence advertisers and sponsors almost the world over. There are enormous sums of money to be won by both men and women in these sports, although they each show a more than twofold difference between the earning potential of men and of women. Jack Nicklaus was the top money winner on the United States PGA Circuit in 1976 winning $266,438. Twenty-two men earned more than $100,000. The leading woman prize winner in 1976 on the PGA circuit was Judy Rankin who won $110,614. The top ten tennis players can win up to $500,000, whereas only a handful of women can expect to win more than $100,000 a year.

The need for continued commercial sponsorship if such winnings are to be maintained is obvious. Tennis was one of the first sports in which women's prize money rose to significant levels. But this is a recent phenomenon and is probably due to the large proportion of women competitors and to the efforts of players, such as Billie Jean King, who were prepared to be fairly militant to ensure that women's prize money increased as the popularity of tennis itself increased.

In short, commercial sponsors have recognized the advertising potential in sport and have actively used sports promotion as a component of their advertising schedules. The world's leading competitors can become rich through the exploitation of their talents and consequently enormous incentives exist for these competitors to demonstrate the best of their abilities for as long as possible.

Such sponsorship, usually at a much more modest financial level, is now being given to some women's sports and has undoubtedly been responsible, not only for a rise in standards in the sports involved, but a change in the status of and attitudes to women's sport. The sheer amounts of publicity and television exposure which some top sportswomen now receive emphasizes their professionalism, ability, and hard work as well as their handsome rewards, and yet shows they still retain their essential femininity.

A further significant contributor to the earnings of sportsmen and women are contracts to wear or use a particular brand of sporting goods. For professionals the prize money from such tournaments as Wimbledon, the British Open Golf Championship or the Tour de France is only a start. The commercial endorsements flowing out of victories or eyecatching performance at such events are usually far more lucrative. For amateurs the commercial endorsements have to be less overt and many payments are "under the counter", but they may be very important. Companies will pay handsomely to ensure that their particular trademark or logo on racquet, ski, shirt, or shoe appears on the television screen, particularly if attached to a winner.

At Mexico City, for example, there was a considerable stir over illegal payments to athletes after an unidentified United States athlete discovered ten crisp $50 bills in his running shoes. The United States Olympic Committee reported that eight or ten athletes cashed traveller's cheques for up to $7500 whilst in Mexico. Although the origin of these cheques was traced to West German banks, it could not be determined who provided them. It also seems that such payments were made to athletes from virtually all countries.

For men at least there are other important ways to make money from amateur athletics. The two main sources hitherto have been the United States indoor circuit in the northern winter and the European outdoor circuit in the northern summer. These meetings are very popular and attract relatively large crowds and commercial sponsorship. The major meetings in these circuits are run by professional promoters who have no qualms about making surreptitious payments to ensure that star athletes compete. A world ranked distance runner can attract a fee of $1000 or more, plus expenses (which may include saleable pairs of first class air tickets), for a single appearance. It is not uncommon for a top amateur to be making in excess of $20,000 per year from participating in such meetings. Although this is small in comparison to golf and tennis earnings, as a tax free bonus it represents a considerable spur to top athletes to continue at their best for as many years as possible, and for those not yet at the top it is an enormous incentive to try and make it.

Very few women's events have been included in these meetings. The financial incentives to top women athletes have been small in the past and are still very small compared to those available to men.

2. NATIONAL AND POLITICAL MOTIVATION

The huge audience for international sport has also been recognized by those who have political aims they wish to advance. One example of this was the invasion of the Olympic village in Munich by an Arab terrorist (or freedom) group. Their acts took place in front of a world-wide television audience, and although probably few agreed with their ultimate acts of murder, their determination and their cause were put sensationally and indelibly before all who were watching. There are other examples. The boycott of all events in which South Africa takes part, or even countries who have sporting links with South Africa, is one. The refusal of many countries to play in Israel is another. The black power salute given by black American medal winners at a presentation ceremony in Mexico in 1968 is yet another. Most recently the United States led boycott of the 1980 Moscow Olympics in response to the USSR's political activities in Afghanistan seemed at one stage to have put the whole future of the Olympic movement at stake.

The use of sport and sporting organizations to further political aims is not new. Although the Nazis' first verdict on the Olympics was that it was an "infamous festival dominated by Jews", Hitler and his propaganda chiefs soon realized the immense propaganda potential of the event. Huge state support was therefore provided so that the 1936 Berlin Games should be the biggest and best ever and the German team should be the most successful. The glory in either case, real or imagined, was intended for the Third Reich. (The German team, incidentally, did "win" the 1936 Games.) The cost of staging the Games has continued to increase as ever more lavish facilities are provided in order to enhance the host nation's international prestige.

There are other ways of using international sport for political gain. The classical example is East Germany, which has put an enormous effort into the production of world sports champions. Their attitude is exemplified by the remarks made by the then chairman of the Council of State, Walter Ulbrich, shortly before the first East German team (as opposed to a combined German team) left for the 1968 Mexico Olympics. He said: "Sport is part of the human image in a socialist society. The sports activities of millions of people are a vivid expression of the humanist cultural policy of our socialist state. Sport facilitates the development of young people into personalities with an all round education and the recreation of adults through sports and games improves their health and joy in life, their efficiency and life expectancy."[1] The East Germans maintain that their sporting successes demonstrate the superiority of their political and social system. The rest of the world may frown on or positively abhor some of their methods, but the East Germans themselves believe that they are fulfilling Baron de Coubertin's Olympic ideal. To quote Ulbrich again: "We think that each individual has a right to sport and that it is up to the community to provide, if possible free of charge, such facilities to the adult citizen that enable him to acquire and conserve physical fitness. In doing so he should not be required to adhere to any association or club." This, the East Germans say, is safeguarded by their 1968 constitution, which is probably the first in the world to guarantee the right to sport. Article 18 says that "Physical culture, sport and tourism as elements of socialist culture, go to the all round physical and mental development of the citizens". Article 25 says that "The state and society encourage the participation of citizens in cultural life, physical culture and sport, for the complete expression of the socialist personality and for the fulfillment of cultural interests and needs". Their achievements have been quite astonishing, nowhere more so than in their performances in the Olympic Games in 1968 and thereafter. East Germany is now the third highest medal winner in the whole history of the Olympics, having overtaken countries like Britain and France whose populations are three times the size and which have competed since 1896!

The East Germans believed that the standard of women's sport throughout the world was low in relation to its potential and so they have concentrated on its development. In 1976 in Montreal, East German women won 55.7 per cent of their country's medals compared with an average of 24.1 per cent for all nations (see table 4). In 1980 they won 51 per cent. The dominance of women was particularly apparent in track and field athletics and swimming, two sports in which high level performances can be greatly assisted by rigorous scientifically based training programmes and the provision of high class facilities. Whatever their constitution might say it is clear that East German involvement in sport is aimed to a very great extent at the production of world and Olympic champions. Many events popular with women in other parts of the world,

Table 4. Distribution of men's and women's medals, Montreal, 1976.

	USSR	USA	GDR	Others	All Nations
Men	89	77	39	257	462
Women	36	17	49	45	147
TOTAL	125	94	88	302	609
Women %	28.8	18.1	55.7	14.9	24.1

but for which at the moment there is little international competition, such as marathon running and 1500 metre swimming, hardly occur in East Germany at present.

Russia, too, has used sport for political purposes. Their interest and involvement in sport is clearly motivated by political goals as is shown by a recent editorial in the magazine *Sport in the USSR*.

> The Soviet Union's impressive socio-economic strides are illustrated by the advances in physical education and health protection. All the prerequisites for making today's citizen strong, healthy and active now exist in our country . . . But only 60 years ago the overwhelming majority of Russia's population knew nothing at all about physical fitness. Sport was a privilege of the idle rich.
>
> At the Stockholm Olypics of 1912 the Russian team finished near the bottom of the table in the unofficial points, scoring 15th out of a total of 18 countries. This indicates the sad state of physical education and sport in Russia five years before the Great October Socialist Revolution. At the Munich Olympic Games of 1972, five years ago, Soviet athletes won 50 gold medals out of a total of 196; they outstripped all their rivals by a big margin in the unofficial points tally. The groundwork for these victories was laid long ago in the early Soviet years when the young socialist republic proclaimed its policy of promoting the health of the population and built the foundation of the world's first programme of physical education for all.[2]

The dominance of Eastern European women in general in many sports is quite astonishing — not just in the occurrence of a few stars, but in depth of talent. By January 1978 112 women had run 800 metres faster than 2.00 minutes. Their distribution by country was as follows:

East Germany	38
USSR	28
Bulgaria	21
Romania	9
N. Korea	3
West Germany	3
USA	3
France	2
Australia	2
Yugoslavia	2
Poland	2

Eighty-seven per cent of the women were from Eastern Europe. At the beginning of 1978 the American magazine *Women's Track and Field World* published a list of the ten best performers of all time in the fourteen standard individual women's track and field events. The situation they disclosed is shown in table 5.

Table 5. Best performers in individual women's track and field events.

Best Performers (140)		World Records (14)
East Germany	44	4
USSR	38	6
USA	12	1
West Germany	11	—
Bulgaria	8	—
Romania	7	—
Poland	6	1
Finland	3	—

No other country had more than two women in the list of best performers and Czechoslovak and Italian women held the other world records. In all, East European women held seventy-five per cent of the top performer places and eighty-six per cent of the world records.

In the 1978 European athletics championships Eastern European women took fifteen out of sixteen gold medals, twelve out of sixteen silver medals and fourteen out of sixteen bronze medals, a total of thirty-nine out of forty-eight or eighty-one per cent. East Germany's share was seven gold, six silver, and seven bronze or twenty out of forty-eight, forty-one per cent of all medals. Eastern Europe's domination in depth of other sports including swimming, gymnastics, rowing and others is just as great, as will be documented in later chapters.

The linking of sport and national politics in Cuba is more direct than in any other country. In the late 1950s and early 1960s Cuba wanted to take part in international sport in order to publicize the new Fidel Castro regime and to beat the economic blockade which the USA had in force at the time. In 1960 Cuba came fifty-third of all the participant nations in the unofficial points total and did not win a single medal. Its progression since then has been dramatic, as shown in table 6.

These successes have been achieved through carefully planned coaching along Eastern European lines in a variety of sports. Cuban authorities are certain that they will in future produce great Negro swimmers, as well as great athletes and boxers, despite assertions by sports physiologists that Negroes will never be champion swimmers. They have already gone part of the way by producing one of the five best water polo teams in the world (taking fifth place in the 1980 Olympics).

Table 6. Cuban performance in Olympic Games 1964-80.

Olympiad	Medals Won			Position
	Gold	Silver	Bronze	
Tokyo 1964	0	1	0	42nd
Mexico 1968	0	0	0	23rd
Munich 1972	3	1	18	13th
Montreal 1976	6	4	3	8th
Moscow 1980	10	6	6	3rd

What is particularly interesting about Cuba is that their sporting facilities are as yet neither lavish nor numerous. Cuba possesses few community recreation or leisure centres, few swimming pools outside the pre-revolutionary hotels, no velodrome, ice rink, regattabahn, or indoor diving pool. They possess only one all-weather polyurethane athletic track. Cuba is certainly planning comprehensive sports facilities but their present facilities are mostly elementary or even primitive. The Cuban sports authorities have put their emphasis so far mainly on coaching and sports medicine and, perhaps as important, have ensured that successful sportsmen and women receive national recognition and hero-worship.

In common with the other communist countries, Cuba's sports programmes are ostensibly aimed as much at women as at men. In 1960 its Olympic team was only 12 and there were no women. Its 1976 team of 158 included 28 women. No Cuban women have yet broken any world records in athletics but they had women among the top twenty performers in the world in 1978 in the 100, 200, 400, 4 x 100 and 4 x 400 metres, and javelin. Cuban men were in the top twenty performers in the 100 and 200 metres (Silvio Leonard), 400 and 800 metres (Alberto Juantorena), 110 metres hurdles and triple jump. Women have therefore perhaps a slight edge in achievement in world class athletics.

In many communist and non-communist countries sport has been encouraged as a public health measure. Recreational sport has been seen as an effective counter to many of the so-called diseases of affluence — obesity, heart disease and so on — and it has therefore been actively supported by many governments.

"Sports are the greatest of all preventative medicines. We are struggling to train enough doctors, to build enough hospitals. Until we do and even after, staying well is our biggest goal and athletics are the best pill." So says Manuel Gonzales, director of the Cuban Olympic Committee. Of Cuba's northern neighbour he says: "America's whole Olympic organisation is a disgrace. The world laughs at you. In Montreal the States finished third. If you are not careful you will sink even lower . . . ".[3] Comments such as these on sport as preventive medicine undoubtedly represent the viewpoints of many governments and sports administrators around the world. Unfortunately in many cases the programmes they run *are* an administrative and financial disgrace. Nevertheless the positive encouragement of women athletes represents an important change.

3. PLANNING FOR SUCCESS

With so much at stake, financially, politically and socially, it is hardly surprising that in recent years some countries have adopted well organized and planned approaches to sport at all levels. In these countries the production of sporting champions is no longer left to chance, it has become the objective of extremely sophisticated nationwide programmes. The importance of these national programmes is not that they can guarantee the success of any individual, but that they can enable a large number of individuals to attain the maximum of which they are capable, and can increase the likelihood that some highly successful individuals will be found from any reasonably large group of participants. In most cases these national programmes have been designed for and applied to men and women more or less equally, and, although the reality does not usually match up to the intention, the implications of this for the relative improvement of women are profound.

What contributes to a national's sporting success? The first answer is usually population size. It is argued that the greater the number of competitors in a given sport the better will be the performances of those at the top. At first sight this seems an attractive explanatory theory, which explains the success of the USA and the USSR since World War II as their populations of 208 million and 165 million respectively would provide enormous bases of mass participation. The corollary is that any nation wishing to increase the standard of its sport can do so simply by increasing the number of participants.

The underlying assumptions of this belief are that talent is evenly distributed amongst the population and that any increase in numbers of participants automatically increases the pool of talented performers. Even if these assumptions were true, a programme based on increasing the numbers of participants whilst aiming for high level performances must be extremely wasteful and even counter-productive. A lot of time and resources must be spent on training and running competitions for a large number of modest performers in order to unearth just a few champions. This must be counter-productive if coaches and facilities are limited.

It is now recognized, especially in Eastern Europe, that a key element in any national sporting programme is the early identification and isolation of talented individuals. Available resources can then be concentrated in order to give them maximum benefit. Such a system would be based on as wide a level of participation as possible at the junior level, so that specific evaluation techniques can be used to identify talented individuals and channel them towards the sport or event to which they are best suited. In this way, the best resources can be concentrated on the best performers and so maximum efficiency can be achieved in producing world champions and record breakers.

Talent identification among juniors, therefore, represents the first step in any organized programme for sports development. The top level performers in world sport make up a highly selected group of athletes, particularly in the individual sports such as track and field, swimming, cycling, weight-lifting and the high performance team sports such as rowing. World champions in these sports must possess a high level of innate abilities, must have undergone an extensive training programme tailored to their individual requirements and must have remained relatively free from injury. There is no guaranteed way of making any individual, no matter what his or her physical or psychological make-up might be, into a world champion. Nevertheless, a systematic programme of sports development can ensure that the likelihood of producing world champions from a group of competitors is much enhanced.

Recent policies and achievements of Canada, Cuba and East Germany have already been discussed. Finland is another country in which a high level of success has followed major reorganization and careful planning. After a dismal showing in the European Athletics Championships in 1966 at which for the first time ever they failed to win a medal, a complete restructuring and reorganization of sport was undertaken. New young administrators replaced the old, and systematic financial and logistic support for their stars was introduced. These changes were so successful that Finland rose from twenty-fifth nation in the unofficial list at the 1968 Olympics to sixth at Munch in 1972. Not only did this scheme produce such men champions as Lasse Viren in the 5000 and 10,000 metres and Pekka Vasala in the 1500 metres but it also resulted in the acceptance of female athletes who had previously been regarded as second-rate competitors. For example, Tapani Jeka admits that he only coached Riitta Salin because her husband Ari, the Finnish 400 metres hurdles record holder, insisted. Riitta then won the 1974 European 400 metres championship in Rome with a time of 50.14. Nina Holmen who won the 3000 metres in Rome in a time of 8:55.2 just two days before Riitta Salin's success, was the first Finnish woman to place higher than sixth at the championships. She became a great favourite with Finnish crowds who previously thought that women running such distances were "abnormal". The newly generated interest in women's track and field paid quick dividends as their women were eighth at Munich in 1972 and won four medals at the European championships two years later.

The examples of Canada, Cuba, East Germany, Finland, Russia and others show how important are a systematic approach to sporting development and the right social environment in producing world rank sportsmen and women. Experience has shown that a successful programme must include at least the following:

- a system of talent search to identify gifted performers and guide them into the sport to which they are best suited;

- a systematic programme of training and classification to ensure that all coaches are well versed in all aspects of their work;
- comprehensive and rapid dissemination of the latest findings of scientific research in a usable form to coaches and sports scientists;
- a sports medical organization to monitor athletes' training programmes and assist in the prevention and cure of injuries;
- a system of training stipends or employment to allow sportsmen and women to undertake the rigorous and time consuming training programmes required for top level competition without excessive financial hardship;
- adequate facilities available for training to all those who require them;
- a carefully chosen programme of international competition to give competitors experience at an appropriate level before they are exposed to the stresses of and unreasonable expectations in major international meetings;
- above all an efficient administrative structure to ensure that the above requirements are achieved and maintained.

4. TALENT SEARCH

The levels of performance required from international sportsmen and women are now so high that they can only be achieved by individuals who have undergone a lengthy period of training, often extending over a period of several years. Potential champions must therefore be selected and their training begun before the age best suited for optimal performances in that sport and before physical development is complete. The process of making this selection is therefore very complex and no method can guarantee success. The actual procedures for identifying champions have to be extremely thorough to have any usefulness. In East Germany, for example, the following tests are carried out on children aged between eight and twelve:

- bone x-rays (for prediction of final body size);
- ECG (indicates natural cariovascular endurance);
- anthropometric measurement and somatyping (to allow scientific selection and prediction of body types suitable for particular events);
- pulse rate (to indicate cardiovascular efficiency);
- muscle strength (for example a quadriceps extension test);
- a speed endurance run;
- running style (to indicate natural aptitude for running);
- muscle biopsy (to assess muscle structure);
- a blood test (to assess physiological parameters);
- oxygen uptake;
- range of motion (to assess flexibility);

- skinfold measures (for body fat) and immersion testing;
- capillarization;
- general health;
- personality (measurement of the attitudes and psychological traits favourable to particular events);
- intelligence.

In short, virtually all the biological requirements for high sporting performance are examined. From age eight youngsters scoring highly on these tests and displaying special talent for one or more sports are directed into special sports schools.

In Eastern Europe there is a high degree of co-ordination between the education system, local and national governments, trade unions and industry, and health and recreation institutions. In Russia, for example, overall direction is provided by the USSR Sports Committee whose job it is to see that the entire system of physical education is based on the principal of uniformity and continuity of all links in the system. A detailed physical education syllabus for every nursery, school and college in the USSR is laid down by the USSR Ministry of Education, and all schools are given targets in terms of the sports standards to which it is hoped their children will aspire.

Young people in Russia who wish to pursue a sport seriously after school hours may do so in one of several specialized sports establishments. But they can also attend a full-time sports school from the age of seven which combines a normal school curriculum with sports training. Above these schools come sports proficiency schools and above them higher sports proficiency schools. At the apex of this pyramid is the sports boarding school.

In 1960 in Russia there were about fifteen hundred sports schools with about half a million children in them. By 1975 there were nearly five thousand schools with nearly one and three quarter million children. Their aim is to use the best of the limited facilities available to give special and intensive coaching to young people in a particular sport. A 1966 government resolution stressed that these are "special sports institutions and are intended to train highly qualified athletes". The specialized gymnastics schools, for example, admit boys and girls from seven onwards who are expected to pass from novice to master in six or seven years.

The chief targets for the schools' members are the Olympic sports. Of the thirty-three sports pursued in the schools in 1966 only six were outside the Olympic programme at that time, acrobatics, calisthenics, chess, handball, table tennis and tennis. Handball has subsequently been included. Children are considered for a sports school on the recommendation of their school physical education instructor or at the request of their parents. Attendance and coaching are free. Most of the schools take children at age eleven although swimmers and gymnasts may start at seven and cyclists and skaters may not start until thirteen.

The first sports boarding school was opened in Russia in 1962 modelled on similar schools established ten years earlier in East Germany. They are similar to other special boarding schools (for cultivating mathematical, musical and other artistic talents) in adhering to the standard Soviet curriculum for ordinary schools. But they have an additional study load in sports theory and practice and are normally very well equipped with gymnasia, indoor swimming pools, athletics stadia and courts and fields for a variety of games.

The East German sports schools take children from the age of eight onwards. Selected children are not forced into these schools but their parents are usually persuaded that it is an honour to have their children attend, and if necessary arrangements are made for the family to move to an apartment and jobs close by. Students board at the school and pursue a study schedule organized around their training programmes. More time is provided for PE and sport than at the average school and there is more constant interscholastic competition. Students are provided with tutors and excellent medical attention. They must show steady improvement if their enrolment is to be maintained. For example, if a fourteen-year old runs 4.15 for 1500 metres he might be expected to run 4.06 at fifteen. If such progress is not maintained he is transferred to a normal school where he can continue running at a more recreational level.

The rationale behind such schools is the conviction that talent in sport, as in art, music and mathematics, has to be nurtured. This encompasses training in special skills as well as general fitness training. It is regarded as natural and advantageous to bring together children of particular and specialized skills in sport in a controlled environment at a residential school. They can be served by the best coaches and amenities, given special diets, be constantly under the supervision of doctors and sports instructors and stimulated by mutual interest and enthusiasm. Early specialization, especially in sports such as athletics, swimming and gymnastics is regarded as essential to the attainment of high standards and success in present-day international competition. In accord with both their written constitutions and their unwritten objectives there is virtually no sex discrimination in most of the talent search schemes of Eastern European countries.

Only in Eastern Europe (and perhaps Cuba) are such intensive talent search and training schemes being practised. The United States has its age group swimming programmes and well organized university and college sports programmes. But there is no national strategy involved; each college and university is in competition with every other and although the coaches have vast budgets and well developed support resources in terms of gymnasia, training facilities, scientific advice and so forth, the whole programme is geared to the making of money. Every university's director of athletics must balance his budget, he must fill his football, baseball and basketball stadia, the pool and the track.

Since women do not normally play American football or baseball and since women's teams with but very rare exceptions cannot fill basketball or athletic stadia, the financial and material support for women's sport in the

USA has always been very much lower than for men. Women have had long and bitter battles through state and federal courts to try and obtain anything like equality of treatment in those sports they do compete in. In many sports up until ten or fifteen years ago women were not so much discriminated against as just ignored altogether, largely because of the financial and social structure of much sport in America.

Talent search schemes in most other countries are quite rudimentary or non-existent. Canada, West Germany, Great Britain and others are trying to initiate such schemes, of varying degrees of efficiency and comprehensiveness. In most Asian and African countries they are non-existent. One wonders what achievements men and women from these countries might be capable of if they were chosen and trained on scientific bases from a sufficiently early age to enable them to develop their full potential.

5. COACHING AND COMPETITION

It is now rare to find any self-coached athletes at the top of the sporting hierarchy. In many sports success depends on a careful blend of training and competition, and the coach is the person responsible for producing this blend so that athletes can produce their best at major international meetings. Throughout Europe and America the central role of coaches has been recognized and sophisticated training courses have been established for them, although the length and rigour of these courses varies markedly from country to country. For example, any sports coach in the Soviet Union or East Germany must have undertaken a four-year degree course, whereas the minimum length of training required in most western countries is between 120 and 150 hours.

In Eastern Europe coaching has become a thorough, carefully planned exercise which integrates many of the components necessary for success in any sport. In Russia top performers in high performance sports have urine and blood samples analyzed, electrocardiographs taken and so on, every forty-eight hours during the competitive season. It is considered that the coach cannot coach properly without this information. This presupposes, of course, not only that the coach can get the information but that he can understand it. There has to be, therefore, a close working relationship between coaches and sports scientists and much effort is expended by sports authorities to see that it exists. The coach has a team of specialists including experts in biology, bio-mechanics, psychology, physiology, sports medicine and so on ready to assist in analyzing and suggesting solutions to any problems which might arise. The progress of any athlete is carefully monitored by such teams and if necessary training programmes are adjusted according to their recommendations.

The success of the coach also depends on his knowledge of the particular sport, its special requirements and its particular teaching methods. Hence coaches' training courses include specific components directed at individual requirements and any active coach has a continual stream of information available with which he is expected to keep himself familiar. Also available are banks of data on the strengths and weaknesses of opponents and rivals of his own athletes. For example, East Germany's prime hope for the 1976 Olympic marathon, Waldemar Cierpinski, was told by his coach that American Frank Shorter was likely to initiate a series of hard surges about midway through the race. He did so, in fact, at twenty-three kilometres! To what extent information of this sort contributed to Cierpinksi's win in the Montreal marathon is, of course, impossible to tell, but it certainly all helped.

The role of the coach is now so important that many countries take large numbers to major international meetings. The Soviet team had seventy-three coaches at the Montreal Olympics, East Germany had twenty-two, Canada had fifty, Cuba had twenty-five and Poland had thirty-one. In contrast to these countries, all of which had relatively advanced sports support programmes, the number of coaches named by the USA was three, France two, Great Britain one and West Germany four. The presence of individual coaches in any official capacity was clearly not considered important by these latter countries, although it is possible that some were included in the team officials. No doubt also many personal coaches were able to be present in some "unofficial" way.

Despite the immense concentration on coaching in many countries with scientific preparation, scientific aids and all the back-up facilities now provided, the ultimate relationship between coach and athlete remains an almost mystic one. Franz Stampfl, one time coach to Oxford University and associated with the planning of the first four-minute mile, wrote: "The coach's job is twenty per cent technical and eighty per cent inspirational. He may know all there is to know about tactics, technique and training, but if he cannot win the confidence and comradeship of his pupils he will never be a good coach." He described the coach as " . . . guide, philosopher and friend, counsellor and confessor, a prop at times of mental tension."[4] Mary Peters, writing of her relationship with her coach, Buster McShane, at a crucial point during the 1972 Olympic pentathlon said: "It can be quite uncanny this relationship between coach and athlete, but his confidence flooded into me. He knew every thought and doubt that had been going through my mind and it was suddenly as though his brain had been supplanted into mine."[5] It is doubtful if this sort of human chemistry can be investigated or understood in any meaningful way by anything we currently understand as science. It re-emphasizes, though, the importance of human factors in sporting achievement.

Most of the famous coaches, Cerutty, Lydiard, Stampfl, Tabori, van Aaken in athletics, Talbot, Counsilman, Carlisle in swimming and all the team sports coaches have been men. Indeed in most countries the number of women coaches is very low. Van Aaken is showing what he can achieve with women long distance runners and most swimming coaches will coach women. Franz Stampfl's careful coaching of some Australian girls is now bearing fruit and Mary Peters recounts how much she owes to her coach, Buster McShane. But until most prominent men coaches are as willing to coach women as men, or until outstanding women coaches emerge, women will suffer a marked, if indeterminate, disadvantage in striving for supreme performance. The lack of women coaches probably also reduces the number of women taking up and continuing in high level sport, but again by how much is not known. Unfortunately, many men coaches still have Percy Cerutty's attitudes to sportswomen:

> Any sport for women should have been kept to the Victorian era when nobody took it seriously. Their efforts are ridiculous and sometimes lowering when compared with the performances of men.
>   There is no place for women today in the hard competitive grind of competition like the Commonwealth, Olympic or European Games. Women running, jumping or throwing was all right when it was the province of schoolgirls.[6]

These remarks were made in the early 1960s!

The importance of coaching and competition is very evident in a country like Australia which is not overendowed with either. In Australia there are a small number of very knowledgeable and competent sports coaches. But many have gone abroad and these have left enormous gaps in all sports. In track and field athletics the deficiencies have become glaringly obvious in recent years, most noticeably in field events.

Australia has no national coach or coaches training scheme and all coaches are amateurs. A National Coaches Association was formed in 1975 supported by the Rothman's National Sports Foundation but as yet it has failed to gain recognition by the Australian Athletic Union (AAU). It has however instituted a national coaches training and accreditation scheme, the results of which should become apparent in the near future. There is an urgent need for Australian coaches to travel overseas in order to gain experience with the world's best coaches, so that new ideas and methods can be brought back to Australia, and for international coaches to be brought to Australia to provide courses for locals. The amateur status of Australian coaches makes this very difficult since it is so expensive and so difficult to arrange the necessary rather lengthy periods of time off work. The result is that Australian coaches cannot keep abreast of the latest technical developments in coaching. There are, incidentally, few women members of the Australian National Coaches Association, although the AAU has just appointed a woman as first technical director of coaching.

One of the problems of distant countries such as Australia, or countries just beginning international athletics, is that it often seems pointless sending low standard athletes to major international competitions such as Olympic, Commonwealth or area games. And so it may be − in the short term. But if no other opportunities exist for international experience there can be little incentive for athletes to improve. They end up in a double bind: their standard is so low that there is little hope of selection in major international teams and since there is little hope of selection then there is no incentive for them to improve. The relative isolation of Australia from the rest of the sporting world and the current impoverished state of Australian sport compounds these difficulties. Men of quite high achievement by world standards are omitted from teams to major games largely for financial reasons. The American indoor and the major European summer meets are available to top class Australian men; Australian women don't even have this opportunity for international travel and competition.

The only possible way out is through dual meets with other countries in which competitors are fielded in every event. At present not even this opportunity exists in Australia nor does it seem likely that it will come about in the near future, despite regular requests for trans-Tasman meets with New Zealand.

Nevertheless, improvements are taking place in Australia, although hardly in a systematic way. Gael Mulhall, for example, lifted her own best performance in the shot put from about 14 metres to a new Commonwealth record of 17.68 metres at the Commonwealth Games in Edmonton. Her training partner, Beverley Francis, has thrown 16.42 starting from a similar best performance. Gael won the shot in the 1978 Commonwealth Games and was second in the discus, Bev was fifth in the shot. None of their performances were good enough for the top ten women's performances during 1978 however.

These two throwers are being trained by Franz Stampfl at Melbourne University. They are undertaking a lot of weight training and have achieved weightlifting feats which would be beyond the ability of most men. On 7 October 1978 at the Victorian power lifting championships three Australian girls, no less, broke the women's power lifting record. Pam Mathews, primarily a javelin thrower, bench pressed 95 kilograms as did Gael Mulhall. Bev Francis bench pressed 107.5 kilograms. The previous record held by Cindy Reinhardt of the USA was 92.96 kilograms.

These girls have available to them an able and knowledgeable coach willing to train them, weight training facilities at the university and the best of Australia's competitive conditions and opportunities. Equal advances might be expected in other events if similar fortunate circumstances prevailed.

Selected competition undoubtedly represents a major source of motivation for high performance sportsmen and women. Statistician Richard Szreter analyzed the average performance of the best ten athletes in all track and field events for every year between 1951 and 1961 inclusive and then compared the rate of progress achieved in each year relative to its predecessor.

He found that the three Olympic years headed the list of improvement years and that the post Olympic years fell at the bottom of such rankings. According to his figures shown in table 7 the three Olympic years yielded an "average of averages" improvement of 1.21 per cent compared to the corresponding figure of 0.25 per cent for the other eight years. The average performance level in track and field events improved markedly every Olympic year. The absolutely astonishing athletic season of 1980 in which almost twenty world records were broken is an example of the same phenomenon. The sporting world is steadily

Table 7. Improvements in overall athletic performance 1951-61: percentage improvement in each year over that of previous year (average of ten best performers in each event).

Year		Per Cent Progress
1956	Olympic Year	1.35
1960	Olympic Year	1.25
1952	Olympic Year	1.03
1955		0.79
1954		0.72
1958		0.57
1959		0.27
1953	Post-Olympic Year	0.18
1951		0.05
1957	Post-Olympic Year	−0.16
1961	Post-Olympic Year	−0.44

Source: International Athletics Annual, 1962.

moving to a position in which there are major championships every year (World Cups, World Championships, Spartakiads) in each of which there are gradually increasing opportunities for women. The stimulus for supreme performance is now both greater and more continuous than it has ever been, especially for women.

6. REWARDS AND INCENTIVES

In order to achieve any sort of success in their chosen sport, sportsmen and women have to continue the daily grind of hard work and pain which constitutes training and they have to face up to the stress of competition and the inevitable traumas of occasional failures and defeats. The hard and relentless work that modern training entails is unlikely to be maintained unless the individual concerned has a pleasant and easily accessible place to train, adequate facilities and a competent coach. Without these many will not persevere with hard regular training or will be discouraged by their defeats and failure to progress. In either case they may well drop out of competitive sport before their full potential is reached.

Despite the fact that sports development programmes exist in many countries which provide facilities and coaches, few countries have training centres which are really much more than adequate, certainly not outside the few major cities. And usually the better the competitor, the better the support he or she will get. This means that in a few countries the top athletes will get adequate support and the rest much less than that. In hardly any countries will such facilities be equally available to men and women or have the supervised nurseries which many women athletes require for their young children.

Probably the most important thing about training is the sheer amount of time involved for world class performers. The training schedules of top swimmers and athletes often involve a commitment of up to six hours a day, five or six days a week, often with competition on the non-training days. The time involved alone makes such commitments extremely difficult for someone who has an otherwise normal life to live, centred around family, education, career and so on. Whatever are the physical determinants of swimming ability related to age, one important reason why top swimmers are so young is the virtual impossibility of maintaining their enormous training loads through early adult life.

Gael Mulhall, the Australian and Commonwealth discus and shot put record holder at twenty-two years of age trains for four and a half hours a day as well as holding down a full time job. She gets up at five o'clock every morning and begins training at six o'clock with ninety minutes of running and stretching exercise. She works from eight until noon and then has another ninety minute training session — this time with weights. Work then follows until four-thirty and then another training session until at least six-thirty. Home for a meal and bed by nine o'clock completes the day.

This regime is quite typical in the amount of training undertaken by would-be contenders for international sporting honours. The question is how long will Gael be able to keep up this dedicated regime of heavy training, a full time job and restricted social life? The dropout rate, particularly amongst girls and young women, in sports such as athletics is very high, and Australia has seen a number of very promising athletes discontinue this sort of punishing regime. The demands on young swimmers are, if anything, even greater than young athletes and the "dropout" rate or early retirement among swimmers is correspondingly greater.

Some individuals in western countries who possess a remarkable desire to succeed have managed to find an independent means of support for themselves while devoting their full time efforts to training. One such is current Olympic 800 metres champion and multi-world record breaker Steve Ovett whose parents supported him. But this opportunity is not available to the majority of competitors in amateur sport and there is therefore an urgent need for systematic financial support on an individual basis. In many countries, both communist and non-communist, prominent and promising sportspersons are supported by the state in such positions as student, journalist, policeman or member of the armed forces. Whilst in receipt of a normal income their duties are so arranged that maximum time can be devoted to their training.

Other solutions to the problem include the United States collegiate scholarship system although this has, at least at present, a number of drawbacks. The number and quality of scholarships offered to girls is low; sports facilities outside the colleges are poor and consequently many athletes retire when they finish their college courses, which is often well before they reach their peak. Added to this there is in the USA a social attitude which tends to equate sport with youth and which therefore produces a strong barrier to continued participation into more mature years. Graduate athletes are not eligible for inter-scholastic sport of any kind and generally find very little organized competition outside the professional sports of baseball, basketball, gridiron and tennis. For those who do still compete in amateur sport there is the added expense of paying for the use of training facilities, equipment and medical treatment should that become necessary. In all of these things women are subject to the myriad further frustrations and discriminations which still abound in western societies.

Many western countries have adopted a system of classification of sportsmen and women through which they are directly allocated stipends to cover training expenses. For example, in West Germany a promising sixteen or seventeen-year old athlete may receive a training allowance of about $100 a month and such support continues through into their careers as senior athletes if they in fact make the grade as international performers. Annegret Richter, a record breaking West German sprinter, was believed to be receiving about $60 per week in the early 1970s to cover her equipment and training expenses as well as to travel to selected competitions.

In Great Britain former European shot put champion Geoff Capes was sponsored by the Meat Board and received a supply of meat free of charge each week. This was worth $25 or so per week, since top class strength event competitors are notoriously enormous meat eaters, usually in the (largely erroneous) belief that it is essential to maintain their weight and strength. In Canada a system of support for elite athletes has been working for several years which gives considerable grants-in-aid to nominated individuals each year. In 1973–74 nearly $1 million was allocated under this programme. Top Canadian swimmers receive an annual government grant of up to $7000 for education, accommodation, transportation and other expenses. They know that, in addition, they will be taking part in at least a dozen trips to international meets around Canada or abroad.

Programmes such as these are being used to persuade athletes to continue with highly competitive sport after leaving school or college. But it is hardly likely that such material support is a sufficient incentive for most competitors. Their efforts need to be directed towards a concrete achievable goal if they are to be worthwhile. Not every athlete can aim for Olympic success, so a programme of competition of carefully graded and increasing standard should be available for all. This is not so easy to achieve when major sporting organizations are dependent on the activities of sponsors and entrepreneurs who do not find the activities of sportsmen and women at the club and local level of any interest. Governments may be more sympathetic but this is not always the case if short term rewards of medals and/or international prestige are not forthcoming.

It is quite clear that the long term health of any sport can only be assured by appropriate financial assistance and planning at the grass roots. That means in schools, in local clubs and regional organizations, and it means support and training for coaches and officials as much as for the competitors themselves. It also means that goals of equality of treatment and opportunity between the sexes could be set by those formulating the plans and providing the assistance. The structure of sporting organizations and society in general in some countries has allowed this to happen, in others it seems a very difficult situation to bring about.

Top. The evolution of technique in the hi
jump. Although the high jump has been
women's Olympic event since 1928, not un
the 1950s did women stop using the highly i
efficient scissors jump. Men had largely aba
doned this technique in the 1900s. **Top le**
Photograph shows Dorothy Tyler of Brita
who won a gold medal at the 1948 Olympi
and broke the Olympic record clearing 0.0
metres (5 ft 6¼ ins). The height to which t
centre of gravity of the body has to be rais
above the bar is illustrated in this shot. T
Romanian Iolande Balas used another inef
cient technique, the eastern cutoff but rais
the world record from 1.75 metres to 1.°
metres between 1956 and 1971. The strad
technique is widely used by women today, b
they also took up the flop with great rapidi
after its introduction in the late 1960s. (Cred
BBC Hulton Picture Library.) **Top right.** Pho
graph shows Japanese girl Tamami Yagi cleari
1.90 metres (6 ft 2¾ ins) in October 1978,
centimetres above her own head. The grea
efficiency of this technique is apparent fr
the closeness of the body's centre of gravity
the bar. The astonishing progress of wome
high jumping is discussed in pages 149-
(Credit: Allsport/Tony Duffy.) **Bottom.** T
evolution of women's swimming. **Bottom rig**
An illustration from the *Graphic* of London
October 1900, showing the start of the Rave
bourne Challenge Cup. The caption informs
that this event, part of the annual festival of
Ravensbourne Swimming Club, was won
Miss Thorpe, lady champion of Yorksh
from Miss Cudlipp of the Portsmouth Lad
Club. Other competitors included Miss Grah
amateur lady champion of Scotland and M
Hilson of Jersey. So women's swimming
widespread and well organized at this ti
although not part of the Olympics until 19
The fastest time for the event incidentally
1 minute 31.4 seconds. The 1980 world rec
for 100 metres (109 yds 1 ft) was 54
seconds. (Credit: BBC Hulton Picture Libra
Bottom left. Kornelia Ender, one of the E
German swimming stars shown here using
new "grab" start for spring events at the Eu
pean Swimming Championships Vienna 19
Her times in the mid 1970s were as fast
men's only a decade or so before. (Cre
Allsport/Tony Duffy.)

CHAPTER SIX

The Biology of Sex and Sex Differences

1. DEFINITIONS OF SEX

Differences between the sexes affect a great deal of human behaviour. Not only sexual activity and its outcomes, but the jobs we do, our business and leisure activities, the way we treat one another and so forth. Sex seems to be one of those invariants around which the structure of almost all human societies are built. But while sex differences are real enough, they are never absolute or completely clear cut. For instance, men are usually taller than women, but among Europeans there are many women who are taller than a lot of men (figure 3 showed just what proportion); and comparing men and women from different races makes the above generalization virtually meaningless. A high proportion of Nilotic Negro women of East Africa, for example, are taller than all Eskimo or Pgymy men.

Similarly, men are usually stronger than women, but there are many exceptions to this generalization and it takes only a little training for many women to become stronger and have greater endurance than most men. It is the same with many other characteristics which distinguish and differentiate the sexes; there are usually considerable overlaps in expression, reversals of the normal or "western" situation in other races and everywhere evidence that many of the differences can be reduced with training and practice. Can so much social differentiation really be hung on so little and so variable biological support?

The biological mechanisms of sex determination are at first sight quite simple. The cells of our bodies contain and are controlled by the genetic material passed on from generation to generation. We receive genetic material from our parents in the form of twenty-three small threadlike structures or chromosomes contained within the nucleus of each egg and sperm which unite at conception to start us all off. These chromosomes are composed of deoxyribonucleic acid or DNA, which is organized into more or less discrete genes controlling particular characteristics.

The chromosomes can be matched by size and genetic content into twenty-three pairs. Each pair is different from every other and can be distinguished with careful study, but the chromosomes of each pair cannot be distinguished; we cannot tell which came from our father and which from our mother. In females this applies to all twenty-three pairs. But males have only twenty-two identical pairs; their twenty-third pair consists of two recognizably different chromosomes, one called the X chromosome and a much smaller Y. Females possess two X chromosomes.

To produce offspring, eggs and sperm must be produced and it is normally the case that one chromosome of each pair, randomly selected so far as we know, go into each egg or sperm. Each egg normally contains one X chromosome as well as twenty-two others, but two sorts of sperm are formed: those which receive an X and those which receive a Y chromosome. If a Y-bearing sperm fertilizes an egg the resulting individual will have an X chromosome inherited from his mother and a Y from his father. He will therefore grow up as an XY male. Sperm bearing X chromosomes will fertilize an X-bearing egg and they will give rise to XX females. The Y chromosome therefore determines maleness, although precisely how is not clear.

The above describes what normally happens. But occasionally mistakes occur. Sperm or eggs are produced without an X or a Y or with two Xs or two Ys and if these are involved in fertilization, aberrant foetuses are produced which may die and be aborted or survive to be born and grow up as more or less aberrant adults. Sometimes the Y chromosome becomes fragmented so that an X and part Y-bearing sperm may fertilize an egg; or the early processes of division of a normally fertilized egg may go wrong, with the X or Y chromosomes failing to separate correctly in some or all of the cells of the foetus. Individuals who reach adulthood lacking a Y chromosome, that is who are chromosomally XO, manifest what is termed Turner's Syndrome. They are sterile and obvious, if aberrant, females. On the other hand individuals who have one or more X chromosomes in addition to a normal XY male complement are males and may be partially or even fully fertile, but they also manifest some obvious female characteristics and perhaps can and probably have passed as females on occasion. They show what is called Klinefelter's Syndrome.

More common, and certainly more significant from our present point of view, are cases where some of the cells of the body are of normal female constitution, that is XX, and some are normal male, that is XY, or one of the above variants. These are called mosaics and arise as a result of an abnormality very early in development. Depending on the proportions of the cells of the body involved, the individual concerned may develop primarily male or female characteristics and when the number of abnormal cells is low the mosaicism may be very difficult to detect.

In addition to these chromosomal errors in sex determining mechanisms, the normal hormonal influences may go awry. Pregnant women may be inadvertently given male sex hormones or they or their developing babies may suffer a pituitary malfunction resulting in over-production of male hormones. In either case female embryos will be masculinized. There are also certain specific genes which will effect sex alterations by altering pituitary function during early embryological development; chromosomally XY individuals then develop as apparently normal but sterile females. A recent survey in Canada showed that about one in four thousand phenotypic males may in fact be genotypic females and that one in two thousand phenotypic females may be genotypic males. In addition various embryological upsets, surgical accidents during circumcision and other early damage to the genitalia may also upset normal sexual development.

Sex distinctions can in fact be made in five different ways: the appearance of the external genitals, the possession or absence of a Y chromosome, the amount of various hormones which are produced in the body; the sex to which the individual is assigned at birth, that is what the doctor or parents thought the baby to be at birth (or sometimes what they wanted it to be irrespective of what it actually was), and finally what the individual regards him or herself to be, that is, their gender (see chapter seven). In most individuals sex assignment on each of these criteria is the same, but there is a sizeable minority in which one or more of these criteria are at variance with the others, or at least ambiguous. Herein of course are the seeds of the disputes of the past couple of decades regarding the sexual status of certain competitors in some sports. Table 8 summarizes these differences in sexual differentiation.

Table 8. Sexual Differentiation.

Criteria	Difference	Identified by
1. Genetic	Presence or absence of a Y chromosome in all or part of tissues of body.	(a) Chromosomal count of cells grown in culture. (b) Buccal smear or other peripheral tissue showing sex chromatin i.e. at least two X chromosomes.
2. Morphological	Presence of ovarian or testis material. Nature of external genitalia.	Microscopic examination of tissue. External and internal inspection.
3. Hormonal	Level of development of secondary sexual characteristics.	Biochemical and physiological.
4. Social	Social behaviours, preferences and direction of sex drives.	Initially by doctors or parents latterly self-identity.

Note: Each of these is capable of subdivision depending on, for example, proportion of tissue with Y chromosomes, morphological differences, hormonal levels, and the particular social behaviours manifest. While 1, 2 and 3 are more or less determined or predetermined at birth, social sex identification or gender role is thought to be essentially neutral at birth. It develops, in part at least, as a result of the society's and then the individual's decisions on the sexual identity by criteria 1, 2 and 3. The influences on gender development and its implications are taken up in more detail in chapter seven.

Less than one per cent of babies are born whose sex is so doubtful that medical tests are necessary to establish to which chromosomal sex they belong. There are about ten per cent or so of adults who live on or across the social, sexual and psychological borderline between the sexes in one way or another and there are an unknown number of sex-chromosome mosaics. All of this poses a number of problems for sports administrators wedded to the notion that there should be absolute distinctions between the sexes. Until 1966 athletes needed only a medical certificate signed by a doctor in their own country as evidence of their sex. A full visual examination was introduced at the European Athletics Championships held in Budapest in 1966 and a chromosome test in 1967, this being fully used on a large scale for the first time at the 1968 Mexico Olympics.

Different sports have different definitions of male and female. The commonest criterion, one which has been adopted by all sporting bodies affiliated to the International Olympic Committee, is chromosomal. Females are defined as possessing only X chromosomes in all of the cells of their body; the possession of one Y chromosome or part of a Y chromosome in even part of their tissues being sufficient to debar them from female events. To qualify for a women's event individuals have to prove their sex on both anatomical and chromosomal criteria to the satisfaction of the controlling authorities.

No longer can sex differences be regarded as fixed, absolute and clearcut. In every phase of sex differentiation — chromosomal, hormonal, anatomical, psychological and social — there are overlaps, ambiguities, uncertainties and changes of sexual identity. Changing medical and social practices will increase their frequency and raise their visibility rather than lower them and hide them. Any definition of sex is an arbitrary one subject to change as social pressures change.

A number of erstwhile female athletes have been affected by this chromosomal definition of sex, among the most prominent of whom has been Eva Klobukowska, one time Polish co-holder of the 100 metres world record and a member of the winning team in the 4 x 100 metres at Tokyo in 1964. She passed a normal medical test at Budapest in 1966 but was disqualified from international competition in 1967 after failing to pass a chromosomal test at Kiev before the Women's European Athletics Cup, being found to have one chromosome too many. Just which one was not identified in the press. Eva's boyfriend said that he was amazed that anyone should consider she was not a woman.

The whole test seems to have been done with maximum insensitivity and this early version of the test may not have been able to identify a Y chromosome very accurately. In 1968 it consisted of collecting cells from the inside of the cheek. In most women about twenty cells in every hundred contain Barr bodies (a densely staining mass representing the second X chromosome). Women with Barr bodies in fewer than ten cells in every hundred were barred from competition. Who knows what injustices were done? The test now uses actively dividing cells in hair roots and is a good deal more sophisticated. Nevertheless, a great deal of unnecessary embarrassment and possible psychological harm was undoubtedly caused to a number of women athletes. It is, after all, their integrity as well as their sex which is being investigated. Olympic athlete Mary Peters describes in her autobiography the actual testing procedures as thoroughly degrading and humiliating. One American swimmer described the testing room as "full of those big-eyed doctors looking you up and down as though they were dying to say 'Flat chested, oh well, we'll see?' ". Marion Lay, a Canadian swimmer, described the scene at the Mexico Olympics " . . . a long line of women awaiting the test in Mexico erupted in reactions that ranged from tension-releasing jokes to severe stress and upset". Even now the tests are one further barrier in the way of women athletes which men do not have to negotiate.

The "strict" chromosomal definition of sex has now been operative for over a decade and during this period women's improvements in all sports, both in absolute terms and relative to men, have been faster than ever. It obviously was not just the chromosomally doubtful females who were doing all the record breaking in the past.

2. SEX DIFFERENCES IN GROWTH AND DEVELOPMENT

Early embryonic development is, in most respects, identical in both sexes. The testes begin to develop about thirty-five days after fertilization and they then begin to produce male sex hormones which accentuate further male developments, including secondary sexual characteristics of physique and physiology. Ovarian changes in female embryos occur a little later in the development sequence. It is the hormones produced by the gonads at these times which are quite crucial for satisfactory sexual development and therefore if for any genetic or embryological reason the testes or ovaries do not develop properly, sexual development will be impaired. Hormonal imbalances in the mother, however caused, may have similar consequences.

At birth males are about 90–150 grams heavier than females. However, babies of the same sex but different race and social class can also differ by as much as this. Difference between first-born and later-borns can also be as great as this, as can differences between babies born to large and small mothers.

Other average differences between the sexes at birth include greater male body length, limb lengths and head circumference. Girls are almost invariably have a greater degree of skeletal ossification and in fact boys remain at only about eighty per cent of the skeletal age of girls until adulthood. These differences are maintained in early growth and, although rates of growth of bone, muscle, and the deposition of subcutaneous tissue differ throughout pre-pubertal development, it is not until the growth spurt of the mid-teen years, and the physiological changes of adolescence accompanying it, that important sex differences become established.

This adolescent growth spurt varies in time and intensity between one child and another but it affects all body systems; it is associated with sexual maturation and, most important of all for sporting performance, full physiological development. The growth spurt occurs in boys on average between about 12½ and 15½ years of age; in girls it is about two years earlier. The precise timing depends on race, class, nutritional levels, climate and heredity. The differences which are established between the sexes have important consequences for sporting preferences and ability during the teen years. These, in turn, greatly influence the choice of adult sports and ultimate ability levels reached.

The difference in adult size between men and women is mainly due to differences in the timing and the magnitude of the adolescent growth spurt. Before this growth spurt boys and girls in western societies differ by only about two per cent in height, after it they differ by about eight per cent. The later occurrence of the male growth spurt allows a longer period of pre-pubertal growth and the spurt itself is also greater.

Many physiological and motor functions change at about the same time as the growth spurt due to the profound muscular growth and associated hormonal changes. These include increases in the number of red cells in the blood, a greater degree of ossification of the skeleton and increases in both relative and absolute sizes of heart and lungs. Strength, skill, dexterity and physical endurance all increase progressively and rapidly throughout adolescence as a result.

Before puberty girls are on average the equal of, and in some respects superior to, boys of the same age in activities requiring speed, strength and endurance. By the age of sixteen the majority of girls have at least entered and often largely completed their growth spurt, having attained more than ninety-five per cent of their adult height, and muscular development. On the other hand many boys do not commence their growth spurt until later than sixteen and at that age rather few boys have reached anything like their adult physique.

The youngest ever athletics gold medallist in the Olympics is West German girl Ulrike Meyfarth who won the high jump in 1968 with a jump of 1.92 metres (6 ft 3½ ins) when aged only sixteen. The youngest swimming and diving gold medallist is Marjorie Gestring of the USA who won the 1936 springboard diving when only thirteen years nine months old. Among the youngest world record holders have been Jenny Turral of Australia who was only thirteen when she set world records for 800 and 1500 metres in 1974, Yulia Bogdanova who was thirteen when she broke the 100 and 200 metres breast-stroke record in 1978 and the youngest of all, Karen Muir from South Africa, who was just twelve years ten months and twenty-five days old when she broke the then world record for 110 yards back-stroke by 0.7 seconds in 1965.

By the age of about fifteen in girls and seventeen in boys the rates of growth and increase in strength are at or below the levels before the adolescent growth spurt started. The rates thereafter decline until maturation is essentially complete in both sexes by about the twentieth or twenty-first year.

3. ADULT SEX DIFFERENCES

Men and women differ in almost every aspect of their biology. There are features for which the average value and the distribution of values differ, but for which there is still a great deal of overlap between the sexes, these include height, weight, brain size, haemoglobin content of the blood, heart and lung size and many others. There are characters which show much clearer differences, including the primary and secondary sex characteristics, skeletal proportions and so on. But even in these traits, as has been shown, overlaps and ambiguities are possible. Figure 9 summarizes some of the anatomical features and figure 10 summarizes some of the physiological differences important in sport.

In making comparisons between the sexes we must always be clear whether we are considering average men and women, or those selected and trained for optimal and extreme performances; that is whether we are considering men and women as they are or as they might be. Merely listing average biological differences between men and women is never enough to explain observed differences in performance. We have to know whether the best men and best women are being selected in the first place, and whether the training, diet, encouragement, facilities, rewards, medical care and so on are those best for each individual involved. We must also recognize not only that there are obvious and important biological differences between the sexes, but that the differences between individuals of the same sex are also obvious and in many respects equally important.

(a) Skeletal Differences

Women's bones are, on average, shorter or smaller and less massive than those of men. This is not itself a disadvantage in many sports and in some, such as long distance running, the shortest sprints, swimming and gymnastics, it may be an advantage. In any case there is considerable overlap between the sexes. Women's arms and legs are proportionally shorter than those of men and their trunks are longer. In Europeans the leg length of men is about 52 per cent of height whereas that of women is only about 51.2 per cent of their height. This difference is of some disadvantage in jumping events and gymnastics, although by how much is not clear.

A more diagnostic skeletal difference between the sexes is that a woman's pelvis is broader and shallower. This causes the thigh bone, or femur, to articulate at a more acute angle than that of men; the upper part is set wider and the bone points inwards a little towards the midline of the body. This results in some mechanical disadvantage in running, since this angle of the femur tends to cause a lateral sway of the body. The rotatory motion of the thighs becomes emphasized and trunk rotation may be introduced to counteract it, together with exaggerated arm movements. All of these result in loss of efficiency when running. But they can be corrected with careful coaching and there is plenty of evidence to suggest that the importance of this particular skeletal difference, although often emphasized, may be much exaggerated. For example, the relationship between width of the hips and running speed has been shown by careful measurement to be very low. And at present women's

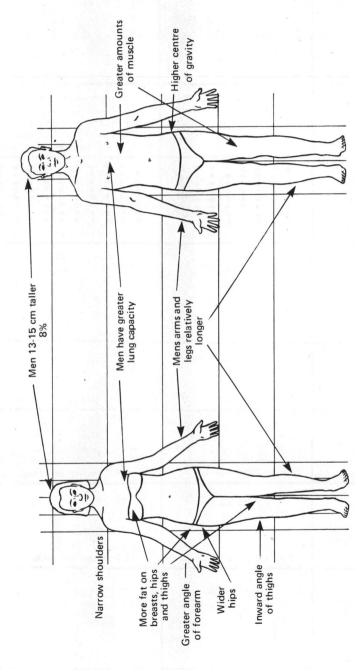

Fig. 9. Some of the more obvious morphological differences between the sexes.

Men 13-15 cm taller 8%

Men have greater lung capacity

Mens arms and legs relatively longer

Greater amounts of muscle

Higher centre of gravity

Narrow shoulders

More fat on breasts, hips and thighs

Greater angle of forearm

Wider hips

Inward angle of thighs

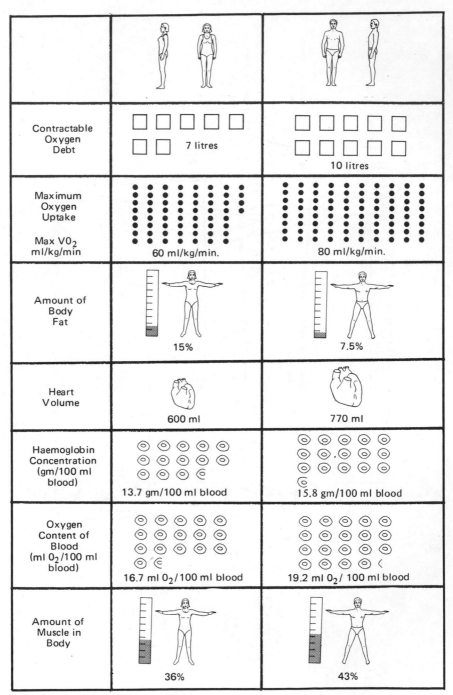

Fig. 10. Some of the more important physiological differences between the sexes. These figures are average values for untrained men and women.

performances are closest to men's in the 100 and 200 metre sprints, whereas these would be expected to show the maximum difference.

Others have gone so far as to say that women may be better runners than men. One study of forty-two top men and women runners found that women had longer strides compared to their height, took more strides per minute and were in contact with the ground less. More subjectively Thaddeus Kostrubala in *The Joy of Running* said that: "Women seem to run with greater ease than men. Their style is easy. The natural style of most 12 to 14 year old girls is almost perfect . . . They roll their feet, their pelvises move. They look at ease and ready to play; in fact they are playing. Is all this because they have not been the victim of male cultural expectation – that of competition?"[1]

Women's shoulders are on average narrower than men's. The upper arm bone, the humerus, is absolutely and relatively shorter and smaller in diameter than in men. Their forearms are shorter and are at a slightly different angle to the upper arm than men's. For these reasons throwing, cycling or rotatory movements of the arm as a whole are more difficult for women, making them tend to throw roundarm and hence less effectively. The speed which can be imparted to a projectile depends on the terminal velocity of the arm which is greater the longer it is, a further plus for men.

This might help explain why javelin throwing is women's worst event relative to men. In the discus, women can compensate with increased body rotation made possible by greater flexibility, which goes a long way towards explaining their much greater relative success in this event.

These skeletal differences are also a handicap in activities involving the support of the body by the arms, as in gymnastics, and in other sports such as rowing and tennis in which the magnitude of arm power at full stretch is important.

The joints and cartilage of the pelvic girdle, vertebral column and foot in women are better adapted to sudden springing, landing and extensions than they are in men and on the whole are far more adapted to physical exercises requiring supple performance and flexibility. These factors, coupled with the lower average strength of women, however, increase their susceptibility to sprains and strains.

Undoubtedly part of the reason for the continued improvement in performance in many sports is a better understanding of the mechanics and physiology of running, jumping, throwing and so on. Much of this has developed with the use of cinephotography and specialized apparatus for analyzing human movement and muscular activity. Since it seems that women have some anatomical disadvantages they are more likely to benefit from scientific analysis of their deficiencies and from expert coaching to overcome them.

(b) Muscular Differences

Women possess, on average, lesser amounts of muscle than do men. This is partly because of their smaller skeletal frames, but muscles also form a lower proportion of female body weight, about thirty-six per cent, than of male body weight, about forty-three per cent. Women, therefore, have a lower muscular strength than do men, although precisely how much lower depends on the muscular function which is being measured; pulling, pushing, lifting or endurance. Nevertheless, so far as is known, muscles of the same size are the same strength in men and women.

Muscle development is stimulated mainly by the male sex hormone testosterone, the production of which is much increased in males during the adolescent growth spurt. This hormone increases the weight of muscle tissue and enlarges the muscle fibres. Female hormones have, by and large, a growth inhibiting effect. Muscle development is also stimulated by exercise and long periods of vigorous usage and this makes it very difficult to compare innate muscular strengths of men and women.

There have been very many studies of the different muscular strengths of men and women. But it is very difficult to find groups of men and women with similar histories of muscle usage and development. If men and women have used their muscles in different ways and to different extents during their lives then their muscular strengths are almost bound to differ and it cannot be said that the reasons are biological.

The muscles in women's arms may develop up to seventy-five or eighty per cent of the strength of men; women's lower leg muscles can develop about seventy per cent of the strength of men; and the muscles of the hand and back are about sixty per cent as strong. Women's strongest muscles are their thigh muscles, which have more than eighty-five per cent of the power of men's thigh muscles. This has led to the claim that of all the aptitudes requiring energetic use of the muscles, dancing is the only one in which women can physically excel. Ballet dancing is certainly one of the most energetic, vigorous and exhausting of all activities but one could hardly exclude women because of that!

The thigh muscles show the smallest difference in power between the sexes, probably because both sexes use their legs to a similar degree in standing, walking, running, climbing stairs and cycling, activities common to both sexes in their pre-adult years. The significance of this is apparent in cycling, in which leg power is probably more important than in any other sport, and the sex differential in some forms of cycling is lower than in most other speed sports (see chapter ten).

This information on the muscular system has to be considered with respect to body size because it is, after all, the whole body which participates in most physical activities. For example, women are relatively poor performers in the jumping events, but when the heights jumped in the high jump are adjusted according to body size the sexes are about equal. The same applies to sprint events on the track. Men's speed per unit of body size is 8.4 and women's is 9.5 metres/minute/kilogram body weight. Women are therefore faster and are presumably generating more muscular power relative to body size.

To compensate for women's generally lower levels of muscular strength they have two important advantages: their endurance and flexibility are greater. The static muscle fatigue patterns of men and women are not significantly different (that is the amount of time which they can exert maximal muscular force). But women's relative endurance is better. Tests in which the subject sustains a submaximal force level at a set percentage of that individual's maximal voluntary contractile strength (MVC) show that in tests utilizing between a quarter and three quarters MVC women are superior. The superiority of women is greater at lower levels of MVC.

Women are much more flexible than men in all parts of their body. They can, for example, usually touch the ground with much more than their finger-tips while keeping their knees straight. This greater flexibility is very important in allowing longer running strides, better hurdling techniques and better kick and arm movements in swimming than would be expected on simple comparisons with men of the same height and weight. This difference is developed early in childhood and is maintained throughout life. It is due largely to women's greater production of the hormone relaxin which is concerned with softening and stretching ligaments, the structures by which muscles are fixed to bone.

(c) Energy Differences

The sexes differ in the three important energy systems providing power, the short and medium term anaerobic ATP–PC and lactic acid systems and the long term aerobic oxygen system.

The Adenosine Triphosphate and Phosphocreatine System

The normal muscular concentrations of ATP and PC are the same in men and women. But because of the smaller amount of muscle in women, the total phosphagens available for use during exercise are fewer. The size of this difference can be ascertained either by measuring the capacity of the oxygen debt, or by measuring anaerobic power.

The alactic acid protion of the oxygen debt is that associated with replacing the total muscular stores of ATP and PC that are depleted during exhaustive exercises. It is measured by determining the amount of oxygen consumed above normal resting levels in the few minutes of recovery from a hard run. Untrained men and women have low values, with training and active participation in sport increasing potential oxygen debt by fifty per cent or more. In all cases the size of the oxygen debt that women can contract is about one-third less than that of men. The differences between men and women are smaller when the values are expressed per unit of muscle mass rather than total body weight.

A stair climbing test measures anaerobic power. A subject runs as rapidly as possible up a short flight of stairs, with the time taken to go from stair three to nine being recorded to one hundredth of a second. The power generated is a function of the subject's weight and vertical distance ascended, divided by the time taken. This indirectly reflects the ability rapidly to utilize the stores of ATP and PC in the leg muscles. The power values obtained for men and women when expressed relative to body weight show very little difference between the sexes, although weight for weight men will probably always have a little more power available for the sprints and explosive events than will women.

The Lactic Acid System

Women have lower levels of lactic acid in their blood after prolonged exercise than do men, which means that less energy has been made available to them. Among untrained men and women the usual difference is fifty per cent or more, but is a little less in active athletes. These differences are based on values per kilogram of body weight and the differences are smaller when expressed per kilogram of total muscle mass. It is just not known whether the difference is an inevitable one due to innate biological factors or whether, and if so to what extent, it is a consequence of the generally more active life that males lead almost from birth.

The lactic acid system is of most importance in events of intermediate time duration such as the 400, 800 and possibly the 1500 metres on the track and the 100 and 200 metres swimming. Women would inevitably produce poorer times than men in these events if this difference in the lactic acid system is an innate one. But particular emphasis on training in this area can make good some or all of their deficiencies.

The Oxygen or Aerobic System

The highest oxygen uptake (max VO_2) that women can attain during physical work is between fifteen and twenty-four per cent less than men. The difference in max VO_2 is smaller when expressed relative to body weight and becomes very small indeed when related to active muscle mass. In practical terms max VO_2 has to be related to total body weight because the total body weight of the athlete comprises the largest part of the workload. Women are therefore at a definite disadvantage in oxygen uptake.

But this disadvantage may be compensated for in women by the greater importance of fat as an energy source. The principal source of fuel in the aerobic cycle is glycogen, but fatty tissue has an energy yield per gram about seven times higher than glycogen. Human heart muscles use fat preferentially and many animals involved in prolonged submaximal exercise, such as migrating birds, also use it preferentially in all of their muscles.

During submaximal work of up to about three hours, fat normally contributes as much as seventy per cent of the energy requirement, this proportion increasing with longer exercise. The importance of fat as an energy source can be varied by diet, workload and training. Well trained men long distance runners have about twenty-two per cent fat mixed in with lean leg muscle, whereas untrained men and lean men sprinters have only about ten per cent of muscle fat. Even well trained women have about ten per cent more fat than similarly trained men and although some of this is subcutaneous, some is intra-muscular and hence useful as an energy source. Precise research data on women athletes are lacking but it is likely that they not only have more fat to act as an energy source but may have more efficient enzyme systems utilizing it. In long distance events they may use more fat and hence preserve more glycogen. They thereby survive long term, aerobic exercise more successfully, a point to bear in mind as being of the utmost importance when actual sporting performances are considered.

In one survey, women long distance runners of national and international calibre were assessed for body composition and cardiovascular endurance. Their mean relative body fat was 15.2 per cent which was about half of that in untrained women of the same age (32.4 per cent) but more than double that of men endurance runners of a similar age. Their max VO_2 averaged 59.1 millilitres per kilogram per minute. This is 16 per cent lower than that of men marathoners of national calibre, but this difference reduced to 7.8 per cent when expressed relative to lean body weight. The three best women runners had an average body fat of 7 per cent and a max VO_2 of 67.4 millilitres per kilogram per minute. These values were nearly identical to the 8.3 per cent and 70.3 millilitres per kilogram per minute found in ten nationally ranked male marathon runners of the same average age.

In all three of the energy systems, then, women have some disadvantages. But the disadvantages are small, can be decreased by proper training and may in one system at least be masked by a greater advantage which hitherto has not been used and therefore not recognized by women.

(d) Differences in Lungs and Breathing

Women have a smaller lung volume and total chest capacity than men, but they require less oxygen because of their lower metabolic rate and their smaller body size. The vital capacity, that is the volume of air moved through the lungs from maximal inspiration to maximal expiration, is lower in women because of their smaller body size, area and height. But vital capacity is still about ten per cent less in women than men of the same size and age. Vital capacity can be improved by training and is an important ultimate determinant of sporting ability. Men tend to breathe more abdominally, that is utilizing their diaphragms. Women normally breathe more in the chest, but training increases their diaphragm breathing. Comparison of a group of men and women long distance runners showed that the men used eighty-two per cent of their VO_2 max in competition, whereas women used seventy-nine per cent of theirs.

The ability to maintain near maximum aerobic power over fairly long periods of time is also important. This ability is related to the efficiency of the oxygen transport system and general body metabolism and individuals with rather moderate maximum aerobic power levels may nevertheless be highly successful athletes. Derek Clayton, the Australian holder of the unofficial world marathon record (from 1969 to 1 October 1981), had a relatively modest VO_2 max of 64.4 millilitres per kilogram per minute. But he could maintain eighty per cent of this value over very long periods of time. The efficiency of the runner probably plays a part in the relationship of performance and oxygen consumption; and this depends upon adequate coaching among other things. A summary of some of the observed sex differences in oxygen transporting power are shown in table 9 (compare also table 3).

Table 9. A comparison of the highest reported results for oxygen transporting power of male and female contestants in various sports.

Sport	Oxygen Transporting Power (ml per min per kg)	
	men	women
Cross country skiing	82	63
Speed skating	79	53
Orienteering	77	60
Swimming	70	58
Downhill skiing	68	57
400 metre running	67	56
Gymnastics	60	43
Table tennis	59	43
Sprinting	56	45
Throwing events	55	38
Volleyball	52	33

(e) Differences in Blood Circulation

Women generally have a smaller heart than men. The heart volume of the average man is about 770 cubic centimetres whereas trained athletes may have hearts up to 1500 or even 1700 cubic centimetres. Female hearts average about 600 cubic centimetres and the maximum value found so far is only 1150 cubic centimetres. But many fewer women's hearts than men's have hitherto been measured and we are therefore much less likely to know the maximum size of women's hearts which can be attained with training.

Women have a higher basal heart-beat rate, and they have a greater and more rapid increase in pulse rate at the beginning of exercise and a much slower recovery on its cessation. In one experiment in which well-trained subjects of both sexes in the same age group performed the same work on the bicycle ergometer, men reached an average pulse rate of 128, whereas women reached

169. In this case fifty per cent of the men's aerobic capacity was being utilized whereas seventy-three per cent of the women's aerobic capacity was engaged.

Oxygen is carried round the body by the haemoglobin found in the red blood cells. Haemoglobin is a large complex molecule, a crucial part of which is iron directly concerned in oxygen binding and transport. This is the main reason why a sufficiency of iron is so crucial in the diet. The average number of red blood cells in women is four and a half million per cubic millimetre of blood, giving a haemoglobin content of 13.7 grams per hundred cubic centimetres. In men there are about five million red cells per cubic millimetre of of blood giving an average haemoglobin content of 15.8 grams per hundred cubic centimetres. After exercise there is a rise of about one million red cells per cubic millimetre in men and a proportionate rise in women. These extra cells are mobilized from reserves such as the bone marrow, liver and spleen and indicate the body's adjustment to meet the demand for an increased oxygen supply. Partly because of these red cell differences, women have about thirty per cent less total haemoglobin in their body than men, although in relation to body weight the difference is reduced to about twenty per cent. Presumably, therefore, the amount of oxygen per unit time they can carry is reduced by a similar amount.

This difference is not inevitable though. The iron balance in women is always more precarious, partly because of blood loss due to menstruation, and with more widespread recognition of this has come more widespread iron supplementation in women.

At a given level of oxygen consumption women have a higher heart rate than men. On the other hand, for a given heart rate men can transport more oxygen during submaximal and maximal work. Women's hearts must pump about nine litres of blood to transport one litre of oxygen during a submaximal workload, men's need pump only about eight litres. The oxygen content of the blood in the experiment in which these values were obtained was 16.7 millilitres of oxygen per 100 millilitres of blood in women and 19.2 in men. Blood pressure, both during the heart's contraction and relaxation, is usually between five and ten per cent lower in women than in men.

(f) Differences in Body Composition and Shape

Most of the physical differences between men and women are very obvious. Men are taller, stronger, tougher, have wider shoulders, narrower hips and so forth. But these are average differences and many women are taller and stronger than many men. In everything that follows this must be remembered, as must the fact that most men have at least part of these advantages because they have always been encouraged to be active, eat well and use their muscles in hard, vigorous activity, whereas women have been encouraged in quite reverse ways.

Men are, on average, between thirteen and fifteen centimetres taller than women and are between ten and fifteen kilograms heavier, an eight to ten per cent superiority in each case. As we saw in chapter three, height confers some advantage in many sports, but just how much is not at all clear. For example, some very short men have competed in Olympic sprint events and many men below average height have won medals. Figure 3 shows that the difference in height between men in the top quarter and the third quarter is between ten and fifteen centimetres and that the tallest twenty-five per cent of women are as tall as half the men. Were height to be the most important determinant of sprinting performance, women would equal the speed of many men Olympic competitors and be able to win the occasional medal. This they cannot yet do and hence the reason cannot primarily be height.

The most consistent man sprinter in the 1972 and 1976 Olympics was Jamaican Don Quarrie, finalist in the 100 and 200 metres at both Olympics and 200 metre silver medallist at Montreal. The most consistent woman sprinter was East German Renate Stecker, gold medallist in 100 metres and 200 metres at Munich, silver medallist in the 100 metres and bronze medallist in the 200 metres at Montreal. Irena Szewinska won the 1976 Olympic women's 400 metres; Fred Newhouse won the silver medal in the men's 400 metres at the 1976 Olympics. Their physiques are shown in table 10. There are only minor differences in height and weight but major differences in performance for each of these pairs.

Table 10. Comparison of physiques of men and women Olympic medallists.

	Height	Weight
Don Quarrie	1.75m	70kg
Renate Stecker	1.70m	70kg
Irena Szewinska	1.76m	63kg
Fred Newhouse	1.75m	67kg

Among the top ten performers in track and field athletics in 1976 there was considerable variation in height and weight. Figure 11 shows for four events the tallest and shortest, heaviest and lightest men among these top ten and the tallest and heaviest women. In three out of four cases for both height and weight a successful woman equalled or exceeded the value of one of the successful men. The largest medal winner in the discus in the 1976 Olympics was not Mac Wilkins, the men's discus gold medal winner, but Maria Vergova, women's discus silver medallist, 117 kilograms to 116 kilograms. Again, whatever was responsible for the difference in performance between top men and women it obviously could not be just height or weight.

The high jump is one event where height might be expected to make a very big difference to performance. Most high jumpers, both men and women, are well over average height. Most of the men are more than 1.95 metres and most of the women more than 1.75 metres, a difference rather less than the difference in 1980 world records (2.01 v 2.36 m). Many assume that it is the height

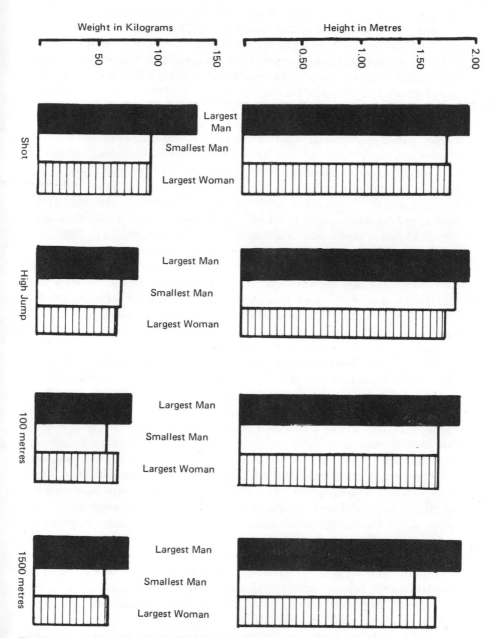

Fig. 11. Morphological variation among the ten most successful athletes of 1976. The tallest/shortest and the heaviest/lightest men in a number of events are compared with the tallest and heaviest women in that event. It is clear that morphological differences alone cannot account for the performance differences, since the women often equal or exceed the height/weight of one of the top ten men.

difference which is responsible for the record difference. But the man who broke the men's world indoor high jump record in 1978, American Franklin Jacobs, is only 1.73 metres. Until he was eighteen Franklin Jacobs had never done any athletics and competed in his last year at high school when the basketball season had finished. Only then was his incredible high jumping ability discovered. Two years later in January 1978 Jacobs jumped 2.28 metres at an indoor meeting in Maryland. Up to two days prior to the meeting he had been hobbling on crutches with chronic knee trouble. Partly because of his late start in athletics Jacobs' technique, although based on the Flop, is unique. As one writer put it he does not really jump over the bar, he sort of flails over it backwards. But whether in spite of or because of his technique, he can jump nearly sixty centimetres above his own height. The top four women high jumpers in 1978 were Sara Simeoni (1.77 metres), R. Ackerman (1.75 metres), B. Holzapfel (1.83 metres) and Ulrike Meyfarth (1.88 metres). If these women could jump only fifty centimetres above their height they would be jumping, 2.27, 2.25, 2.33 and 2.38 metres respectively, close to or better than the men's record. In October 1978 Tamami Yagi cleared 1.90 metres to set an Asian record. She is only 1.64 metres tall and she therefore jumped twenty-six centimetres above her own height. This is the best performance by a woman yet. Photograph 10 shows Ms Yagi making this jump using the flop technique. Maybe women will never jump as high as men, but it is obviously not just their lower height which is keeping them so far behind at present.

Women have a lower centre of gravity than men. Men's centre of gravity is at about 56.7 per cent of their height above the ground, whereas women's is at about 56.1 per cent of their height above the ground. This is probably a disadvantage in the jumping events and possibly also in some gymnastic exercises. In some events it may be a positive advantage, however, since women may be that much more stable and be less easily upset or deflected in running. Wind resistance is reduced for one thing. The effect of this is proportional to the square of the speed and hence is most important in the sprints. A small body is also an advantage in long distance races because there is less weight to propel. Successful men marathoners and long distance runners are mostly rather slight, and women are now achieving notable successes in these events.

Women's limbs are on average shorter and their trunks proportionately longer than men. The thigh shows the greatest difference between the sexes. In women it is shorter and set at a different angle but it is on average three centimetres greater in girth than a man's thigh, mainly due to the accumulation of fat during years of puberty. The shorter, thicker thigh in women tapers rapidly and at the lower part is scarcely, if at all, larger than that of a man. Men's thighs tend to be a column, women's thighs tend to be conical. This emphasizes, somewhat, the slight inward set of the thigh bones due to the greater width of the pelvis in women.

Women have about ten per cent more fatty tissue than men, stored in the breasts, on the hips, buttocks and elsewhere, as well as a rather thick subcutaneous layer, which allows women to withstand heat and cold better than men. This may be of advantage in some sports in that women are able to maintain a more even and generally lower level of normal metabolism and thus devote more of their metabolic effort to the sporting task in hand. Women's breasts are probably a disadvantage in most sports requiring vigorous activity and are at the very least in most sports merely extraneous tissue to be carried around. In swimming, though, rounded breasts may aid the passage of water over the body and hence be an advantage. The greater body fat of women in general leads to less drag which, in turn, leads to women requiring about twenty per cent less energy expenditure per unit of distance swum. The greater amount of fat in their thighs also means that their legs are more easily held horizontal in the water, which increases the efficiency of their leg action. It is also clearly more efficient to move the body through the water when it is horizontal than at an angle.

Some of this fat is inert but some, as already remarked, can be utilized as an energy source during events of long duration and this must confer some small advantage on women competing in them. With all these advantages it comes as no surprise that in the ultra long distance events, such as swimming the English Channel, women are at least equal, and possibly superior, to men. The longest event regularly swum in the pool, the 1500 metres, sees women closer in performance to men than in the shorter events.

It is not just in swimming that the advantages of women at these longer events are apparent. In long distance cycling and above all in long distance running, women have in recent years demonstrated their enormous unfulfilled potential; their performances in marathon running have been quite astonishing, more so in even longer events. In 1967 sixteen women participants completed the one hundred kilometre run organized annually at Biel, Switzerland. Among the 1162 men who entered only 749 finished. All 16 women qualified for the silver medal given to those who finished the course in less than twenty-four hours. One of the women who subsequently ran in this race was seventy-four years old and she finished inside sixteen hours.

The 1973 Pacific AAU hundred mile championship in the USA was won by a woman, Natalie Cullimore, who covered the distance in eighteen hours. This was slower than her best time but two hours faster than the only male finisher. The women's fifty mile world record is still slower than the men's although it is coming down, but the way this distance is run by women is probably an important indicator of what might happen in the future. In 1971 the record was seven hours five minutes and thirty-one seconds. In 1974 it was lowered to six hours fifty-five minutes by Eileen Waters, who finished her run by completing the last mile in six minutes thirty seconds, which is a pace faster than run by any man at the conclusion of this distance.

The record in 1980 stood at six hours twelve minutes and twelve seconds compared to the men's record of four hours fifty-three minutes and twenty-eight seconds which represented a superiority of 26.9 per cent. Women have been active in the longest races of all — the twenty-four hour endurance events and the 1980 record held by Sue Ellen Trapp is 123 miles 675 yards (198.5 kilometres). The men's record is held by Stan Cottrell with 167 miles 440 yards (269.2 kilometres), a 26.3 per cent superiority. (A complete listing of men's and women's long distance running records are given in table 23.) Faced with this and other astonishing achievements at long distance running, who would still maintain that the longest officially recognized competitive distance for women should be 1500 metres?

(g) Differences in Capacity for Improvement

Training affects all the systems of the body, modifying and often reducing the average differences between untrained men and women described above.

Muscular strength of both men and women increases following weight training. Normal college age women show greater increases in strength than men of the same age for most muscle groups. This is to be expected if much of the normally observed sex differences are due to the effects of greater muscular usage in men. Weight training usually results in significant losses of body fat and gains in lean body weight and hence, overall, little change in total body weight. The gains in lean body weight tend to be a little less and losses of body fat tend to be a little greater in women than in men.

Gains in muscular strength are usually accompanied by an increase in the size of individual muscle fibres, although the strength of muscles increases three times faster than their increase in size. This increase is less in women anyway, partly because muscular growth is stimulated by the hormone testosterone, which is at much higher levels in normal men than in normal women.

In one study forty-seven women and twenty-six men volunteers took part in a ten-week programme of intensive weight training, attending two days per week and forty minutes per session. Assessments of strength, body composition and anthropometric measurements were made at the beginning and end of this study period. Men and women made similar relative gains in strength and absolute gains in body composition. The men were stronger than the women in all muscle groups, although the women had a greater leg strength when expressed relative to lean body weight. Additional muscular development was confined basically to the arms and was much greater in the men.

In another study strength, body composition and anthropometric measurements were made on seven women throwers before and after six months of training. Five of the women carried out strength training with near maximal loads three days per week using dumbbells, barbells and legpress, together with a programme of team sports and technique drills. After six months these five increased their bench-press strength by 15—44 per cent and half-squat strength by 16—53 per cent. The two who did not weight train showed little or no strength gain. Lean body weight increased only in the largest woman and in the two who did not weight train, while fatty tissue decreased in those who weight trained and increased in those who did not. Upper arm girths increased by an average of 2.9 per cent in all the women regardless of strength training; but thigh girth was essentially unchanged in them all, increasing by an average of only 0.4 per cent. To re-emphasize the point, strength in these women increased by up to 50 per cent with virtually no increase in muscular size.

All of this counters one of the main objections which both men and women have most forcibly made in the past against women taking part seriously in strenuous competitive sport. As exercise physiologists, Carl E. Klafs and Daniel D. Arnheim put it in their book: "Excessive (muscle) development is not a concomitant of athletic competition . . . Contrary to lay opinion participation in sports does not masculinise women."[2] Women, in other words, will not inevitably end up as musclebound he-men (or she-women).

Other training programmes such as running, jogging, swimming and cycling bring about similar physiological changes in men and women, although the precise gains in physique and performance in any individual case depend upon the frequency of training, the duration and intensity of the training programme and such individual factors as genetic potential and medical history.

The changes found after such forms of training include significant increases in maximal capacity of the oxygen system, that is, maximal aerobic power, increases in total blood volume, heart volume, maximal cardiac output and stroke volume and total haemoglobin content of the blood. There are also significant increases in the accumulation of lactic acid in the blood following maximal exercise. Most of these changes, while similar in men and women, result in smaller differences between the sexes after training compared to before. Because of differences in starting points and body volumes exact comparisons are sometimes difficult to make, but figure 12 shows the differences between men and women, before and after training, for some of these important factors.

Increased amounts of training, and the increased efficiency of training, are among the most important reasons why sporting performances have improved so markedly since the war and are still rapidly improving. Since physiologists have identified the energy systems important for runners, for example, athletes and coaches can concentrate on improving the aerobic or the anaerobic systems, depending on the event or events for which they are specifically training, conscious that the activities required for each are quite different.

The athlete most associated with lengthy and very arduous training schedules is the Czech Emil Zatopek, so successful in the immediate post-war years. He set a pattern which first men and latterly women athletes have followed, and the willingness and opportunity for women to undertake such arduous schedules must be an important contributory factor to their recent successes, especially in the longer distance events.

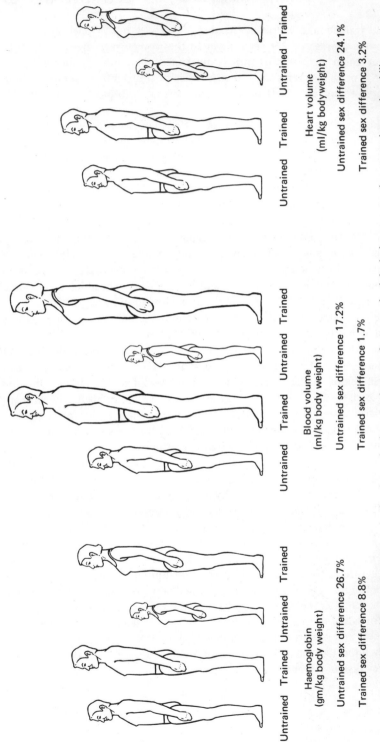

Untrained Trained Untrained Trained

Haemoglobin
(gm/kg body weight)

Untrained sex difference 26.7%

Trained sex difference 8.8%

Untrained Trained Untrained Trained

Blood volume
(ml/kg body weight)

Untrained sex difference 17.2%

Trained sex difference 1.7%

Untrained Trained Untrained Trained

Heart volume
(ml/kg bodyweight)

Untrained sex difference 24.1%

Trained sex difference 3.2%

Fig. 12. The differences between trained and untrained men and women for some physiological parameters important in sporting ability. In each case the value for untrained men is set at one hundred per cent. The values for trained men, untrained and trained women can then be assessed by comparing the heights of the respective figures. It is obvious that the differences between trained men and women are much less than between untrained men and women. Notice too, that the values for trained women exceed in each case the values for untrained men.

(h) Differences in the Nervous System and Specific Abilities

The brain is heavier and larger in men than in women but there is considerable overlap in the distribution of the sexes. In Europeans the average male brain weighs about 1425 grams, the average female brain about 1265 grams, but there is no real significance in this difference since brain size is highly correlated with body size. In proportion to the overall size of the body the size of the female brain is as big as the male in all races.

There are a number of sex differences in mental and motor abilities, but the distributions, as usual, show a great deal of overlap between the sexes and, with the exception of colour blindness and possibly spatial ability, there has been no demonstrated relationship between different behaviour of the sexes and innate or structural features of the nervous system or its receptors.

Some of the differences between the sexes in abilities which may have some consequences for sporting performance are summarized below. Many have rather little relevance for the sports with which we are primarily concerned, but they all add something to the conclusions we can draw about specific abilities and their effects on sporting performance differences.

Perceptual Speed

Perceptual speed is the ability to respond quickly to small differences in stimuli. It is measured by, for example, speed in recognizing similarities or differences between pairs of names or numbers. Females show consistent superiority on tests of perceptual speed at all ages. On one standard test, the Minnesota Clerical Test, only about sixteen per cent of men workers in the general population reach or exceed the median of women.

Reaction Time

Reaction time, that is the time between the presentation of a stimulus and the beginning of the response, is usually slightly less in men than in women. The differences are very small however, and are largely because men practise activities requiring fast reactions more than women. Athletes of both sexes who are in high level competition have faster reactions than non-athletes, and sprinters have faster reactions than distance runners. Isometric weight training improves reaction times by between six and thirteen per cent in both sexes. The common finding of a faster reaction time in men has been challenged by the results of a recent study of Chinese students. The mean speed of reaction of female athlete students was 0.4 per cent faster than male athlete students. The reaction of both male and female athletes was more than four per cent faster than non-athletes of the respective sex.

Movement time may or may not be related to reaction time. It is that period of time between the start of recordable movement and the completion of that movement. Men register a faster movement time than women, although the response to a visual stimulus seems to be about the same in men and women. Between the ages of about six and twenty there is no noticeable difference between the sexes in movement time, which suggests that the persistent effects of practice are responsible for the slight advantage of men later in life.

Motor Abilities

Men are superior to women in most kinds of motor behaviours. This difference is evident even during the preschool years, but is greatest during adolescence when girls definitely fall behind boys in motor development. Boys continue to improve in motor skills with age, but among girls there is little relationship between age and performance once adolescence is reached.

Women seem to be superior at learning simple motor tasks, perhaps because of their advantage in manual dexterity. Women reach their peak performance in skills such as reaction time and speed of movement at an earlier age than do men, which is consistent with sex differences in rate of development. The ability of women to learn motor tasks as well or better than men suggests that some of the discrepancy found in adolescence is due to differences in motivation and interest rather than differences in actual ability.

Spatial Ability

Men have, on average, better spatial ability than women as measured by the ability to visualize and solve three-dimensional problems. Evidence that this is genetically determined is not conclusive and some at least of the sex difference in spatial ability is due to differences in practice, training and socio-cultural expectations.

Visual Ability

It has been suggested that women may have more restricted or less efficient vision than men and that this may explain some of the lower performance levels of women in ball games. One study in Florida of men and women athletes showed that both vertical and horizontal fields of vision of athletes were superior to non-athletes. There were no sex differences within either athletes or non-athletes except in the vertical range. Women demonstrated a greater high vertical range of vision.

All in all it would seem that there are very important, if not overriding, influences of social factors on the sex differences of special abilities. Women in western societies are discouraged from taking part in a wide range of vigorous activities and contact sports. Change this and the mechanical ability, memory, motor and spatial abilities required to pursue them will probably develop in women to about the same level as in men.

(i) Psychological and Personality Differences

There are usually large differences between the sexes in interests, emotional and ethical attitudes, in styles of thinking and personality characteristics, although, as always, there are considerable overlaps between them. Men show greater aggressiveness and a much greater desire for achievement and acceptability, women show lower aggression and have much lower achievement motives. They also show more symptoms of neuroticism and instability. Typical masculine interests are adventure, outdoor and physically strenuous occupations, machinery and tools, science, physical phenomena, inventions, business and commerce. Women are more interested in domestic affairs, in aesthetic objects and occupations.

The problem with all these differences is to distinguish those which are products of socialization, that is, brought about by the current values and attitudes of society, from those more firmly rooted in biology and hence more difficult, although not impossible, to alter or eradicate. As philosopher John Stuart Mill wrote more than a hundred years ago: "What is now called the nature of women is an eminently artificial thing, the result of forced repressing in some directions, unnatural stimulation in others. It may be asserted without scruple, that no other class of dependents have had their character so entirely distorted from its natural proportions."[3]

One feature of women's sport which is not unexpected in view of these differences is the very high dropout rate in the late teens and early twenties. Women who remain often continue high class performance as long or longer than men and have a correspondingly higher likelihood of success. Mary Peters won the Olympic pentathlon at Munich at her third appearance when aged thirty-three; Beryl Burton born in 1937 was still the top British woman cyclist in the late 1970s, when her daughter was beginning to challenge her; Miki Gorman won the Boston Marathon twice in 1974 and 1977. Between these victories she had given birth, at forty, to her first baby. Stella Walsh, outstanding performer at the 1930 Women's World Games, won the United States Women's Pentathlon Championship with a record score in 1951 when aged forty.

The implications of all this for the fiercely competitive world of modern sports are obvious enough. Women, in general, wish to participate in different sports to men and are less fired by competitive spirit than men. These are only generalizations at best and are clearly of decreasing validity at the present time. Many of the findings just summarized are a consequence of the sex role socialization processes which women have in the past undergone, but these socializing processes are changing rapidly at present. Furthermore, the very successes which sportswomen are currently having are accelerating these changes in just those areas of importance to them. In other words the stereotypes of women's sporting behaviour are changing and are becoming similar to men's. The more women are encouraged to compete and to expect success, the more they will actually achieve.

(j)   Differences in Reproductive Systems

Women's reproductive system is mainly internal and therefore much less susceptible to injury than men's. The internal organs are not subject to any particular stresses in the contact or jumping events. However, two important processes occur in women which have no counterpart in men and which might confer some disadvantage: menstruation and childbirth.

The menstrual cycle involves a number of hormonal and physiological changes over a month or so, culminating in a period of blood loss if pregnancy has not occurred. During the 1930 track and field championships in Prague a survey showed that twenty-nine per cent of the competitors produced their best performance during menstruation, in sixty-eight per cent menstruation had no effect and in only three per cent was there some reduction in efficiency. Another survey of competitors in the 1952 Olympics suggested that menstruation itself decreased sporting performances by significant but variable amounts in about thirty per cent of women. On the other hand twenty per cent of women reported that their performances were better during menstruation.

The body fluid content changes appreciably during the menstrual cycle, reaching a maximum during the days immediately preceding menstruation. There are many studies which show that women have a higher risk of accident during these days due to so-called premenstrual tension. This premenstrual tension may adversely affect their performance in sports requiring a high degree of motor co-ordination or concentrated mental effort, but this tension is analogous to arousal and may confer some advantage in events requiring sheer muscle power such as putting the shot. And at least one survey of women athletes has shown that they produce their best performances during the immediate premenstrual days.

The effect of the menstrual cycle on training has not been thoroughly investigated. Some authorities recommend only light training during menstruation, others suggest that no departure from routine training is necessary. Surveys of sportswomen show that while most will compete during menstruation, many will not train or at least not vigorously. Overall the menstrual cycle probably makes women's performances a little more variable than those of men. With the advent and widespread acceptance of the birth control pill which can be used to control the time of menstruation, no woman need now worry about menstruation during major competition, although any effects that the pill itself might have do not seem to have been carefully investigated.

This conclusion on the relative unimportance of menstruation on sporting activity seems realistic from current biological knowledge. But biology and biological knowledge are often irrelevant in what people actually believe. Consider the following comment:

> . . . too much activity in sports of a masculine character causes the female body to become more like that of a man. This holds good not only in regard to the outward appearance but in regard to the genital organs for they tend

to decay. The monthly preparations for proliferation, which were previously normal is disturbed and may even cease altogether; the power to proliferate may be lost.

This was written by one S. Westermann in a book published in America in 1939 entitled *Sport: Physical Training and Womanhood.*[4]

Dr Eduardo Hay, Professor of Obstetrics and Gynaecology at Mexico University, carried out a survey of sportswomen and menstruation. In the *Olympic Review* for November/December 1977, he reported:

> One athlete broke a national and Central American record during her menstrual period . . . She informed us that her period came the day before the competition and she thus considered herself in a position of inferiority . . . The only way to fight this was to force the pace right from the start but she was still keeping up this maximum effort at the end of the race.
>
> During our research at the Olympic Games we came across a young athlete who had taken part in three swimming competitions the same day. She won two gold medals in the relay and an individual race, moreover improving the Olympic and world record and all this during her menstruation.[5]

The first quotation offers what seems to be authoritative biological evidence in support of one viewpoint. But despite its apparent authority it is now known that the opinion is rubbish. The second gives an example of what actually happens.

Pregnancy and childbirth is the second female phenomenon without any male counterpart. Many examples show that women perform most sports without a noticeable decrease of performance during the first three months of pregnancy: three medal winners in the diving at the 1952 Helsinki Olympics were pregnant at the time they competed; ten of the twenty Russian medal winners at the 1956 Olympics were pregnant at the time they won their medals; Sandra Davis, an American runner, is reported to have finished one marathon when she was four weeks pregnant and another when she was eight weeks pregnant; rowing and discus throwing competitions have been won by women up to four months pregnant. Dr Gyula Erdelyi, a Hungarian, studied 172 female athletes with children. She found that two-thirds of the athletes continued their usual sports activities during the first three to four months of their pregnancies and that the quality of their performance did not decrease during the first trimester, although it did thereafter and most, but not all of the athletes, then stopped their sports. One athlete referred to by James Fixx in *The Complete Book of Running* went out for a four-mile run two hours before her first child was born. She had apparently miscalculated the due date and did not realize that her feeling of malaise came from being in labour.

Labour and delivery, incidentally, appear to be better for athletes. Caesarian section was fifty per cent less frequent in one group of seven hundred athletes than a control group and labour itself was considerably shorter.

Other women runners report running throughout their pregnancy, and recommencing shortly after. An American long distance runner, Marcia le Mire, says:

"I ran for nine months of my first pregnancy, with complete approval from my doctor, and seven months with my second pregnancy. Distances ranged from three to seven miles. I also began running again shortly after delivery (one and two weeks)." She also says: "I ran a marathon (3:53) when my first child was ten months old and still nursing."

The short term effects of childbearing are of course a lowering of performance simply because of the interruption of training during late pregnancy and after the birth, but as Roberta Angeloni, a top Canadian middle-distance runner and a columnist for *Sports and Fitness Instructor* writes, "Without doubt pregnancy does have some effects on the quality and quantity of sports performance, just as sports performance affects the pregnancy. But most of the literature suggests that the effects are positive and to the benefit of the mother-athlete." One recent study of fifteen world class athletes found that four gave up competitive sport after childbirth, six created new world records and the others improved on their previous performances. Another survey showed that forty-six per cent of the female athletes who participated in the Tokyo Olympics, and who continued athletic participation after childbirth, bettered their results by the end of the first year after childbirth; thirty-one per cent more bettered their results between the first and second year after childbirth.[6]

There have been many famous women athletes who have competed with great success after the birth of one or more children. The great Dutch athlete, Fanny Blankers-Koehn, for example, who held at one time or another twelve world track and field records, was a mother before breaking the 100 metres, 220 yards, 80 metres hurdles and pentathlon world records and winning four medals at the 1948 Olympics. She was also, incidentally, pregnant during the Olympics and withdrew from the long jump and the high jump at which she was at the time world record holder partly for that reason. Photograph 5 shows Fanny Blankers-Koehn in the 1948 Olympic 200 metres final. She continued running for some weeks after the Olympics and resumed her career in 1949, winning three golds and a silver at the 1950 European Championships. British cyclist, Beryl Burton, was world champion for some track events and British record holder for many road events after becoming a mother. One of these long distance road records was superior to the men's record at that distance (see p. 186 and figure 26). Pat McCormick, one of the most successful divers in history, won both the springboard and highboard events in the 1952 Helsinki Olympics. She repeated this double triumph at the 1956 Melbourne Olympics which were held only five months after she had given birth to a son. Mary Rand won a bronze medal in the long jump at the 1962 European Championships only a few months after the birth of her daughter and went on to win the Olympic long jump gold medal with a world record jump at Tokyo in 1964. She had competed, prior to motherhood, in the same event at Rome in 1960 unsuccessfully. All in all, it is better to regard pregnancy, as one authority put it, as "an intensive day and night, nine month period of physical conditioning because of the increased demands upon metabolism and the entire cardiovascular system". As American runner Miki Gorman said: "Compared to having a baby the marathon is easy".[7]

4. THE SIGNIFICANCE OF THE SEX DIFFERENCES

Every one of the biologically influenced differences between the sexes described above probably makes some contribution to differential sporting ability between the sexes. Some of them are relatively unimportant in sport; others are obviously significant. What this book does question is the overriding importance of these biological differences and the assertion still commonly made that they cannot be overcome.

The evidence which leads us to question their importance and their inevitability comes from a number of directions. First, there are marked and continuing improvements in women's performance in a wide range of sports (see chapters eight to ten). Second, there are the demonstrable effects of entirely social factors on performance (see chapter five). Third, the physical and psychological differences between the sexes that are normal in western societies have changed in recent years and look like changing even more in the future; in some other societies in the world, furthermore, they are much less pronounced or even virtually non-existent. Fourth, there are examples of high sporting achievements despite marked and even massive biological disadvantages, examples where tremendous biological differences exist between competitors but performance differences do not. Fifth, there are some intangible psycho-social factors, and finally there is evidence from athletes' preparation for particular events, or rather lack of it.

(a) The Inconstancy of Sex Differences

In all populations there is considerable overlap in the distributions of height and weight of the sexes, and a very great deal of variation within the sexes. Some of this variation is directly associated with social and environmental factors. In Britain, for example, the difference between men in the highest socio-economic class and those in the lowest is about ten centimetres in height and between ten and fifteen kilograms in weight. These differences are about the same as the average differences between men and women in the same class. In other words, some at least of the average sex difference may be due to the same things producing the class differences — and few would suggest that they are primarily biological.

The sex differential in height also varies in different races. For example, some American Indians show an average sex difference of less than five centimetres, while some African Negroes show an average sex difference of close to twenty centimetres. Bushmen women are an average of four centimetres taller than the men and Afghanistan and Druse women are as tall as their men and as strongly developed.

The sex difference in height may be related, at least partly, to food intake, since in many societies the men traditionally take the larger share of available food. Mundugumor women are as tall as men, they do all the fishing and traditionally eat as much as they please before taking the catch to the village. A survey of skeletal characters in five groups of American Indians showed that the women were larger and closer to the men in size when the diet for the whole group was ample. The women were relatively smaller on a restricted diet.

One country in which physical characteristics have been monitored since the war is Japan: the mean height of older Japanese schoolboys has increased by between eight and nine centimetres whereas that of girls has increased by between ten and eleven centimetres. These changes have been particularly noticeable in urban areas and are probably related to calcium intake. Urban Japanese now drink much more milk than they used to, whereas rural Japanese still depend largely on rice for their calcium. The greater equality in dietary habits seems to be responsible for the greater relative growth of girls.

The differences between males and females in other areas of their somato-types (overall bodily proportions) also vary between ethnic groups. Among the Manus of the Admiralty Islands there are no systematic differences in somatotype between boys and girls; men and women both tend to have broad shoulders and chests, heavily muscled limbs and little subcutaneous fat, a situation very different to that of European racial groups. On the islands of Bali, men and women lack the differentiation of physique that is normal in other cultures. They are not markedly different in height and both sexes have broad shoulders and narrow hips. Women have very little breast development.

Clearly there is a great deal of socio-economic and cultural influence on secondary sex characteristics and general physique. Systematic changes in these socio-cultural factors in western societies may underlie a good deal of the current sporting improvements by women. It is quite certain that some of the improvements in the performance of both sexes can be attributed to the increased height, weight and muscular development which have taken place in developed countries more or less throughout this century.

One of the most important differences between the sexes is haemoglobin concentration in the blood. The concentrations differ partly because of women's lower dietary levels of iron and partly because women lose a small but important fraction of their iron every month through menstrual loss. One study in Japan found that about ten per cent of the women athletes belonging to various college sporting clubs were anaemic. Those found to be anaemic were given courses of iron preparation, vitamin C and glycerosphosphate of lime for up to two months. The number of red blood cells and the amount of haemoglobin improved in all of them and they all improved their performances, especially high jumpers and middle distance runners. What, one wonders, would be the result of surveying all women athletes and treating them this way?

In some societies what we take to be the normal behaviours and psychological outlooks of the sexes are reversed. The best known examples are those reported by Margaret Mead from New Guinea. Of three tribal groups in that country, Dr Mead claims that one, the Tchambuli, show a relationship between the sexes which is the exact opposite of what we accept as usual. In both the others there is little difference in temperament between the sexes. In the Arapesh the behaviour of both men and women is uniformly gentle and un-aggressive, and what we should describe as maternal and passive; the Mundugomor are (or were) headhunters and both men and women aggressive and "masculine".

(b) The Effects of Specific Disadvantages

Throughout the history of sporting achievement there have been many outstandingly successful athletes, both men and women, who have had what are apparently major biological disadvantages such as small heart size, low haemoglobin count, muscular abnormalities, injuries and other features which might have been expected to forever disbar them from competing at all, let alone at the highest levels of competition. If such major disadvantages can be overcome, cannot also the often smaller and subtler sex differences?

The American Harold Connolly was the 1956 Olympic hammer throw champion and a long time world record holder. He suffered from a number of physical defects including combined upper and lower paralysis of the left brachial plexus and an atrophied and partially paralyzed left arm. He suffered a broken left arm at birth, he had broken it four times before he was fifteen and by the time he was fully grown it was about ten centimetres shorter than his right. However, using a modified and highly personal technique, he had a long and outstanding career in competitive hammer throwing.

Another great field event specialist was the American Al Oerter. To his credit is the unique achievement of winning four consecutive Olympic gold medals in the discus 1956–68. At Tokyo in 1964 Oerter was forced to compete with a special harness round his neck because of a cervical disc injury. He was also suffering from injuries to his ribs following a fall and he was heavily bandaged because of this to prevent internal haemorrhaging. He could not train for more than a week before the discus final and competed in great pain against doctor's orders. and yet he won!

On the track, too, there are many similar examples. The American woman sprinter, Wilma Rudolph, won three gold medals at the 1960 Rome Olympics. At the age of four she had lost the use of her left leg after contracting double pneumonia and scarlet fever and was confined to bed for two years. She had still not been able to walk properly by the time she was eight. A very successful marathon runner of pre-war years was accidentally discovered to have a combined aortic and mitral valvular defect due to an earlier bout of rheumatic fever. The New Zealander Murray Halberg, a world record holder at two miles and three miles and Olympic 5000 metre champion in 1960 had a deformed and partly atrophied left arm as the result of a rugby accident which failed to heal properly when he was seventeen years old.

In the 1948 London Olympics British cyclist Reg Harris came second in the 1000 metre sprint and the 2000 metre tandem. Harris's was a remarkable performance because he had just recovered from a broken neck and was riding in pain from a broken arm. Harris is altogether a remarkable competitor. He won the world amateur sprint title in 1947 despite having suffered severe war wounds. He turned professional after the 1948 Olympics and won the world professional sprint championships in 1949–50–51–54. He also set many world records some of which stood for more than twenty years. He caused a sensation when he came out of retirement in 1974 to compete in the British professional 1000 metre sprint and an even greater sensation when he won it! Harris was then aged fifty-four and able to beat men half his age.

At the Helsinki Olympics in 1952 and at Stockholm in 1956 the most successful horsewoman in the equestrian events was Lis Hartel. This was despite the fact that she suffered from extensive quadripareses of poliomyelitic origin. Another polio victim competing in the 1952 Olympics was the American Walter Davis who won the high jump. He had contracted polio at eight years of age and had spent five years in a wheel chair and many more walking on crutches.

Oliver Halasy was a member of the 1948 Hungarian water polo team. Before the war he had been a medal winner in European 800 metre and 1500 metre freestyle events. But Halasy had no left foot, having lost it in a childhood accident. The gold medal winner in the 1948 Olympics for rapid fire pistol shooting was the Hungarian Karoly Takacs. In 1936 he had competed in this event in the Berlin Olympics using his dominant right arm. In 1938 his right arm was blown off by a hand grenade while he was serving in the army. By 1948 he had become sufficiently proficient with his left hand to win the event, a feat which he repeated in 1952 at Helsinki.

The most fantastic story of all concerns someone who, it must be admitted, is unlikely ever to make the highest levels in international athletics. It involves the twenty-year old Canadian Arnie Boldt who has only one leg, having lost his left leg above the knee in a farm accident when he was three years old. Arnie Boldt competes in the high jump and won this event in the Olympics for the handicapped in 1976 with a jump of 1.86 metres. On 30 December 1977 he jumped 2 metres at Saskatchewan, a height which was jumped for the first time by men with two legs in 1912 and by women in 1978. He hops to the bar with a fast approach and uses a forward dive to clear the bar. Who would dare put much weight on biological disadvantages to explain women's inferiority with this example before them?

(c) The Importance of Psycho-Social Factors

Commenting on performances in the 1964 Tokyo Olympics a noted German commentator, Karlheinz Gieseler, secretary general of the Deutscher Sportbund, said that: "Roughly speaking, the winning performances resulted from about 70 per cent physical ability and about 30 per cent human qualities".[8] Ernst Jokl, a noted sports physiologist, once wrote that: " . . . there is a creative phenomenon which is continually revealed in painting, music and literature and which is categorically different from the standards of physics".[9] He believes that something akin to this creative phenomenon, certainly a rather poorly understood psychic state, is involved in supreme sporting achievements.

The athletes themselves say much the same thing. Jesse Owens, who in one afternoon in 1935 broke six world track records and in 1936 at Berlin won four Olympic gold medals in the 100 and 200 metres, 4 x 100 metres relay and long jump, said that: " . . . technical and mechanical ability and robust physical strength alone do not make a winner . . . success is achieved by the human being as a balanced whole, as a marvellous, mysterious puzzling combination of mind and will power and courage and vitality".[10]

Roger Bannister, the first sub-four minute miler and subsequently a distinguished neurophysiologist, seemed to recognize this when asserting that: " . . . the narrower and more limited our lives become, the more vitally necessary people will find it to satisfy their longing for freedom in the hazard of their athletic performances". He went on to explain that these demand irrevocable decisions and that, as he put it " . . . the efforts of a whole lifetime seem to be crowded into a few minutes. The more experienced he is — and this is the real gain, the sooner he will learn how to pour all his energy, physical and mental into the profound happiness of a few moments."[11]

In one respect women currently have an advantage over men in this area. An editorial in the journal *Cycling* as long ago as 22 December 1949 showed why:

Sir Adolphe Abrahams, honorary Medical Adviser to the British Olympic Association, once explained the beating of a previous best time as being entirely psychological. What has been done by man can be equalled by man and perhaps bettered! . . .

[Women] have two incentives. The current women's best and the performance of other humans who happen to be men! Women, by capacity of heart and lung should be 30 per cent less efficient than men. Marguerite Wilson, who got much nearer than this, demonstrated that she was exceptional in her sex. But might not some of the supreme consequences of her will have been due to the examples of the speed performances she had before her in the male sphere?

In some sports the differences between men's and women's performance is probably still too great for this effect (if genuine) to operate. In others, notably some cycling and swimming events, it may well be a real phenomenon. Loa Olaffson set her unofficial world best performance for 5000 metres track race in a mixed event so it certainly works in athletics. And the achievement of women in mixed long distance road races are continually confounding and astonishing their critics. Perhaps the closer women's performances come to men's the more rapidly will they approach for this reason.

(d) Preparation for Particular Events

Among the most astonishing phenomena in international sport are those of athletes breaking records and winning medals in events at which they had never or only rarely before competed. The most striking examples are from track athletics, occurring in virtually every event from the 100 metres sprint to the marathon. Of course, the individuals concerned are all highly trained with a great deal of natural ability, but it suggests how much unrecognized potential there is among male athletes. A few examples make the point. The 1948 Olympic marathon winner Delfo Carbrera from Argentina had never run a marathon before. Nor, at least officially, had the 1952 Olympic marathon winner Emil Zatopek. For the winner of the Christchurch Commonwealth Games marathon, Ian Thompson, the British selection trial was his first race longer than ten miles. A picture of innocence, he won the race in two hours twelve minutes. Thompson did nothing out of the ordinary for his training and in Christchurch he had not yet mastered the basics of taking a drink on the run.

These examples are not restricted to men. In October 1978 Norwegian Greta Waitz received an invitation to run in the New York City Marathon. Despite the fact that she had never before run in a marathon, she accepted. The conditions for the race were far from ideal — much too hot. Commented three times race winner Bill Rogers: "The race was tougher this year because of the weather", veteran British long distance runner Ron Hill said: "It was pretty bad. There were guys sweating before the start". Despite all this Greta Waitz finished an astonishing 104th overall in a field of about eight thousand finishers. Her time was two hours thirty-two minutes thirty seconds, just over twenty minutes behind Rogers, the men's winner. This was a new women's world record beating the previous best by two minutes eighteen seconds.

Conventional wisdom requires that preparation for marathon running takes at least two years with training schedules involving 150 to 200 kilometres a week. All the textbooks say that at least one long run of 30 or more kilometres should be included in a pre-marathon training regimen. Greta Waitz followed none of this advice. Nor did America's Julie Brown, breaker of the American women's marathon record in 1978. She describes her race preparations as follows: "I turned my ankle in a cross country race last November (1977) and the ankle was weak from being strained. Then I broke it and continued running on it and I think I came back a little too fast. The other leg was the one that got the stress fracture." The last injury kept her in a cast for much of the summer. She then ran in the Nike–Oregon TC Marathon on 10 September after just seven weeks' training. She slashed nearly ten minutes from her own best performance and broke the American record by ninety-four seconds. What might she do with a full two years training?

At the other end of the distance spectrum are the sprints. The 1948 Olympic 100 metre champion was the American Harrison Dillard. He was world record holder and hot favourite for the 110 metres hurdles prior to the 1948 Olympics but fell in the final of the American trials and failed to qualify. He entered the 100 metres trial and qualified as third string, going on to win the Olympic final. The 1960 Olympic gold medallist in the 400 metres was American Otis Davis. He was a twenty-six year old mediocre basketball player when first persuaded to take up running. His performances at 200 and 400 metres were modest and it was on the strength of a couple of local victories that he made the AAU trials where he finished a moderate third. He went on to win the gold medal essentially as a novice twenty-eight year old unknown.

At 800 metres the best example is Britain's Ann Packer. She was selected to run in the 400 metres at Tokyo in 1964 where she started favourite but finished second. Having also achieved a qualifying time in the 800 metres, merely, so she said, to make up Britain's team in that event, she participated and went on to win in world record time. The final at Tokyo was only the seventh 800 metre race of her career, which included three in Tokyo and the one earlier in the season when she had achieved the qualifying time. All her training and all her ambitions were directed to the 400 metres. However, the 800 metres competition took place after the 400 metres and Ann Packer knew that the Olympic 800 metres final was the last race of her athletic career. She was determined to avenge, as she put it, her own second place in the 400 metres and the fourth place of her fiance, Brightwell, in the men's 400 metres. All this contributed to her determination, her lack of nervousness, the unimportance of failure and just the right juxtaposition of internal psychological and personality phenomena with appropriate external conditions necessary for supreme sporting achievement.

The 3000 metres steeplechase is among the most gruelling of all track events. The winner of the 1968 Olympic steeplechase was the nineteen year old Kenyan Amos Biwott. He ran his first steeplechase only about ten weeks before the Olympics, taking up the event when he failed to make the Kenyan team in the 5000 metres. In 1968 Kenyan Kip Keino had won the 1500 metres and come second in the 5000 metres. In 1972 at Munich Keino was second in the 1500 metres, but could not run the 5000 metres because of the programme arrangements. He entered the 3000 metres steeplechase, an event he had run only four times before, and won it, despite a very poor hurdling style, in a time only two seconds outside the world record. When Henry Rono added the 3000 metre steeplechase to his collection of world records in 1978 it was only the thirteenth steeplechase he had ever run. His technique at the water jump was to land with both feet in the water because, he had been told, it was safer that way. As everyone says, the steeplechase record could go a lot lower when he learns some barrier technique.

Karen Rossley of East Germany broke the world record for 400 metres hurdles in 1977 in what was only her third race at this event. In East Germany in 1977 only four women ran the event, among them Rossley, world record holder at 55.63 and Barket Klepp, ninth fastest ever with 56.98. The shape of things to come may be indicated by American athlete Sandra Farmer who at the age of fourteen won the AAU junior 400 metres hurdles record in 58.90. This was only her fourth 400 metres hurdles race. When a greater proportion of women take up this event seriously the standards are sure to improve markedly.

These successes demonstrate what unrecognized potential there is among even top class athletes. They pose two questions. First, how much more potential is there among women, who are so consistently told that they have less potential than men anyway? Second, what unrecognized potential is there among women for events in which at present they do not often compete — the long distance events, steeplechase, walks and so on. The performances by women in events fairly new to them, such as the marathon and the 400 metres hurdles, demonstrate quite conclusively that there is indeed a great deal of unexpressed potential among sportswomen.

CHAPTER SEVEN

The Sociology of Sex and Sex Differences

1. SEX AND GENDER

In chapter six the biological differences between the sexes were considered. Several biological criteria for identifying the sexes were shown, and also how to take into account what individuals themselves think and how societies identify individuals as male or female. This encompasses the notion that there are important differences in those social traits which define masculinity and femininity in society. These social traits include behaviours and attitudes — both of the individuals themselves and of the rest of society towards those individuals. Together they make up the sense of identity for individuals, they define the expectations of society.

Sex is determined, not always precisely, by biological factors and in most cases is decided at conception. The acquisition of gender, on the other hand, only begins at conception, gets more rapidly underway at birth and continues throughout life. While in some respects gender is the result of an interaction between biology and sociology, in other respects it is predominantly a social phenomenon.

From the time children first become aware of themselves as individuals — at about eighteen months on average — until the time of their maximum participation in sport they are exposed to gender stereotyping. They are treated differently by parents, they recognize the differences between their parents in work habits, body size, strength and so on. They find they are treated differently at school and in order to gain acceptace as adolescents they find they have to conform to sexual stereotypes. Not only is their sexual apparatus different but they find their patterns of sexuality are expected to be different by their parents and peers. By the time of maturity and marriage their sexual and domestic destinies are seen to be different.

By the time they have become parents themselves, whether or not they agree with the sexual stereotyping which has led them to where they currently are, they have a clear idea of what is typically masculine and what is typically feminine behaviour and they pass these expectations on to their own children.

Just as there is considerable variability and overlap among and between men and women for their primary and secondary sexual characteristics so there is similar variability and overlap among their gender traits. Masculinity and femininity are not all-or-none traits, they are not even the extreme end of a single spectrum. They are a confusing, sometimes contradictory, set of traits which our society at the present time has identified as stereotypically associated with males or females. The various traits identified as defining masculinity and feminity are of the sort shown in table 11. For the first eight of these traits and many others like them, both men and women express a clear preference for the masculine behaviour. For a smaller range of behaviours, including the last four listed, both men and women prefer the feminine behaviour.

Table 11. Some of the traits defining masculinity and femininity.

Feminine	Masculine
Not at all aggressive	Very aggressive
Very emotional	Not at all emotional
Very submissive	Very dominant
Very passive	Very active
Not at all adventurous	Very adventurous
Not at all ambitious	Very ambitious
Almost never acts as a leader	Almost always acts as a leader
Very illogical	Very logical
Very tactful	Very blunt
Very gentle	Very rough
Very quiet	Very loud
Very neat in habits	Very sloppy in habits

The curious fact is that various occupational groups differ in their masculinity–femininity scores. Among men, engineers and professional sportsmen have the most "masculine" averages; journalists, artists and clergymen the least "masculine". Among women, domestic employees are the most "feminine", athletes and doctors the least "feminine".

Masculinity and feminity scores also vary with age. Twelve to thirteen year old girls are more feminine and sixteen to seventeen year old boys more masculine than any other age groups.

I have emphasized that the sources of our gender identities are to be found at the present time within our present societies. Other societies and other times have different images of masculinity and femininity. It is part of the argument of this book that our own ideas are in the process of changing, partly in response to changing biological realities demonstrated by improved performances and partly through social change quite outside the sports arena.

2. PATTERNS OF SOCIALIZATION

Socialization is the basic social process through which individuals learn and internalize the attitudes, values and behaviours appropriate to the society in which they live and which are expected of them as responsible participating members of that society. It is a life-long process which is carried out through such agencies as the family, peer group, school, church, media and the multitude of social organizations to which individuals belong and with which they come into contact.

Socialization is a unique experience for each individual depending on that individual's genetic makeup, personal experiences and the way these interact with social processes. Socialization begins very early: there are significant differences in the way a mother treats a boy or girl as early as six months; fathers teach their sons and daughters different motor skills before they begin school. At home and kindergarten during a girl's early years she is told not to be rough or competitive. At primary school only certain sports are offered her and she is told to avoid others if she is to be a real girl. Hence a choice is more or less forced on her and if she still persists in choosing masculine sports she may suffer from conflicts extending into her adulthood. As a girl becomes more proficient her level of personal investment increases and the long hours of practice may isolate her socially. Personal conflict and stress increase as it becomes necessary for her to convice others of her femininity. This tension and conflict increases further if she has chosen a sport that is regarded by society as primarily a masculine one.

Boys get a much better deal. Incentives such as praise, recognition, status and prestige seem to be much more available for them than for girls in sport. Susan Brownmiller in *Against Our Will* says that: "There are important lessons to be learnt from sports competition, among them that winning is the result of hard, sustained, serious training, cool, clever strategy that includes the use of tricks and bluffs and a positive mind set that puts all reflex systems on 'go'. This knowledge and the chance to put it into practice, is precisely what women have been conditioned to abjure."[1]

The taboos, mores and value systems of traditional western society have tended to suppress what natural competitive drives women might possess and to enhance those of men. Values such as getting married and raising a family have been substituted for participation in competitive athletic pursuits. Men and boys have always received massive reinforcement from society to be competitive, whereas women and girls have received massive discouragement.

As American long distance runner and one time women's world mile record holder Francie Larrieu put it: "Social pressure — that's the hardest thing we women in track have to overcome. People who see me training are always asking, 'aren't you a little old to be doing this kind of stuff?' It's very distressing. You would think I was still playing with dolls or something."[2] Chi Cheng, one time holder of the women's 100 and 200 metres world record, who was originally from Formosa but was a student at California State Polytechnic College at Pamona, was asked how she dealt with this conflict. She replied that she took every opportunity to show off her femininity in public and that athletes are like other women in bed even though the public conceives of them as masculine.

"The public sees women competing and immediately thinks they must be manly — but at night we're just like other women."[3]

Social pressures exist for men too, of course. Men are encouraged to be aggressive, self-reliant, competitive and above all successful. These traits are often in conflict with those required of a lover, husband, father or normal integrated member of society. But they are even more in conflict with what is expected of women's role in society. Sportswomen are at one and the same time imitating and striving after what is seen as a male role in society, attempting to modify that role somewhat in order to accommodate themselves within it and trying to retain their femininity.

All this is beginning to change. In many countries, formerly negative incentives for women such as criticism, reproof and often downright derision are being replaced by positive incentives such as enhanced prestige, status and recognition for competitive and successful athletes. And the attitude in which sporting success on the one hand and family life and motherhood on the other were regarded as mutually exclusive is, happily, fast disappearing. In other words there is developing an accepted sportswomen's role which can be adopted in addition to or instead of the more typical feminine role. In the world of tennis, for example, Margaret Court alternates both roles, whereas Billie Jean King has been a leader in legitimizing the athletic role for women. When Margaret Court won her first Wimbledon championship as Margaret Smith in 1963, she spoke of her lack of fulfilment in the role of world tennis champion. She retired shortly after and opened a boutique in Perth in Australia. Only after her marriage did she make her tennis comeback and she continued to compete with success after her first child was born. Billie Jean King, on the other hand, has been at the forefront of attempts to equalize opportunities and rewards for women tennis players and, although not downgrading her feminine role, she has not emphasized it in public.

This trend towards a lessening of the conflicts on sportswomen emphasizes the more positive aspects of the socialization process — the identification with, modelling of behaviour on, and basing career aspirations on particular individuals. This is partly the hero worship mentioned in the introduction to chapter five, but involves also the influence of friends, brothers and sisters and others of the individual's own age.

Until now girls have had few women sports heroes on whom to model themselves. The more women do succeed in the world of sport, the more will those of the younger generation follow in their footsteps; girls will see more of their contemporaries taking up sport and maintaining their interest in it. They will then be that much more likely to take part themselves, to get involved and stay involved.

When Wilma Rudolph became the first American black woman to compete successfully in the Olympic Games she influenced the socialization of millions of young girls. Likewise did Billie Jean King when she defeated the admitted male chauvinist Bobby Rigg on the tennis court. Norway's Greta Waitz hopes to be an inspiration for other female athletes, and with her tremendous fame in Norway she undoubtedly is.

Princesses may win the BBC's Sports Personality of the Year, as did Princess Anne for her horseriding in 1971, but so too do many women commoners, like Mary Peters for her 1972 Olympic triumphs. And Mary Peters has told us of the enormous influence that Maeve Kyle, Thelma Hopkins and Mary Rand had upon her at various stages of her career. All of these women must, in their different ways and in their different spheres, have influenced very many girls in the generation below them. There are undoubtedly still very important differences in the socialization of would-be sportsmen and would-be sports-women but, like so much else, the position is changing rapidly.

3. AGENCIES OF SOCIALIZATION

(a) The Family

The first and, many believe, the most important socializing agency is the family. Differential treatment by parents from the moment of birth has been shown to establish different play patterns for boys and girls before their first birthday. One of the most important ways that boys are encouraged in their greater competitiveness, aggressiveness and independence is through sport. Boys are encouraged to play with cricket bats, footballs, baseball bats and so on more than are girls; and the establishment of clubs and leagues for the under sevens and under nines is almost entirely for male-oriented sports of football and cricket.

A general finding is that high parental primary involvement in sport and high parental value for sport both increase the degree of sports role socialization in children. Since in most societies at present it is fathers who are primarily involved in sport, they are the most positive socializing influence. They are more likely to have been involved in sport when younger, are more likely still to participate in, officiate or administer sport and are also more likely to be involved indirectly through attending matches, watching on television, reading the sports pages and gambling. They will transmit their positive attitudes to sport particularly to their sons. Far fewer mothers are involved in sport to the same extent as fathers so they offer much less of a role model for their daughters. And the sports in which mothers are interested are fewer in number – primarily tennis and netball. Those girls whose mothers had always played sport, and continued to either play or show a keen interest in sport, were involved in a wider variety of sports including many non-traditional female sports and saw no incompatibility with their conception of being female.

The socio-economic class and ethnic group in which the family is located has a strong influence on sex role learning in the family. Working class husbands and wives exhibit a much clearer differentiation of tasks and hence more positive sex role models for their children than do parents in middle and high economic status families. Children of such families show less sex role identification with members of their own sex. Girls, therefore, more readily participate in a wider range of sports and are encouraged and given the financial support to do so.

Similarly different ethnic groups have different traditional views of the sex roles. To the extent that many migrant groups and ethnic minorities in the USA, Western Europe including the UK, and Australia have more traditional and conservative views on the female sex role, the sport opportunities for girls in such communities are very limited. This is in addition to the discrimination which the whole community suffers so that sporting facilities and opportunities are overall much less than for the dominant groups.

(b) The Peer Group

As children grow up they become more and more exposed to the values and standards of their peer group. The maintenance of status among their peers is an important contributor to the development of self confidence in young people, as well, of course, as being of enormous importance in determining their values and behaviour. Thus if a child's peer group places a high value on sport, that child is more likely to become involved in sport than a child whose peer group puts a low value on sport.

It has consistently been found that sporting ability is one of the most important characteristics for adolescent boys. They desire it for themselves and confer high status on those who have it. Among boys of all ages, sport is the most popular topic of conversation.

An Australian sociologist W. F. Connell describes the situation in admittedly very sports-orientated Australia of the mid 1950s.

> Sporting events, results, records or performances, and sporting personalities are clearly the most popular material for conversation for all male adolescents. Any stranger can feel fairly sure of a warm and well informed response if he should open his conversation with a Sydney adolescent on some aspect of sport.[4]

The situation for adolescent girls is quite different. They seem to be more concerned with the status to be gained from good looks and attractive clothes. While being good at sport seems to be an attribute highly ranked for males by males, and for males by females, it is valued very low for females by females and for females by males.

Although boys can receive considerable peer group recognition from success at sports, girls do not. For a girl to get peer group recognition she must conform to the sex role behaviours expected of her by her peer group, and by society in general. These do not normally include primary involvement in sporting activities.

(c) The School

Students enter school having already acquired very different values from their families, from their peer groups and from the media. For most boys sport is already important and enjoyable to them. For most girls involvement in sport, particularly physically demanding and/or competitive sport, is neither important nor enjoyable.

In the primary school female teachers are numerically over-represented. These females themselves had negative experiences in school sport and physical education as students. Many also feel that they are not adequately trained to teach physical education classes or coach sports teams. Teaching sport is also seen as of very low status and by women primarily as a masculine task. Hence those people who might be expected to redress the imbalance between the range and availability of sports for boys and girls outside school, not only do not do so but reinforce the negative association between sport and females in young children's minds.

By the time children enter high schools many of their attitudes are already well formed. Sport and physical education has its own place in the curriculum and its own specialist teachers. Although the curriculum is designed for *all* children and often has very lofty objectives formulated in terms of the development of physical, social, intellectual and emotional attributes, in practice things are usually rather different. There is often a concentration by teachers on those of greater ability and an emphasis on the competitive aspects of the subject, both of which reinforce negative aspects towards and inadequate feelings about sports involvement. In other words previously acquired attitudes and values are usually considerably reinforced and nothing is done to redress the imbalance in socialization about sport which is mediated through non school agencies.

(d) The Media

The influence of the mass media as a socializing agent is of immense importance. The media coverage of women's sport and women in sport is in most countries quite appalling. It is considerably less than the coverage of men's sport; it frequently concentrates on the women involved as either freaks or sex objects; and it often trivializes women's activities, reducing the serious sporting content and emphasizing the clothes worn, the "social" and sexual nature of the game and so on.

First, consider the total level of coverage in the popular media. Most sport covered in national newspapers and on television is basically men's sport — horse racing, football, cricket, baseball, motor racing, boxing and so on. Even though women participate in some of these, they are almost totally ignored in media coverage. Sports such as golf, tennis and hockey which are important for both men and women are presented very largely as men's sports. It is men's tournaments and matches which are covered most consistently, extensively and prominently. Men's events are referred to as "the major event", "the big one", or less emotionally but even more inaccurately as "The Open Championship" or "The National Title", when women are not even allowed to enter! Sports such as netball which are largely women's sports are hardly covered at all, despite the fact that their level of participation may be almost as great as that of the most popular men's sports.

A number of surveys have documented this poor coverage of women's sports. For example a monitoring of NBC sports programmes in the USA between August 1972 and September 1973 found that there were 366 hours of live sport broadcast. Just one hour, the Wimbledon Final, was of women's sport. In one May week in 1980 in the major cities of Australia a total of 200 hours 39 minutes of sport was broadcast on television. Of this women's sport received 5 minutes, no less, which was deemed sufficient to cover the story of "Women's Olympic Immortals"!

These figures on Australian television come from a recently completed survey of media coverage of women's sport.[5] It is worth quoting a few more of the findings of this study:

- Less than two per cent of the sports pages were given over to covering women's sport and this included the simple listing of results from all sports.

- Three times as many men's sports as women's sports were reported and four times as many men's sports as women's had their results listed.

- There was a vast imbalance between men and women in action photographs (ninety per cent to eight per cent), but an even greater imbalance in non action graphics (ninety-three per cent to seven per cent). Many of the latter photographs of men were headshots of footballers and jockeys, whereas of women they were often of scantily clad cheer leaders or models.

This enormous imbalance in coverage suggests to the readers that women's sport is just not important. This sort of media coverage provides few strong incentives for women to take up or continue sport and fewer heroes for them to worship or role models for them to emulate than for men. The lack of action photographs of women reinforces the image of passivity, and many of those that are printed tend to add to rather than dispel the idea that sport for women is more of a diversion than anything serious. Many of the action photos in the Australian study, for example, were of women joggers, but they were printed on the fashion pages and seemed to be more concerned with selling track suits than illustrating sportswomen.

But this inequality of treatment extends into the specialist sporting press. Most of these publications are in any case exclusively for men's sport, but those covering men's and women's sports continue, in most cases, to give women very unequal treatment.

* *Track and Field News,* the premier athletics journal in the USA, produces an annual special edition featuring lists of top performers in all events, athletes of the year and so forth. Until 1975 this covered only men's athletics. In 1976 and 1977 the magazine produced a much less substantial women's annual edition. It is now increasing its coverage of women's events and the imbalance

in the annual editions is becoming much less. Nevertheless in its forty-eight monthly editions from 1977 to 1980, women were featured in its major cover photo just six times — four of these being the women's annual editions.

The Association of Track and Field Statisticians produces a substantial annual volume giving world, Games and area records, one hundred deep world best performances and other very valuable statistics (which have been heavily drawn on in chapter eight of this book); but its coverage is of men only and there are no immediate plans to change this. In *Sports Illustrated,* the USA's premier general sports magazine, just 1.4 per cent of the pages of articles in 1970 were on women's sport and 8.2 per cent of the pictures were of women.

Journalists and editors say they are only reflecting sport in the real world and catering to the expressed wishes and interests of their readers. It is doubtful if the imbalance in interest and demand of their readership is as extreme as they make it seem; they are always well behind changes in public opinion in this field and there is hardly ever any expressed intention to try and change things so that coverage of sport for the millions of women who do participate is anything like adequate. Not that ignoring women's sport is restricted to the popular media. In thirteen American college level anthologies and textbooks published in the 1970s on the sociology of sport, only three have a separate chapter, or section in a chapter, devoted to female involvement in sport.

The second charge is that when media do report women's sport they trivialize it by treating the participants as sex objects, freakish exceptions (if they are successful), objects of fun (if they are not), or merely advertisers' models.

A recent article in a serious Melbourne newspaper, *The Age,* was canvassing the possibility of women playing Australian Rules football. It was illustrated by the photograph of a women with naked breasts and wearing only footy shorts and socks. Another recent article, this time in a Sydney paper, on highly success-ful Australian golfer Jan Stevenson runs: "Australia's Jan Stevenson was nominated today as the sexiest swinger in golf. Her sinuous body movements remind us of Marilyn Monroe . . . The sexy kid from Sydney is a 23 year old suntanned blond with an enticing smile and 110 pounds laid out just right on a 5 foot 5 inches frame."

An example of the media treating sportswomen as freaks was the prominence given at the time to the remarks of Dr Ludwig Prokop, the chief sex-tester at the Mexico Olympics. He commented that after testing 911 girl athletes he was convinced that sports made them ugly and that they had hard stringy bodies and in some cases hair on their chests. Is it any wonder that women subjected to these sex tests felt degraded and that there might be reluctance on the part of potential world class women athletes to expose themselves to such physical and verbal ill-treatment?

Subsequently there have been the continued snide remarks and unflattering photographs of East European women saying in effect that if to win women have to look like "that", then western women ought not to bother.

An article on women in sport published in 1973 *Sports Illustrated* suggested that: "Behind the myth that participation in sport will masculinise a woman's appearance there is the even darker insinuation that athletics will masculinise a woman's sexual behaviour."[6]

In general, women in sport are evaluated from a viewpoint of what is pleasing to a white heterosexual male. Those women who depart from this norm are singled out as being too muscular, too masculine, as "tomboys", or even "butch" and "dyke".

Treatment of sportswomen as objects of fun is exemplified by a story from a Sydney tabloid, the *Daily Telegraph,* quoted in the recent Australian media survey. A non-gimmicky photograph of a woman soccer player was accompanied by an article, the first half of which said:

> If you could judge people by the clothes they wear, pretty 16 year old Jamie Michelle Rosman wouldn't rate with the champions. Jamie's fashion wouldn't earn her any space in the pages of Vogue, but it hasn't cramped her style on the soccer field. Jamie's playing shorts are comically baggy and at least two sizes too big. And her ankle-high socks are hardly de rigueur on the international football scene. Yet the nasty scar on her shin didn't result from a kick on her unprotected shin. It came when she tripped over a garbage can one night. Suffice to say this delightful young lady is different. In more ways than one. She is the youngest member of the Australian women's soccer team.

Finally, women's sport is trivialized by advertising and other means. The John Newcombes, Bjorn Borgs, Jack Nicklauses and similar stars of the male sporting world can capitalize on their well publicized skills and successes to sell sporting goods, rackets, balls, sports clothes and so on, and on their general fame to sell a wide variety of products. There are few women in such favourable situations. Anonymous women are frequently used in decorative, usually passive roles as adjuncts in selling sports accessories. Even in apparently identical situations, the sexual emphases are different. A typical advertisement was one which appeared in the now defunct British magazine *Sportsworld.* A man and a woman were featured in tracksuits. Beneath the man the caption ran: "Top training and fitness tips from Arsenal's goalkeeper." Beneath the woman was the caption: "Get in great shape with Viv Noves – top international model gives tips on keeping a trim figure."

In many countries women are claiming the right to participate in hitherto all male teams – soccer in England, football in Australia, baseball and even gridiron in the USA. Using newly enacted anti-sex discrimination laws, women and girls have been taking male dominated sports organizations to court. Most of these suits have been unsuccessful, which in itself is discouraging enough, but the actions have often drawn very revealing comments concerning male attitudes to women's participation.

In the United States, Federal Judge Barron P. McCune, in ruling in 1973 that the Avonworth Baseball Conference has every right to bar a ten-year old girl from playing Little League Baseball, said: " . . . the 45-pound girl's admission to Little League play would downgrade the team she joined talent-wise, inhibit the play, complicate the task of getting fathers to volunteer for coaching and managing duties and greatly embarrass the boys who had to sit on the bench while a girl was on the playing field."[7] In another American court case quoted in Carol Oglesby's book *Women and Sport* the judge said that: "The present generation of our younger male population has not become so decadent that boys will experience a thrill in defeating girls . . . Athletic competition builds character in our boys. We do not need that kind of character in our girls, the women of tomorrow."[8]

In the face of this massive ignoring, misinterpreting and belittling of their role in sport to which women are exposed from the start of their sporting lives, it is not surprising that women are often reluctant to take part at all, or to take sport seriously, or to compete to the best of their ability, or to make much attempt to win any events in which they do compete. They are encouraged by various subtle and not-so-subtle pressures not to take their own sporting achievements too far or too seriously. They are forced to play what two American writers call "The Femininity Game" and describe as follows: "Sooner or later nearly every woman plays the femininity game. The rules are simple: you win the game by losing all the others — tennis, volleyball, chess, you name it . . . The equipment is looks and charm, the power base, men. If you want to get a man and keep him, you let him win."[9] Annie Oakley, when doing the same thing, is made to say by Irving Berlin in a less serious vein: "You can't get a man with a gun." A popular women's magazine (*Dolly*) said much the same thing but in a slightly different way:

> Outdoor sport can lead to the indoor variety, so it is worth pursuing, both as a spectator and sportswoman. Sport is marvellous for health — all the fresh air and exercise for taut muscles, trim bodies and stamina.
> Don't agree to a round of tennis, golf etc., if you're hopeless at it. It will bore him rigid or exasperate him to the point of breaking the racquet/club over your head. If you're the sportswoman of the year type, let him "just" win. He'll love the battle.[10]

4. BODY IMAGES AND SELF IMAGES

There is one particular aspect of sexuality and gender which is of overriding importance for athletic sports — the body itself and the public and private images we have of it.

One of the complaints of women in our societies today is that they are seen as sex objects — the Marilyn Monroe, Brigitte Bardot, Raquel Welch model — and evaluated in the extent to which they approach these archetypes. Alongside this and associated with it, is a model of passivity, helplessness and physical incompetence. Almost everywhere in the mass media women are presented as attracting men partly through particular sexual attributes of their bodies and partly through a studied dependence on them in most things physical and active. With few exceptions, projections of female sexuality in the past have totally avoided anything involving dynamism, strength, muscular development and co-ordination.

While the values male sexuality expresses are often the direct opposite of these — strength, co-ordination, resourcefulness and dominance — they are also rather more varied. The images of Frank Sinatra or Robert Redford are hardly the same as Bjorn Borg or Rudolf Nureyev, but just as sexually attractive.

The prejudices about what is beautiful and sexual for each gender are very deeply ingrained and are therefore very difficult to alter. But in the past these images have been mostly a record of the way that men — male artists, clothing designers, film makers and photographers — have seen and depicted both men and women.

But women are now beginning to demand a say in formulating images of sexuality and are seeking to expand the range of meanings female sexuality can express to equal the range male sexuality has always expressed, to add dynamism and strength, for example, to the conventional attributes of poise and grace.

Dorothy Harris, sports psychologist at Penn State's Centre for Women and Sports in the USA says that: "Women have to become secure enough to throw out the old concepts and develop themselves to whatever extent their genetic endowment will allow. Fitness is my only aesthetic standard."[11] Nevertheless, the labels of "unfeminine" and "butch" flung at strong and competitive women have been sufficient to turn many young girls permanently away from serious training. While they were growing up, the choice for most women was made abundantly clear: be sexual or athletic, but do not presume to be both because one option eliminates the other.

The extent to which these public images of the body are also private images has not been very fully investigated. When women are asked to describe their personalities they most frequently choose words and phrases such as weak, fearful, desirous of friendship and harmonious relationships. Men, on the other hand, describe themselves as competent, intelligent and motivated by power and personal accomplishment. Research in which high school girls were given balance co-ordination and power tests, to measure physical performance, together with a semantic differential test and a draw-a-person test designed to reveal the individual's body concept, showed a significant correlation between the two.

Neither the concept of self image nor of body image is stable and unchanging. As individuals grow and mature in body, mind and personality, their images of themselves also change, but the differences between the sexes remain fairly consistent. In both sexes there are individuals who are fat (endomorphy), muscular (mesomorphy) and lean (ectomorphy). But for males the "ideal" body type leans towards mesomorphy and for females it tends towards ecto-morphy. This differentiation is reinforced by mass media which project males as strong and muscular and females as curvaceous and voluptuous.

Concepts of appropriate body images are developed at a very young age and strongly influence the activities in which boys and girls participate. Boys in primary schools equate fitness with "having muscles, being able to run fast and jump", whereas girls equate fitness with being "skinny". A study of the relationship between strength and status in high school girls found that stronger girls were regarded as having less status by girls of their own age than were girls who were not as strong. Strength, as we have seen, is essential for success in many sports but tends to be devalued in girls.

Traditionally, the whole thrust of school and college sports and physical education programmes has been to reinforce the cultural stereotypes of body image. This is less true now than it was and it is less true in Eastern European than in Western European countries, but it is still of profound significance.

Attempts to change this particular aspect of sexual differentiation are among the most important of all the changes designed to improve women's participation and performance in sport. Chapter eleven reviews recent developments in this area.

5. THE ALLOCATION OF RESOURCES

At all levels of sport, from the primary school to major international competitions, females receive less financial support, have fewer opportunities, receive less coaching and have more obstacles put in their way than males.

The circumstances of women's sport vary in detail from country to country, and as a generalization the above is probably less true for Eastern European countries than elsewhere. But details of the financial support for sport in general and women's sport in particular are not readily available for these countries.

In all countries, discrepancies in the allocation of resources begin at the school level and increase as sport becomes more serious and more expensive. Australia is a highly sports-conscious nation with very successful women swimmers, tennis players and athletes; yet its discrimination against girls in schools is quite severe. In its most populous state, for example, New South Wales, the Primary School Sports Association offers eighteen (funded) sports at regional and state levels, ten of which are boys only, four are girls only and four are mixed. The same is true of high school sports. The boys' sports association offers twenty-three sports and the girls' eighteen at the regional and state levels.

Although the New South Wales Girls' Sports Association is aware of at least some of the unequal opportunities provided for girls, attempts to change the situation have been thwarted by the assumptions of other influential bodies concerning the appropriateness of girls' or boys' sport. It took more than a year of argument, for example, to have water polo accepted as a regional girls' sport, despite the fact that it had already been accepted as a suitable local school sport for girls.[12]

In addition to their official funding from the State Department of Education, the Boys' Combined High School Sports Association receives grants from a number of outside organizations. The Rugby League and Lawn Tennis Associations, the Packer Cricket Organization and businesses such as the Colgate Palmolive Company and the Bank of New South Wales provide grants of money or equipment. In 1978, money grants alone were approximately $18,000. The Girls' Secondary School Sports Association receives no outside financial assistance, not even from the Lawn Tennis Association which is concerned as much with women's tennis as with men's. Because they received no outside financial assistance, the GSSSA applied to the Education Department for increased funds. In 1978, they received an extra $1,000 which was hardly sufficient to keep up with inflation.

The Primary School Sports Association also received outside grants. Although this is not differentiated by sex, the bulk of its outside funds are for boys' sports, for example $7,000 from the Rugby League.

Sport is also an important activity amongst tertiary educational institutions, nowhere more so than in the United States. Indeed, in the USA much non-professional sport is almost entirely confined to high schools, colleges and universities.

Opportunities and facilities outside these educational bodies are very restricted, although increasing slowly. The promotion of sports meetings outside the college circuits is also heavily dependent on commercial sponsorship and the continuing conservative image of sports as rugged male-oriented activities has been and still is very important in this context.

Despite the availability of the university athletics (sports) scholarships for men, with their often modest academic requirements, many would-be sportsmen are probably excluded for want of a university place and many sports careers are interrupted or terminated prematurely when courses are completed (or not completed). While this may not apply to the very top sportsmen, it is probably important in the case of more modest performers and perhaps much potential talent is missed, particularly in the case of students attending high schools without good sports facilities or coaches. There are many examples of champions being "discovered" while at university, rather than recruited through the scholarship system, and so there are probably very many who are not "discovered".

But the scholarship system has in the past hardly applied to women in America, and so who knows how many potential women world beaters never even get started in athletics or other sports? One of the very few institutions to give women's track scholarships in the past has been Tennessee State University. From there have come the famous Wyomia Tyus, Wilma Rudolph, Edith Maguire, Martha Watson, Iris Davis and others, all members of the so-called Tennessee Tiger Belles who have been so successful in women's sprinting at the Olympic Games and elsewhere since about 1960. This just shows what other colleges might have done. The victorious United States women's 4 x 100 metres relay team at the 1968 Olympics is shown in photograph 7. Its members were all from Tennessee.

In the last few years a number of institutions have started to award women's athletics scholarships. Although still few in number these will undoubtedly have important effects on the standards of women's performances. But in the crucial areas of general financial support and the provision of facilities the differences between the sexes are most glaring and the effects most profound.

The financial imbalance of sport in the USA is typified by the difference in the sports budgets of the major universities. The University of Southern California, for example, a large but typical American University, spent in 1975 about $2.5 million on its men's inter-collegiate sporting programme and $11,000 on its women's programme. In 1974, Ohio State University spent $43,000 on women and $6 million on men, and the University of California, Berkeley, spent $50,000 for women and $2.1 million on men. In 1976 the average budget for men's sport in a number of large midwestern universities was $3,760,000 while that for women was $259,000 − about seven per cent of the funds.

In testimony before the United States Senate, Donna Lopiano, Director of Intercollegiate Athletics for Women at the University of Texas at Austin, said: "My operating expenses budget for women's athletics is not even equal to the yearly phone bill of the U.T. men's athletic program. The seven sport women's program operates on a total budget of $128,000 compared to the $2,400,000 for men's athletics."[13]

Changes are now taking place in the financial field it is true, but often agonizingly slowly. For example, North Carolina State's athletic budget for women increased from $20,000 to $300,000 in four years and the number of scholarships for women has increased from none to forty-eight in that time. Ohio State's budget for women increased to $300,000 in 1976−77, Indiana's increased from $2,500 in 1970−71 to $185,000 in 1975−76. Other colleges and universities show similar recent changes, but differences of tenfold and more in the financial provision of men's and women's university sport are still usual.

This slow and often minor improvement in funding for women's sport is being fought all the way. The University of New Mexico's men's sports programme in 1970−71 was $527,000, the women's programme was $9,150. In December 1972 the president of the university made national headlines by stating that he had set as a top priority the expansion of women's athletic programmes: " . . . even if it means a cutback in some areas of men's athletics". The actual increase which resulted was to $35,000 in 1973−74. Of this the men's athletic director was quoted as saying: "I think it's fine but I'm going to battle anything that will take money from our own programme". The football coach said: "I'm all for supporting women's athletics but there must be some-place to draw the line on fiscal responsibility". And the basketball coach referred to women as: " . . . dipping into my pocket ever since I learned about them on a farm in Indiana".

In a congressional hearing in 1975 it was reported that American universities spent less than one per cent of their total sports budget on women. By 1976 that figure had increased to a little over two per cent! In 1973 Senator John Tunney of California introduced into the United States Senate the Amateur Athletic Bill. This bill would have given a lot of control of sport to the federal government, and would have created a national foundation with as much as $50 million a year for sports development. In the light of pre-existing legislation, notably Title IX (see page 116), there is no doubt that a great deal of the development would have had to be in women's sport. Not surprisingly, perhaps, the bill was opposed by the AAU, NCAA, USOC and various other sports bodies. The bill was never enacted.

This financial imbalance in treatment of course has major consequences in terms of provision of coaching and facilities. It is a wonder that American women have been as successful as they have in international sport considering the discrimination against them.

Carin Cone, the 1956 Olympic backstroke champion, recalled seeking a place at a university that offered swimming. Applying to Duke University she received a reply from the director of admissions: "You're fully qualified academically to enrol at Duke. As to that interesting hobby of yours, our women's pool is open from 5 to 6 p.m. on Tuesdays and Thursdays."

At the University of California, Los Angeles, the allocation for men's sport in the early 1970s was $2.9 million, for women's, $20,000. In 1964 two UCLA students, swimmers Donna de Varona and Marilyn White, who won medals in the 400 metres individual medley and 400 metres freestyle respectively at Tokyo had to enter as unaffiliated competitors because their university had no separate swimming programme for women. Swimming is now one of ten sports offered to women, men have eighteen. Scholarships for UCLA's 800 or so athletes totalled nearly $500,000 with another $400,000 or so divided among the 31 full time male coaches employed in the early 1970s. But the 10 coaches who work with UCLA's 175 women athletes are not paid. They are full time students or staff who coach in their spare time. And they have no funds at all for recruiting.

Facilities for major women's sports are almost always inferior or non-existent in most institutions and where they are shared with men, it is always the men's teams who have the major usage and priority at all times. Women are assigned the least favourable courses, courts or playing areas; and they are rarely given prime time in the use of stadia, pitches or pools. This, of course, is a world wide phenomenon. In a wide range of sports women can be "associate" members of clubs which allows them the use of facilities at specified midweek times and usually carries no voting rights.

A recent pamphlet issued in the USA, entitled "What Constitutes Equality for Women in Sport",[14] reviews the present situation in American colleges and universities. Among the many examples of discrimination there listed, the following are typical: men but not women may receive academic credit for participating in intercollegiate athletics; women's teams commonly have to pay for their own transportation and meals, while universities commonly pay first class air fare for men's teams; in some university stadia women are not allowed in the press box, so that they cannot adequately cover events in which women's teams are competing.

When the United States Olympic Federation was making training arrangements for the 1972 Olympics, the men's facilities were chosen to parallel the climate and conditions of the actual competition in Munich. The women's team, however, was given a training locale where the heat and humidity made preparation extremely difficult. During the 1968 Olympics one of the American women's team was expelled for what officials termed "misconduct involving a member of the opposite sex" — a member of the American men's track team. He was allowed to stay. She had to go home.

In December 1978 one of the USA's top women distance runners, Jan Merril, ran in a mixed two-mile indoor race. In a field of forty to fifty men she finished fourth in 9:38.9 which was 0.5 seconds faster than Francie Larrieu's American and World indoor record. In January 1979 she ran against nine men in another two-mile race and finished fifth in 9:31.7. Neither of these times will be ratified as records because the AAU does not accept women's times in mixed races. Their argument for not doing so is that women gain an unfair advantage by being pulled along by faster men!

American runner Linda Huey wrote a book in 1976 describing her school and university experiences of the 1960s.[15] Of her school days in California where she first became interested in sport, she writes:

> Just about every aspect of the school programme indicated that girls' sports were less important than boys'. The home made green shorts and white blouses that we wore took a real beating during the course of a year. They were our tennis uniforms, our hockey outfits, our basketball and track uniform all wrapped in one. The boys received a different team uniform free for each sport, complete with name, number and the Leigh High green and gold stripes.

The financial imbalance permeates every aspect of the sport from facilities for training to prizes for winning. Concerning this Linda Huey makes the following observation:

> Poor organization is only one of many examples of the track world's double standards when it comes to men and women. Many times I've seen Billy Gaines go home from a track meet with a television, a tape player or a stereo after winning the 60 yards dash. Yet Patty Van Wolvelaere or Cherrie Sheppard, both top hurdlers, received bouquets of roses after their victories.

But it is not just a case of financial discrimination; attitudes are as much if not more important. At track meets, she says:

> . . . with the press and spectator attention focused on the men, women often encountered a condescending attitude from officials. Mary Decker, one of America's best middle distance runners, was once forced off the track by an

official who told her "You don't belong on the track now little girl". If Decker's coach had not intervened she would have missed the race in which she set a new world record in the 1,000 yards.

Incidentally, at that athletics meeting at which she had broken a world record and been voted the Most Valuable Woman at the meet, Mary Decker received as a prize a pen and pencil set. The Most Valuable Man, Dwight Stones, got a television set!

Even the textbooks in the United States are patronizing and out of date in their treatment of women's athletics. For example, one book on women's track and field athletics written in 1969 by two university coaches[16] makes no mention of events longer than 800 metres, nor does it discuss 400 metres hurdles or 4 x 400 metres relays. Yet in 1969 women were regularly running these events as well as 1500 metres and 3000 metres and had already begun their assault on even longer distances. Other authoritative and presumably high selling books designed for the British and American markets have similar short-comings. Not that other countries are any better in this respect. The premier sporting reference book in France,[17] although published in 1973, says that women run only 800 and 1500 metres. It makes no mention of 3000 metres for women nor the fact that women have taken up marathon running in large numbers and with remarkable success, despite French women being in the forefront of world marathon running. In Britain in 1961, Ian Buchanan published his *Encyclopaedia of British Athletic Records*.[18] Despite the book's claim to be an encyclopaedia and despite the fact that women's athletics had been going in Britain since 1891, women's records are not included. The standard history of athletics, covering the years 1864–1964, Roberto Querci-tani's *History of Track and Field Athletics*,[19] makes no mention at all of women's athletics. I have already mentioned the scant treatment that women's sports gets in American books devoted to social aspects of sport in general.

Some of the more outrageous manifestations of discrimination in the USA may change in the near future. In 1972 the United States Congress enacted an Education Amendments Act which contained the following as Title IX: "No person in the United States shall, on the basis of sex, be excluded from participation, be denied the benefits of, or be subjected to any discrimination under any educational program or activity receiving federal financial assistance."

In June 1974 the United States Department of Health, Education and Welfare announced that it intended to enforce fully Title IX. Women were to be entitled to the same facilities and opportunities as men. The National Collegiate Athletic Association protested to Health Education and Welfare that its enforcement regulations were deficient and showed "an appalling lack" of knowledge about college athletics. Early in 1975 the Department of Health, Education and Welfare issued provisional guidelines favourable to women, although calling for "equal athletic opportunity for both sexes" rather than equal funding. The male athletic establishment immediately sent a delegation to the President arguing that if the proposed rules went into effect, men's athletics would be decimated. In testimony before a United States Senate subcommittee the president of the NCAA, John A. Fucack said: "Bluntly put, directors of athletics fear that if significant sums are diverted under Title IX from sports which are today revenue producing, the quality of the particular athletic program in question must diminish, or be restricted."[20]

Certain other compromises were allowed to creep into the regulations putting into force Title IX and the final situation has yet to be resolved. Colleges were given a three year period in which to meet the required standards for women's athletics, a period which expired in July 1978. The NCAA in 1977 brought a suit against the Department of Health, Education and Welfare endeavouring to keep the government from imposing Title IX regulations. In a memorandum to its members justifying this move the NCAA stated: "The NCAA believes that NCAA member institutions should have the right . . . to determine their legal or other obligations with respect to the provisions of equality of oppor-tunity, free from interference by the Federal bureaucracy." The judge hearing the suit dismissed it saying the NCAA didn't have grounds to bring a suit because it had not been hurt by Title IX.

Michigan State University runs men's and women's basketball teams. During the season the men used to receive three or four pairs of gym shoes, the women received only one pair. Doctors were always present at men's games but not at women's. The women had to wash their own uniforms. They practised in a gym with a warped floor and inadequate heating and travelled to their away matches in station wagons. The men travelled by bus and plane.

In 1978 the women filed complaints with the Federal Department of Health, Education and Welfare and the Michigan Department of Civil Rights. The immediate results were that heat was turned up in their gym and laundry was provided. Some of their other complaints were investigated.

They also took a suit to the United States District Court requesting $16 a day for meals and that they be billeted two to a room (as were the men). The judge granted their request. He did so under the equal protection clause of the fourteenth amendment to the United States constitution. In view of the pre-varication over other anti-discrimination laws, especially Title IX, this seems to be a most significant decisions.

In 1972 the Association of Intercollegiate Athletics for Women (AIAW) was organized as the women's equivalent of the men's National Collegiate Athletic Association (NCAA). Most colleges in the country now belong to AIAW, which governs intercollegiate competition in seven sports: golf, bad-minton, gymnastics, track and field, swimming and diving, volleyball and basket-ball. Initially AIAW banned competitors on athletics scholarships but in 1974 this policy was changed and there are now more than sixty colleges offering women's athletic scholarships. This is still, needless to say, well below the number offering men's athletic scholarships, but is considerably greater than a few years ago. At the same time as it mounted its legal challenge on Title IX, the NCAA, on legal advice, proposed to extend its own rules governing intercollegiate athletics to cover women's sports, thus endeavouring to take control from the AIAW. The final outcome of all these wrangles has yet to be decided. The co-publisher of the authoritative American journal *Swimmers World* is in no doubt about the importance of Title IX for his sport. Reviewing the past decade in the January 1980 issue, he wrote:

Before (the enactment of Title IX) there was virtually nothing in the schools. This has to be *the* most important factor in the resurgence of our girls after the last Olympics. It gives girls opportunities to compete in school they never had before and, combined with our age group program, has brought us back to the fore again. Title IX has been the great emancipator.

CHAPTER EIGHT

Track and Field Athletics

1. BIOLOGICAL EXPERIMENTS

Every athletic event is a rigorous biological experiment — how fast or how well can some activity be carried out under uniform specified conditions. Women were told in the past that they would perform so hopelessly that they were not allowed to take part in the experiments. They were also told that some of the experiments were rather dangerous and for that reason alone they could not participate in them. But some women refused to accept this. They argued that it was unscientific to arrive at such conclusions without a formal gathering of the evidence. In any case they felt that if men got enjoyment from marathon running, hurdling, long jumping or whatever, why shouldn't women? At present, therefore, track and field athletics is part of a giant biological experiment, a battleground between the sexes and one of the most popular sports in the world. In each of these three aspects, though, it is changing very rapidly and any conclusions we come to now may be invalid within months.

The specified conditions for flat running races and jumps are the same for men and women, although the actual conditions under which they occur cannot be precisely identical. Wind, temperature, humidity, altitude and track surface, for example, all affect performance. Men probably compete more frequently at high altitude, a marked advantage in some events, and on the pick of the world's tracks. Any small bias in conditions are therefore likely to be in their favour. In the throwing events women's implements are lighter than men's but they have all remained the same weight during most of athletic history and so changes in the relative performances of men and women can still be studied.

Although all the physical variables are carefully controlled and, with the exceptions mentioned, are virtually uniform, the variables of the social environment are not controlled and vary markedly from country to country and from time to time. Therefore social factors are likely to be responsible for any systematic differences in performance at different places and times. The difficulties of trying to assess the changes in the social environment of women's athletics are very great. It includes such tangible things as financial support, number of coaches and so on, and intangibles such as attitudes and incentives. But the very meaning of these terms varies from country to country. A four minute mile or an eleven second 100 metres means exactly the same thing in Russia or America or wherever. But we do not know that coaches have the same powers, status or respect or even that they do the same job in different countries. Therefore, although funding, coaching, status, number of competitors and so on have all increased in recent years, we cannot be sure that these mean the same thing or have the same effect in different countries. Sociological research on sport in different countries has hardly begun and so we can never be sure that what seem to be equivalent advances in the organization, support and acceptance of women's sport in different countries are in fact so.

Men's athletics in its modern form dates back to the 1850s and was truly international by the time the Olympic Games were re-established in 1896. Women's athletics began in a small way at local and national levels at around the turn of the century and they have had international contests for just over fifty years. But full recognition, their acceptance into major competitions and their participation over the whole range of events open to men, has always been and is still tenaciously fought by male dominated national and international controlling bodies. Financial support and hence development of clubs and facilities has always been and still is at a much lower level than for men. Girl's athletics in schools have been, until recently, almost derisory in many countries if not ignored altogether. And the number of coaches in women's sport and their levels of expertise have always been much lower than those of men's coaches.

Partly for these reasons women's performances have always been inferior to men's. But inferiority of performance has itself been used as a justification for this discrimination and so the cycle has been repeated. Despite all this, women's performances are fast approaching those of men in many events. Even in those events where biological disadvantages seem most important, such as jumping and throwing, the performance differential between the sexes has been declining for many years and is still declining as fast as ever. Accompanying these improvements in performance have been improvements in the organization, encouragement and financial support for women's athletics and a widening of opportunities through the number of international meets and events in which they can participate. It is not known which is cause and which is effect, but it is doubtful if one could change without the other.

2. THE HISTORY OF WOMEN'S ATHLETICS

Athletics itself can be said to start with the Olympic Games and similar celebrations of the ancient world of the Greeks and Spartans. Sexual discrimination in sport also began then, since most of these sporting occasions were strictly segregated. So strict in fact that it is reported that in some meetings women were forbidden even to watch upon pain of death.

From the time of these ancient Games until the nineteenth century, women's participation in sport was virtually nil. Their physical activities were confined to such things as horse riding and dancing. In the nineteenth century women began playing croquet, lawn tennis, archery and a little golf. But it was not until the growth of mass secondary and later tertiary education that women's sport really got under way, being given great impetus by the enormous popularity of bicycle riding at the turn of the century.

Track and field athletics was developed by men essentially for men and throughout its history the sport has been administered both nationally and internationally largely by men in the interests of men. Many of the events developed out of military activities of the ancient and not so ancient world and assumed their modern form in the mid-nineteenth century, largely in the universities and armed forces of Britain, Europe and North America, institutions in which women were very under-represented.

The Olympic Games were re-established in 1896; the International Amateur Athletics Federation (IAAF) was founded in 1912 with seventeen countries affiliating and this immediately became the recognized governing body of the sport, formulating uniform rules and ratifying world records.

All of this occurred before the first national women's governing body for athletics was founded in any country, an event which took place in France in 1917 when the Federation Feminine Sportive de France was formed with three member clubs. In the same year the American Physical Education Association appointed a committee on women's athletics (which in America means sport in general), although it was not until 1922 that a National Section for Women's Athletics was formed in the USA. The Austrian Amateur Athletic Association was another early mover in this field. It organized women's national championships on 27 July 1918. Austria, Belgium, Czechoslovakia, France, Finland, Germany and the Netherlands all held national championships in 1921.

In Britain, the first official recognition of women's athletics was the inclusion in the 1919 Inter-Services Championships of a 440 yard relay for teams from the women's services. The Women's AAA was formed in Britain in 1922, the year after an international body, the Federation Sportive Feminine International (FSFI) was formed in which France, USA, Great Britain, Czechoslovakia, Italy and probably Switzerland were represented. This organization provided the stimulus for many of the early women's international meetings held in the 1920s and 1930s and it continued to be the premier women's athletics body until 1936, when it handed over full control of international women's athletics to the IAAF.

In thinking of these formative years of international athletics, say 1890–1920, the position of women in society at that time should be remembered. In most countries women did not have the vote, although the suffragettes were fighting hard for it; there were no women's trade unions; there were no family planning organizations or information readily available; there were no labour-saving devices in the home (other than domestic servants for upper class women) and most women worked long hours in domestic service, office, shop or factory before marriage, and long hours in the home rearing large families after marriage.

There was, in other words, little recognition of what we would now call women's rights or women's liberation. The whole feeling in society as to what it was right and proper for women to want to do and be able to do was very different then from what it is now.

Wherever and in whatever sport women competed they had to maintain a proper sense of decency and decorum. Lengthy skirts had still to be worn for tennis, for example, which as a result was played by women from virtually a standing position. Women swimmers had to be more comprehensively covered by their costumes than men and the style of shorts and vests which were regarded as necessary for women track and field athletes were hardly appropriate for any form of free-flowing human movement. One serious suggestion at this time concerned the need to widen the goal in women's lacrosse from six to fourteen feet in order to accommodate the goalkeeper's billowing skirt! Another problem in the early years was selection of women swimmers. Since it was considered indecent for men to look too searchingly at women in bathing costumes, and since there were no women selectors, women swimmers could not be carefully evaluated and therefore could not be selected. Since women swimmers competed in the 1912 Olympics, this terrible problem was, somehow or other, overcome in at least a few countries!

Women's track and field athletics began as an international sport in March 1921, when a women's international meeting was organized in Monte Carlo in which just over one hundred women from five nations took part: France, Britain, Switzerland, Italy and Norway. The track events at this meeting were 60 metres, 250 metres and 800 metres with 300 and 800 metres relays and a 74 metres hurdles race. It is not clear why these rather odd distances were chosen. The field events were long and high jumps, shot and javelin.

In October 1921 an international women's match between France and England was held at which 100 yard, 300 metre, 1000 metre, 800 yard relay and 100 metres hurdles races were run. It was immediately after this that FSFI was formed to perform the same functions for women's athletics as the IAAF performed for men's.

In April 1922 the second Monte Carlo meeting took place, this time with seven countries represented by three hundred competitors. The second congress of the FSFI was then held which ratified women's world records and decided to organize a Women's Olympic Games. Under pressure from men, however, this name was changed to Women's World Games. These were held later in the year in Paris with five nations represented, and included on the programme were 300 and 1000 metre events, now seemingly recognized as the logical reduction for women of the long standing men's 400 and 1500 metre events.

The Second Women's World Games were held in Gothenburg in Sweden in 1926, the number of countries participating having doubled to ten and the number of events increased to thirteen. In five years, therefore, women's athletics had grown from almost nothing to become a major force on the sporting scene, with a programme almost as varied as men's and approaching theirs in level of participant support. One of the competitors in these second Women's World Games, shotputter Miss Godbold of the USA, is shown in photograph 13.

Alice Milliat, who in 1917 had founded the French Women's Federation, approached the International Olympic Committee (IOC) in 1919 to have women's track and field in the 1920 Olympic Games. Baron de Coubertin's reaction was to suggest that all women's events be removed from the Olympic Games. Women renewed their application for the 1924 Olympics but it was again rejected. The then president of the IOC, Count Henri de Baillet-Latour of Belgium, tried to prevent a women's track and field programme from being introduced in 1928, but was defeated on a majority vote. No doubt the vigorous opposition to women's participation had a good deal to do with the fact that their first programme in Amsterdam was a tiny one of only five events, 100 and 800 metres, 4 x 100 metres relay, high jump and discus, and their admittance was only provisional anyway. Clearly women had had to compromise and sacrifice a lot merely to gain admittance to the Olympics. What should have been an occasion marking a period of acceptance and expansion of women's athletics had quite the reverse effect, a drastic reduction in the number of events open to them. The second Olympic Games in which women track and field athletes took part were held in faraway Los Angeles; the number of women attending showed a marked decline (see table 13). Altogether the admission of women to the Olympics resulted in a great deal of the impetus of women's athletics being lost.

From that time the women's Olympic track and field programme has gradually expanded to its present size of fourteen events (compared to men's twenty-four), although fierce opposition has marked every stage of this expansion. The introduction of new women's events has usually been contested on quite irrational grounds and are still being so opposed. In 1930 the IOC president Count Baillet-Latour suggested to the Olympic Congress in Berlin that women be permitted to participate only in "aesthetical" events which he identified as gymnastics, swimming, skating and tennis.

So fierce, in fact, was the early opposition to women participants and so restricted was the women's Olympic programme that women maintained their own World Games until 1934 with a much larger number of events than in the Olympics. The Third Women's World Games, in which seventeen nations competed, were held in Prague in 1930 and the Fourth (and last) Women's Games, in which nineteen of the twenty-six FSFI member countries were represented, were held in August 1934 in London.

But who today knows of this vigorous early period of women's athletics? Sporting histories and encyclopaedias commonly say that the reason there were so few events for women in early Olympiads was that women's athletics was in its infancy. In fact the Olympic movement did a great deal to restrict what had previously been very vigorous growth. Not only was the first programme only five events but, as previously recounted, the 800 metres was immediately removed, not to reappear for thirty-two years, because of the way women had given their all in the race. It was not until 1972 that the number of track and field events for women equalled the number on the programme of the Second Women's World Games in 1926, almost half a century earlier!

The London Olympics of 1948 should have been a triumph for and a marvellous postwar send-off for women's athletics. A promise made in 1936 by the IAAF to increase the women's programme was finally put into effect (three new events were added) and Dutch multi-world record holder Fanny Blankers-Koehn was one of the undoubted personalities of the Games in winning four gold medals. However, at the USA versus Commonwealth match held in London in August, after the 1948 Olympics, women were given a token two events on the programme, neither of which counted towards the match result.

Since the second world war women's athletics has been tied to men's at the international level. Its development has therefore been largely controlled by men and dominating all else has been the Olympic Games, which have had an enormous influence on the standards of women's athletics. The list of events as they are introduced (and not introduced) into the Olympics is very revealing of men's attitudes (see table 12).

Table 12. The introduction of Olympic athletic events: a male-female comparison.

	Men		Women
100 metres	1896		1928
200 metres	1900		1948
400 metres	1900		1964
800 metres	1896		1960 (also run in 1928)
1,500 metres	1896		1972
5,000 metres	1912		
10,000 metres	1912		
Marathon	1896		
110 metres hurdles	1896		1972[a]
400 metres hurdles	1900		
3,000 metres steeplechase	1920		
4 × 100 metres relay	1912		1928
4 × 400 metres relay	1908		1972
20,000 metres walk	1956		
50,000 metres walk	1932		
Long jump	1896		1948
High jump	1896		1928
Pole vault	1896		
Triple jump	1896		
Shot	1896		1948
Discus	1896		1928
Javelin	1906		1932
Hammer	1900		
Decathlon	1912	Pentathlon	1964

a. 100 metres hurdles. This event replaced 80 metres hurdles which had been run from 1932-68.

Prior to 1948 there were only three track events for women, none longer than 100 metres. When the women's 800 metres was reintroduced in 1960 their world record was nearly 15 per cent worse than the men's, 2 minutes 5 seconds compared to 1 minute 45.7 seconds. By 1978 the women's record had improved 8.75 per cent to 1 minute 54.95 seconds, whereas the men's record had improved only 2.15 per cent to 1 minute 43.44 seconds. The 1978 difference between the performances was just 10.01 per cent. When the women's 400 metres was introduced in 1964 their record at 51.9 seconds was 15 per cent worse than the men's record of 44.9; the difference between the records in 1978 was just 10.78 per cent, 48.94 versus 43.86. When the women's 1500 metres was introduced in 1972 their world record was more than 17 per cent worse than the men's record; six years later, the difference was down to 10.09 per cent. The women's world record for the 3000 metres in 1978 was 10.85 per cent below that of the men's record. Is it not likely that, given the stimulus of Olympic competition, the women's performances would improve in this event to the same extent as did their performances in the shorter distances when they were introduced into the Olympics?

The 3000 metres for women was included in the European Championships for the first time in 1974. The current world record of 8:27.12 was set by Ludmilla Bragina during the USA–USSR match in August 1976. After the match Bragina said: "I trained really hard all winter. If others can emulate the same intensity and volume of work and give me a bit of competition, the world record could be between 8:10 and 8:15 within a couple of years".[1]

But why draw the line for female competition at 3000 metres? The best performances by women at 5000 metres, 10,000 metres and in the marathon are each about thirteen per cent below those of men (see table 15). In other words women's standards in these events relative to men are now better than were the 400, 800, and 1500 metres events when they were introduced into the Olympic programme. Furthermore the number of women participating in these longer events is increasing very rapidly, and improvement in performance will probably be even faster than in the past. On any rational criteria the whole track programme from 100 metres to the marathon should be thrown open to women.

There have been and still are many other curious anomalies. The 4 x 400 metres relay for women was not introduced until 1972, although the 400 metres had been run since 1964. There is no women's 400 metres hurdles in the Olympics, even though it is included in the European Championships, the World Cup and several international matches. The long jump was not introduced until 1948, although the high jump had been on the Olympic programme since 1928. There are no walking events despite the fact that walking is a thriving sport for women in many European countries.

But even if all these missing events were introduced into the Olympics there would still be gaps in the women's programme. There is no women's triple jump, pole vault, steeplechase or hammer throw in any national or international championship. One reason commonly given for not introducing them is that there is no tradition of women competing in these events. But this is not a reason, it is just a hangover from the past. Women can compete in these events as safely and as capably as men and have every right to do so.

The time is past when the Olympics can be regarded as a male preserve which happens to be graced by women on the periphery. Women's claims for new Olympic events must be regarded as of first priority. Table 13 shows the increasing overall level of participation of women in the summer games. In the 1976 Montreal Olympics women formed one-eighth of all competitors, but in those sports where they have their own competitions, namely athletics, swimming, gymnastics, fencing, archery, volley-ball and canoeing, their proportions were much higher.

One of the major stated concerns of the International Olympic Committee at present is that the Games are becoming too large and expensive to mount. They are therefore seeking to reduce not increase the number of events and have an almost built-in excuse not to introduce any new women's athletics events. Nevertheless, in 1976, six rowing events for women, women's handball and women's basketball were introduced, but so too were four additional men's canoeing events, an additional men's rowing event and an additional men's speed skating event. In 1972 men's handball and various judo, wrestling and weightlifting categories had also been introduced. Women's hockey was, at last, introduced in 1980. The argument about reducing the size of the Games therefore rings a little hollow.

The introduction of new competitions, world championships, cups, area games and the like is providing other routes by which new women's events may gain international acceptance. It is the IAAF which will sanction new women's events in these competitions. The past actions of that body with respect to women's athletics should therefore be looked at.

The recognition of women's world records by the IAAF is a similar sorry story to that of the introduction of women's events into the Olympics. The details are set out in table 14. The omissions and inconsistencies of this list, the lack of correspondence with the women's Olympic programme and the failure to recognize the realities of women's actual athletic achievements are so obvious as to require no further comment.

There is a rather unpleasant story concerning the initial recognition of women's world records by the IAAF. In 1934 a joint committee of IAAF and FSFI had been set up to investigate a possible merger. The FSFI, having originally proposed to hold the Fifth Women's World Games in 1938, offered to stop its work and wind itself up provided that the world records they had accepted were also accepted by the IAAF, and that an extended women's programme was included in the Olympic Games. The FSFI did in fact disband in 1938 having received these assurances. The IAAF accepted in 1936, after the Berlin Games, the recommendation for an extended Olympic programme (which because of the war only came into effect in 1948 and was only three

Table 13. Women in the summer Olympic Games.

Year	Place	Number of Female Participants[a]	Percentage of Total Participants	Number of Countries with Female Representatives	Number of Events for Female Athletes[b]	Percentage of Total Number of Events
1900	Paris	12	0.8	5	3	3.5
1904	St Louis	8	1.3	1	3	3.4[c]
1908	London	43[d]	2.1	3	5	4.5
1912	Stockholm	55	2.2	10	6	5.6
1920	Antwerp	76[d]	2.9	12	11	6.8
1924	Paris	136	4.4	20	11	8.4
1928	Amsterdam	290	9.6	24	14	11.5
1932	Los Angeles	127	9.0	17	14	11.1
1936	Berlin	328	8.1	26	15	10.4
1948	London	385	9.4	33	19	12.7
1952	Helsinki	518	10.5	41	25	16.8
1956	Melbourne	384[e]	11.5	37	26	17.2
1960	Rome	610	11.4	45	29	19.3
1964	Tokyo	683	13.3	53	33	20.1
1968	Mexico City	781	14.1	53	39	22.7
1972	Munich	1,299	17.7	61	43	22.1
1976	Montreal	1,261	14.9	59	49	24.7

a. The total number of participants and number of women involved are difficult to determine precisely, because of non-competitors, non-arrivals and boycotts among those listed as intending participants. Different authorities therefore quote different numbers.

b. The "Number of Events for Female Athletes" column does not include sports events open for males and females and the same goes for the column on "Percentage of Total Number of Events". For full details of the events as they were introduced see table 41.

c. About 380 so-called "Olympic events" were held in 1904 in St Louis. This peculiar situation has not been satisfactorily dealt with by any Olympic historians to date.

d. The figures for female participants in 1908 and 1920 include seven and twelve figure-skaters respectively, as this sport was part of the Summer Games at that time.

e. Figures for 1956 also include the equestrian competitions in Stockholm.

Table 14. IAAF official world records and their date of recognition.

	Men	Women	
60 metres		1933	
100 metres	1912	1934	
200 metres (straight)	1896	1935	
200 metres (turn)	1951		
400 metres	1900	1957	
800 metres	1912	1928	
1,000 metres	1913		
1,500 metres	1912	1967	
2,000 metres	1918		
3,000 metres	1912	1971	
5,000 metres	1912		
10,000 metres[a]	1911		
4 x 100 metres	1912	1936	
4 x 200 metres	1919	1932	
4 x 400 metres	1911	1969	
4 x 800 metres	1926	1969	(Between 1933-68 a 3 x 800 relay record was recognized)
4 x 1,500 metres	1919		
110/100 metres hurdles	1908	1969	(Between 1934-68 an 80 metres hurdles record was recognized)
200 metres hurdles (straight)[b]	1898	1969	
200 metres hurdles (turn)[b]	1959		
400 metres hurdles	1908	1973	
High jump	1912	1932	
Pole Vault	1912		
Long jump	1901	1928	
Triple jump	1911		
Shot	1909	1926	
Discus	1912	1936	
Javelin	1912	1932	
Hammer	1913		

a. The IAAF also recognizes men's records at 20,000 metres, 25,000 metres, 30,000 metres and for the one hour run, and for track walks at 20,000 metres, 30,000 metres and 50,000 metres. For none of these events are women's records recognized. At its meeting in Montreal in 1979, the IAAF did vote to recognize women's records at 5,000 and 10,000 metres.

b. In 1977 the IAAF ceased to recognize either men's or women's records at this distance.

extra events anyway). They did not accept all the FSFI world records, however, and records for some events such as the 400 metres, 1000 metres and the various walks were long delayed or are still not recognized.

Unofficial records exist for many of the events missing from the IAAF list, but women holding them are denied the official recognition, the award of plaques and the general status that go with approval by the world's athletics governing body and which are automatically awarded to male record holders. In encyclopaedias and sports books it is the official list of record holders that are published and rarely the unofficial lists of best performers, so that the women's athletic programme looks more sparse than it actually is.

One factor which has markedly complicated the history of track and field athletics in Britain and the commonwealth countries has been the class difference between men's and women's athletics. Men's athletics in Britain was, until the 1950s, largely an upper class activity. It had long been dominated by the aristocracy, with such figures as Lord Burghley and Lord Killanin prominent, and by Oxford and Cambridge Universities, whose intake was heavily from the middle and upper classes. In the three Olympiads from 1920–28, ten Oxbridge athletes won track medals and five others reached finals, an astonishing domination of British athletics. This tradition was maintained in postwar years with such athletes as Roger Bannister, Derek Johnson, Chris Chataway, Chris Brasher and many others maintaining Oxbridge domination until the mid 1950s. Only when Arthur Rowe, Gordon Pirie, Derek Ibbotson, Peter Radford and others came on the scene in the late 1950s was there any working class break-through into British men's athletics.

In contrast when the Women's Amateur Athletics Association was founded in 1922 its members were mostly secretaries, shop assistants, schoolteachers and the like. The number of women in Britain's universities has always been much lower than men and in the 1920s they were very few indeed. Women's athletics has always had a very working class flavour in Britain and women have had to suffer class as well as sex discrimination as a consequence. The resources of working-class girls to finance their sport are much lower than those of middle- and upper-class university-backed males. The WAAA, for example, did not appoint its first coaching organizer until 1947 and the financing of overseas tours by women's teams or individual women has always been a major problem.

Less obvious but probably as important is the sex-class relationship between administrators and athletes which has exacerbated the difficulties of that always difficult relationship. Many questions of priority, regarding such things as the choice of events in matches and the numbers of women allowed to travel to overseas matches and competitions, have been settled in the past on grounds of sex-class prejudice rather than on athletic ability. As men's athletics in Britain has gradually lost its upper class image, the position of women's athletics has been more realistically appraised and more fairly supported. Between 1960 and 1976 British women won three gold and six silver medals at the Olympics, British men won only two gold and five silver medals from their larger pro-gramme, and since nothing succeeds like success, this has ensured continuing reappraisal of and changes in women's athletics.

Some of these class differences and attitudes undoubtedly occur in other countries with similar consequences. The principal founder of the modern Olympics was Baron Coubertin and the nobility and aristocracy have been prominent in the International Olympic Committee ever since. In parts of the British Isles religious and sectarian prejudices are added to those operating against women. This is particularly the case in Ireland, divided since 1921 into Northern Ireland within the UK and the independent Republic in the south. The Republic is largely Roman Catholic and the hierarchy in the church have often held very conservative views on both religious and secular issues. A future Archbishop of Dublin, when head of a famous boys' school before the war, threatened to withdraw his school from athletics if the national body let in women. Among his reasons were that the women would be undressing on the sides of the track and this would be an occasion of sin for the men athletes.

In the immediate postwar years, however, many famous women athletes including Fanny Blankers-Koehn and June Foulds ran in Dublin before enthusiastic crowds. Fanny Blankers-Koehn ran after her 1948 Olympic triumphs and won 100 and 200 yard races off scratch. They inspired Irish girls to compete in track and field competitions; there was consequently a big surge forward in the sport and for two years girls' athletics events became a feature of Irish sports meetings. Then suddenly in 1951 girls' athletics stopped in the Republic completely. The former headmaster, now Archbishop of Dublin, let it be known that he did not approve and athletics administrators gave in rather than confront the church. The result was that for ten years potential girl athletes in the Republic had no opportunity to compete. A few, like Maeve Kyle, moved north. As well as being the most capped player in the history of Irish women's hockey she ran 10.8 for the 100 yards, a time not yet beaten in Ireland. But most women athletes, not surprisingly, just gave up.

Women's athletics continued in Northern Ireland and produced, among others, Thelma Hopkins who broke the world high jump record in 1956 and won a Commonwealth gold and an Olympic silver medal, and Mary Peters, Olympic pentathlon champion and world record breaker in 1972 and Commonwealth champion in 1974. The success of Northern Ireland girls had repercussions in the south. In 1961, despite continued ecclesiastical opposition, women's athletics was again launched there and has since grown remarkably and produced many outstanding athletes. The organization of women's sport in Ireland, both North and South, continues to be plagued by religious and now political divisions concerning such issues as the establishment of all-Ireland organizations, Irish championships and the like. There are, no doubt, continued restrictions on girls' sport in the more conservative schools.

The question is, how many potential women champions and record holders were completely lost to athletics in Southern Ireland and to what extent did women in Northern Ireland fail to reach their full potential through lack of competition from their southern compatriots? We shall never know. Nor shall we ever really know how many other countries were and still are similar to the Irish Republic in their attitudes to women's sport; certainly many of the

Islamic and Hindu countries are similar. India, for example, has produced a number of notable male track and field athletes and the Indian subcontinent countries are prominent in a number of men's team sports, especially hockey and cricket; but who can name a single sportswoman from India, Pakistan, Bangladesh or Sri Lanka?

Restrictions on girls from these cultures exist outside these countries. It seems most unlikely that the Asian communities in Britain will produce any sportswomen in the near future because of the social and cultural attitudes to women that these communities hold. The contrast with Britain's West Indian community is pronounced already. Women's sprinting in Britain is now largely dominated by girls of Caribbean descent and there are also many prominent black women field event athletes. In this, they have undoubtedly been strongly influenced by the important part that sport has always played in transplanted black communities, since it has been such an important avenue of upward social mobility and financial reward for them.

Despite the prominence of black women athletes in the USA, the UK, Cuba and the West Indies, the athletic potential of women in Africa has hardly yet been touched. There are two separate traditions for them to follow. Blacks of West African origin, both men and women, in America, in the West Indies and now Britain, have concentrated on and been highly successful in the sprints up to the 400 and occasionally the 800 metres and the high and long jumps. But the great successes of African men (but not women so far) in the long distance events have been mainly by East Africans: Tanzanians, Kenyans, Ugandans and Ethiopians. There may be some racial factors responsible for this difference or it may be the effects of tradition but, whichever it is, when African women become fully involved in athletics, performances in *all* events may be revolutionized. In 1978 all the principal men's track event records were held by black athletes, 100–400 metres by Afro-Americans, 800 metres by an Afro-Cuban and 1500–10,000 metres by a Tanzanian and a Kenyan. Not one women's record at that time was held by a black athlete.

The history of women's athletics in Eastern Europe is clearly divided into pre- and post-war phases. In pre-war years, women's athletics in most Eastern European countries was run similarly and had similar processes and problems to women's athletics in Western Europe. Czechoslovakia was certainly represented in the early days of FSFI but never produced any Olympic medal winners. Hungary and Poland appear among the medal winners of pre-war Olympics. But two of Poland's medals come from Stanislawa Walasiewicz who, as Stella Walsh, lived most of her life in the USA, and Hungary only ever won one medal, in the high jump. The other East European countries did not take part in international athletics.

Russia played no part in the Olympic movement and little part in international sport of any kind during the inter-war years. Although great social and economic changes were taking place in that country, it was not until 1952, when Russia re-entered the Olympic movement, that their effects on sport could be evaluated. Other countries, notably Poland and Bulgaria, did not reappear in the Olympics after the war until 1952 and East Germany was not represented as a separate entity until 1968, when the previous all-Germany team was split between East and West. In Montreal, Russia had the second largest athletics team, Poland the third largest and East Germany the fourth largest, including the largest women's team.

Sport in Eastern European countries differs in important ways from other countries. Its objectives are set, its administration is largely controlled and its financing comes directly or indirectly from the state. There are school, college, army, factory and union sports clubs, but they all operate within overall policy guidelines and objectives defined by the state.

Sport is viewed by the governments of these countries as an instrument of political, social and economic policy. For the state to provide sports facilities, training programmes and so forth is thought to be a good thing in itself, especially insofar as it can be used to rectify inequalities in society and help in the establishment of an egalitarian and classless society. But it is also valued for its contribution to improving and maintaining the health of people in the community, the development of community spirit and as a substitute for many of the individual consumer luxuries which the governments cannot or will not provide.

Sport is also used as a positive instrument of foreign policy. Success is used to advertise the virtues and successes of their political system, particularly in what is seen as the contest with the capitalist powers for the allegiances of the developing and non-aligned countries.

The degree of central direction and encouragement in these countries has allowed the development of master plans for various sports, which include such things as national talent seeking, special sports schools, national coaching schemes, national grading and merit schemes and so forth. The directors of the various plans, the national coaches and other officials know that they will be backed by the full resources of the state and they exercise a good deal of political authority.

The products of all this activity, sufficiently talented individuals, are found jobs as journalists, army officers, youth leaders and so on, where their expertise is used in discovering fresh talent, training and providing leadership and inspiration for the next generation. Of course they are also ensured sufficient time to train and compete and very often are more than adequately rewarded financially and by the provision of housing and consumer durables. The availability of these perks must be a continual incentive to younger sportsmen and women.

Women's sports are obviously as important as men's in achieving the social and political aims of the governments in Eastern Europe. Hence, although women's sport definitely receives a better deal in Eastern Europe than elsewhere, it is not just abolishing sex discrimination itself which is the objective in encouraging and providing facilities for sportswomen: it is also one of the best ways of showing the superiority of the socialist system and promoting individual health and community feeling.

Track and field athletics has always been, and still is in theory, almost exclusively an amateur sport. But in practice now the reality is quite different. The distinction between amateur and professional is blurred in America where track and field scholarships are a form of professionalism. It is blurred in Eastern Europe where sinecure government appointments are a form of professionalism. It is blurred in Western Europe where part-time public relations or salesmen jobs are a form of professionalism. And it is blurred by sports promoters paying inflated expenses for athletics stars to appear. But these arrangements are ignored by the governing body of athletics and, because no money changes hands in a public ceremony at the end of events, and athletes cannot directly advertise the sponsor's wares, the fiction is maintained that athletics is still amateur.

This, too, has worked to the disadvantage of women. In the big money sports of tennis and golf, the financial imbalance between the sexes is, to a large extent, visible and easily documented. This allows visible and vociferous campaigns to remove or reduce the imbalance, such as that effectively carried out by Billie Jean King and others in the tennis world. But if the disadvantage is not apparent, especially if it is not apparent or admitted by either those most disadvantaged or those in charge of the sport, how does one set about removing it?

This brief history of women's athletics shows that comparing the performances of men and women at the present time is still not comparing like with like. The number of women athletes is still much smaller than the number of men, for social not biological reasons. American, Asian and African women, particularly the latter two, are more under-represented than European women. And in probably all countries outside Eastern Europe the resources and encouragement given to women's athletics are much lower than are given to men's. All of these must have profound effects on the levels of women's performances.

3. COMPARISONS OF SPEED AND ENDURANCE

This section presents the hard evidence that women are actually catching up on the track — the world records and other best performances. There are eighteen events which offer comparison, from the 100 metres to the marathon of more than 42,000 metres. Women's world records at the end of 1980 varied from being worse than men's by 8.56 per cent over the shorter to 13.79 over the longer (excluding the special case of the 100/110 metres hurdles comparison). The complete list is shown in table 15, which shows that the average difference for all events was 10.49 per cent.

This position relative to men that women have now achieved is the culmina-

Table 15. Official world records and unofficial best performances in track events at the end of 1980. (The difference is the percentage by which male speed exceeds female).

Event	Male				Female				Percentage Difference
	Name	Year	Time	Speed (m/s)	Name	Year	Time	Speed (m/s)	
100	J. Hines	1968	9.95	10.050	M. Oelsner	1977	10.88	9.191	8.56
200	P. Mennea	1979	19.72	10.142	M. Koch	1979	21.71	9.212	9.17
400	L. Evans	1968	43.86	9.120	M. Koch	1979	48.60	8.230	9.76
800	S. Coe	1980	1:42.40	7.812	N. Olizarenko	1980	1:53.50	7.048	9.77
1,000	S. Coe	1980	2:13.4	7.496	T. Providokhina	1978	2:30.6	6.640	11.42
1,500	S. Ovett	1980	3:31.4	7.096	T. Kazankina	1980	3:52.7	6.446	9.08
Mile	S. Ovett	1980	3:48.8	7.692[a]	M. Decker	1980	4:21.7	6.725[a]	12.57
2,000	J. Walker	1976	4:41.4	6.863	M. Puica	1976	5:35.5	5.961	13.14
3,000	H. Rono	1978	7:32.1	6.636	L. Bragina	1976	8:27.12	5.916	10.85
5,000	H. Rono	1978	13:08.4	6.342	L. Olafsson	1978	15:08.8	5.502	13.24
10,000	H. Rono	1978	27:22.5	6.088	L. Olafsson	1978	31:45.4	5.248	13.79
Marathon	D. Clayton	1969	128:34.0	5.470	G. Waitz	1979	145:42.0	4.848	11.37
4 × 100	USA	1977	38.03	10.518	GDR	1980	41.60	9.615	8.59
4 × 200	Southern Calif.	1978	1:20.26	9.963	GDR	1980	1:28.20	9.070	8.96
4 × 400	USA	1968	2:56.16	9.086	GDR	1976	3:19.23	8.031	11.61
4 × 800	USSR	1978	7:08.1	7.466	USSR	1976	7:52.3	6.775	9.26
100/110H	R. Nehemiah	1979	13.00	8.462	G. Rabsztyn	1980	12.36	8.091	4.38
400H	E. Moses	1980	47.13	8.487	K. Rossley	1980	54.28	7.369	13.27
								MEAN DIFFERENCE	10.49

a. Speed in yards per second.

tion of a little over fifty years' competition. How have they fared over these five decades? In the first place the number of events in which they can compete has increased from about eight events in the early 1920s to today's eighteen regular events. Secondly the longest event of the 1920s was 1500 metres (very rarely run). Today everything up to the marathon is run by women, although events at the longer track distances are very infrequent. Thirdly, as table 16 shows, women have more than halved the deficit in their performance compared to men for those eight events in which they have been competing continuously over these fifty years.

Table 16. World records and performance differentials in the track events 1927-77. (Differences are expressed in per cent by which male speed exceeds female).

Metres	1927			1977		
	Records		Difference	Records		Difference
	Men	*Women*		*Men*	*Women*	
100	10.6	12.2	18.75	9.95	10.88	8.55
200	21.2	25.3	16.21	19.80	22.21	10.85
400	47.3	60.8	22.28	43.26	49.29	11.02
800	111.6	143.7	22.28	103.44	115.94	10.01
1,000	145.8	188.2	22.53	133.9	153.8	12.94
1,500	231.0	318.2	27.41	212.2	236.0	10.09
4 x 100	41.0	49.8	16.67	38.03	42.55	10.52
4 x 200	87.4	112.6	23.67	81.4	91.57	11.11
MEAN DIFFERENCE			21.35			10.64

The question now is whether the next fifty years will see another decline of about half the original difference. In other words, can it be expected that for these eight events women will have reduced the difference to zero by about 2020? Predicting the future is of course a hazardous procedure, but the events of the last ten years or so give a little firmer base for making such predictions. Has the rate of change in these original eight events speeded up or slowed down? What of the changes in all of the other events?

Table 17 gives the necessary figures on this. In the "original" eight events women's performances approached men's at an even faster rate than before. The performance differential declined by about a third in this decade leading to predictions that it will have disappeared altogether by about 1995. When all the events are considered together, if the rate of decrease in performance between the sexes seen in 1968–80 were to be maintained it would disappear altogether by 1995 also!

This is a statistical prediction based on overall averages. It says very little about individual events or groups of events and can take very little account of

Table 17. Changes in performance differential for all track events 1968-80[a]. (Differences expressed in per cent by which male speed exceeds female).

Year	100m[b]	200m[b]	400m[b]	800m[b]	1,000m[b]	1,500m[b]	Mile	3000m	5,000m	10,000m	Marathon	4 x 100[b] metres	4 x 200[b] metres	4 x 400	4 x 800	Mean all events	Mean of the 8 1920s events
1968	11.11	13.64	18.49	13.44	24.58	19.94	16.60	21.30	20.74	24.72	30.85	10.74	12.47	21.72	14.44	18.50	15.55
1970	11.11	13.13	14.00	13.44	15.98	17.64	16.52	18.22	16.47	20.56	29.71	10.74	12.47	16.47	14.55	16.07	13.56
1972	11.11	13.13	14.00	11.98	12.64	13.28	15.64	16.77	16.40	18.96	22.78	10.74	13.11	13.25	13.73	14.50	12.42
1974	11.11	10.85	12.52	11.74	14.11	13.76	14.25	14.56	16.40	18.96	19.74	10.32	13.11	13.25	12.28	13.42	12.19
1976	9.62	10.85	11.02	9.98	12.94	10.09	14.87	10.23	16.40	21.45	19.20	10.11	12.78	11.61	9.26	12.69	10.70
1978	8.56	10.25	10.38	10.01	11.19	10.09	13.04	10.85	13.24	13.80	13.79	10.03	12.24	11.61	9.26	11.91	10.34
1980	8.56	9.17	9.76	9.77	11.42	9.08	12.57	10.85	13.24	13.79	11.37	8.59	8.96	11.61	9.26	10.53	9.41

a. Other than the two hurdles events, which are not precisely identical for men and women.

b. An event which was run by women in the 1920s and for which there exist reliable world best times from these years.

such changes in human actions, interventions and motivations as may occur in the future. Nevertheless, the prediction based on the figures shown in table 17 is so astonishingly at variance with current beliefs regarding women's athletic prowess that further analysis is obviously worthwhile, based on longer periods of time and using groups of events similar in their physical and physiological requirements. The prediction that women will achieve overall equality based on all track events by the turn of the century clearly implies that some events will see equality before then, which seems more astonishing still.

Discussions in earlier chapters have prepared us for the idea that in the longer distances women are throwing off the burden of previous prejudices and capitalizing on some positive biological advantages. Are these their best events? How do they differ from the shorter events? Is it possible to predict in which events women will actually achieve equality first?

Comparisons between men's and women's performances in the sprints and sprint relays can be made from the beginning of women's international athletics in 1921. (All of the women's records are given in appendix B). If the trend in average differences between the sexes of 1921-80 is maintained in the future, women should hold one or more of the world sprint records by 2040! The actual and statistically predicted decline in mean difference between men's and women's world records are the solid lines of figure 13. Continue the straight line on into the future and it crosses the zero difference line in 2040.

A second group of similar events comprises the 400 metres, 800 metres and their respective relays and the 1,000 metres. The relays, as shown in appendix B, were introduced more recently than 1921 but nevertheless a statistical prediction based on all these events can still be made. This says that eventual equality between the sexes will be reached in 2051. Again figure 13 plots the actual mean differences between the men's and women's records and the straight line shows the statistical prediction. Notice that in this case the current women's world records are actually better than predicted. If women keep up their record breaking exploits of the last few years for any length of time then they will catch men well before 2051.

Recent performances by women in these events suggest that rapid changes will indeed occur in the near future. There is a tendency to convert the 400 metres and even the 800 metres virtually to sprint events, trained for by sprinters and run as anaerobic oxygen-debt events. This is already the case for the men's 400 metre race and judging by the domination of the 800 metres for several years from 1976 by Juantorena, a converted 400 metre runner, it is nearly the case for that event. When setting his world record in the Montreal Olympic final Juantorena's time at the halfway mark was an astonishing 50.85 seconds, with the second 400 metres therefore taking 52.59. In a 1977 race in which he ran 1:43.6, he covered the first half in 49.7 and the second in 53.9. In most of the heats at Montreal the first 400 metres was run faster than the second, and of the fourteen fastest races in 1977, twelve had faster first laps. In the final of the European championships in Prague in September 1975

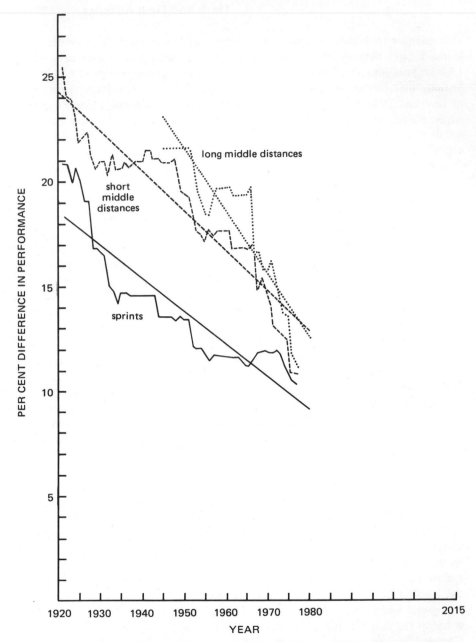

Fig. 13. The decline of the performance differential between men and women in three groups of track events as measured by world records. The sprints include the 100 metres, 200 metres, 4 x 100 metres relay and 4 x 200 metres relay. The short middle distances include the 400 metres, 4 x 400 metres relay 800 metres, 4 x 800 metres relay and 1,000 metres. The long middle distances include the 1,500 metres, mile and 3,000 metres. The lines are the actual differences between the world records of men and women and the regression lines calculated from them. If continued the regressions intersect the zero difference line in 2040, 2051 and 2025 respectively.

Sebastian Coe of Britain clocked a stunning 49.3 and went on to win the bronze medal in 1:44.5. In all these 800 metre races it is speed which counted, the oxygen debt being largely contracted in the first half of the race with the ability to then endure it for the second half being paramount.

The same thing is happening in the women's events, particularly at the present time in the 400 metres. Szewinska of Poland is a recent holder of the 200 and 400 metres world records. At Montreal when setting her 400 metres world record of 49.29 she ran the first 200 metres in a fast 23.1 and the second in 26.19. Marita Koch currently holds both the 200 and 400 metres world records. She ran the first 200 metres of her world record 400 metres race in 22.9 and the second half in 26.04. There is already talk of Marita Koch running 800 metres. The 800 metres and the 1500 metres were both won at Montreal by Kazankina of Russia, who held the world record for both events for some time. (She again won the 1500 metres at Moscow in a major comeback after having a baby.) She also set a searing pace of 55.05 in the first half of the 800 metres Montreal final and ran the second 400 metres in 59.89. Further advances are more likely to come from specialist sprinters, 200 and 400 metre runners moving up a distance like Juantorena, who are better trained to contract an oxygen debt early in the race and then live with it, than from 1500 metre runners like Kazankina. If this argument is correct, there will be continued rapid improvement in the women's 400 and 800 metres in the near future.

The third group of events comprises the mile and 1500 and 3000 metres, the longest women's track events formally recognized by athletics authorities. These events were rare before the war and the 3000 metres seems only to have been taken up by women in the 1960s. Nevertheless a sufficient sequence of comparisons to make a reliable prediction is available: according to this, equality between the sexes will occur in 2025. Again, as figure 13 shows, the actual difference at the moment is below this prediction. Undoubtedly part of the reason for this is that races over these distances were quite rare in earlier years. The pace of record-breaking has undoubtedly increased recently as they are run more frequently. What, one might ask again, would happen to women's 3000 metre performances if this event were put into the Olympic programme?

The final group has the longest events of all: the 5000 and 10,000 metres and the marathon. Women have only been running these events for the last decade or so, a period of time too short to allow firm comparison or predictions. But the changes which have actually occurred in women's long distance running in recent years, particularly in the marathon, suggest that many and more profound changes are still to come.

Although there are earlier reports of women marathon runners, the story of their attempts at this distance really begins on 16 December 1963 at Culver City, California. On that day sixty-seven men runners set off in the Culver City Marathon. As they did so two young women emerged from behind some bushes across the street and set off in pursuit. Although one of these women retired at eighteen miles or so, the other, Merry Lepper, finished the course in 3 hours,

37 minutes and 7 seconds and this therefore has to be regarded as the first women's marathon record. This record didn't last long. Early in 1964 Dale Greig finished the Isle of Wight Marathon in 3:27.45 and the record was broken yet again in 1964.

On 8 May 1967, thirteen year old Maureen Wilton ran unofficially in the Toronto Marathon. She finished sixth in a field of twenty-eight men in 3:15.22. Her average pace for the race was inside 7½ minutes per mile, but she covered the final mile in just over 6 minutes. Her pulse was back to normal two minutes after the race.

The AAU at first banned women marathoners in America but in 1972 at the New York Marathon women were allowed to compete in the same race as men – provided they started ten minutes earlier. The women runners simply sat down on the line at the sound of "their" starting gun and only began to race when the men did. No action was taken by the AAU but ten minutes was added to the women's finishing times, as though they had used the extra time.

The three-hour barrier in women's marathon running was first broken in 1971. In 1974 seventeen women and in 1975 twenty-seven women ran under that time. In 1976 the top ten runners were all under 2 hours 50 minutes and in 1979 the top ten were all under 2 hours 40 minutes (see table 24). In 1978 thirty women marathoners bettered 2 hours 49 minutes and in 1979 more than fifty did so. A glimpse into the future can be had, as always, in the USA. A thirteen year old girl has run a marathon in under 3 hours (Debbie Barrett in a time of 2:55.12) and in 1974 among the ten fastest who were nine years old and under there were two girls.

The number of women marathoners has shown an increase just as their performances have. In December 1977, in Phoenix, Arizona, there were more than 300 women starters in a marathon field of more than 1700. The first woman finisher, Adrienne Beames of Australia, was 69th overall. In Honolulu in 1978 among 3050 entrants in the marathon there were 619 women. Cindy Dalrymple finished 59th. In October 1978 there were more than 1000 women starters among a total of 11,000 for the New York Marathon. The first woman to finish, Norway's Greta Waitz, was 104th overall.

The progression in the women's world marathon record is therefore truly an astonishing one, as shown in table 18.

The three German record holders in this list are all proteges of Dr Ernst van Aaken, the foremost European advocate of distance running for women. Most of the other runners come from the USA. Of the thirty sub–2:49 women marathoners in 1978, twenty-three came from the USA. Others came from Norway, West Germany, Canada, Brazil and New Zealand. It could hardly be said, therefore, that women's long distance running talent has yet been tapped very widely.

A regression curve calculated for women's marathon running compared to men predicts that they will reach equality with men in twenty-seven years from the start of this series in 1963, that is, in 1990. This revolution in performance

Table 18. Women's world marathon record 1963-80.

1963	3:37.07	Merry Lepper	USA
1964	3:27.45	Dale Greig	UK
1964	3:19.33	Mildred Sampson	New Zealand
1967	3:15.22	Maureen Wilton	Canada
1967	3:07.26	Anni Pede-Erdkamp	West Germany
1970	3:02.53	Caroline Walker	USA
1971	3:01.42	Beth Bonner	USA
1971	3:00.35	Sara Berman	USA
1971	2:55.22	Beth Bonner	USA
1971	2:49.40	Cheryl Bridges	USA
1973	2:46.36	Miki Gorman	USA
1974	2:46.24	Chantal Langlace	France
1974	2:43.54	Jacqui Hanson	USA
1975	2:42.24	Liane Winters	West Germany
1975	2:40.15	Christa Vahlensieck	West Germany
1975	2:38.19	Jacqui Hanson	USA
1977	2:35.15	Chantal Langlace	France
1977	2:34.45	Christa Vahlensieck	West Germany
1978	2:32.30	Greta Waitz	Norway
1979	2:27.33	Greta Waitz	Norway
1980	2:25.42	Greta Waitz	Norway

in women's marathon running has been largely unaccompanied by a reasonable programme of long distance track events. As these get under way, even more rapid changes may be predicted.

The popularity of women's marathon running may be due to the enormous rise in popularity of jogging, road racing and "fun runs" in recent years. These "fun runs" and longer races of greater seriousness are run on roads, are usually open to both men and women and are often longer than 10,000 metres. An indication of the upsurge in interest is given by the fact that in Central Park, New York, in 1973, 78 women entered l'Eggs ten kilometre minimarathon. In 1980, 4,007 women finished the race, twenty-two of them in under thirty-five minutes. They certainly provide a perfect springboard to the marathon. It may or may not be significant that there is little in the way of fun runs or a large road racing programme in Eastern Europe, nor any women ultra-long distance runners.

In summary, then, table 19 compares world records to give predicted dates for essential equality of performance between the sexes for the four groups of track events.

As table 17 showed and as figure 13 and the predictions derived from it also show, the performances of women in all running events are still improving faster than men's. Their improvements have been simply amazing. They are now running 1500 metres at the same average speed that they were running 800 metres in the 1950s, and are now running 3000 metres at the same speed

Table 19. Predicted dates for essential equality of performance between the sexes for groups of track events.

Track Events	1980 Mean Difference	Predicted Date of Equality
Sprints	8.52	2040
Short Middle Distance	10.36	2051
Longer Middle Distance	10.83	2025
Long Distance	13.30	1991

they were then running 1500 metres. Most astonishing of all, the speed that women can now maintain running the marathon is faster than they could maintain in the early days of their running 10,000 metres in the late 1960s.

One of the arguments against using world records to make comparisons is that those who break them are very unusual people, hardly typical of average athletes. Records get broken quite infrequently and the picture they give may not be very typical of what is actually happening in the sport. The great popularity of track athletics and the collection of voluminous statistics about its practitioners allows us to overcome this disadvantage. Since about 1950 lists of the top ten, fifty or sometimes one hundred performers have been available for a number of events. These provide a much more continuous, accurate and secure statistical basis for analyzing ongoing trends in performance than do world records. Using these lists comparisons can be made between the top man and top woman, the second man with the second woman and so on. Figure 14 shows some of these comparisons in which the relative performance of the top ten women is expressed as a fraction of the top ten men from all events 100–3000 metres.

In all events women are improving faster than men and the previous conclusion, that in longer events they are improving faster than in shorter, is re-emphasized. If the trends illustrated in this figure are maintained women will achieve equality in the longer distances well before they achieve equality in the shorter distances. The dates predicted for reaching equality, based on the top ten performers in each event, are: 100 metres — 2071; 200 metres — 2088; 400 metres — 2029; 800 metres — 2039; 1500 metres — 1995; 3000 metres — 1996; Marathon — 1988. These dates are similar to those predicted on the basis of world records, a little later for the sprints and rather sooner for the middle and long distances. Because they are based on ten performers every year rather than one every few years they are much more reliable.

The discussion on energy systems in chapter 3 described the distinction between anaerobic and aerobic systems, the former primarily operative in events lasting up to two minutes or so, with the aerobic becoming increasingly important thereafter. Women probably have some advantages over men with respect to the energy available from this system and therefore might slow down less when running over long distances. This can be assessed by comparing the

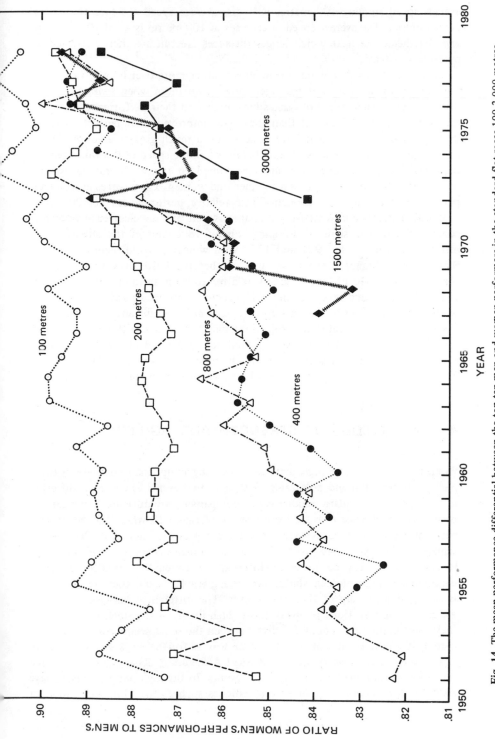

Fig. 14. The mean performance differential between the top ten men and women performers in the standard flat races 100-3,000 metres. Women are improving rapidly in all events. The figures include comparisons up to the 1978 season. Lists of the top ten performers are not available for the longer distances in most earlier years.

100 metres

200 metres

800 metres

400 metres

3000 metres

1500 metres

YEAR

RATIO OF WOMEN'S PERFORMANCES TO MEN'S

average speed running 100 metres with the average speed at which the longer events are run. The average speed of each sex at 100 metres is set at 100 per cent and the mean speed at which longer distances are run are then expressed as percentages of this.

Figure 15 shows that women slow down rather more over long distances on the track than do men, but that men slow down more when swimming long distances. Over the years both sexes have improved their performances at long distances to a greater extent than they have improved their performances at short distances, but women have done so by a much greater amount. These changes are shown in figures 16 and 17, in which the speed of the world record performances in the longer distances compared to the world record performances at 100 metres are plotted for men and women. The changes in women's performances are obvious enough. Their relative performances at 800, 1500 and 3000 metres are now virtually the same as men, and the changes in women's running show little signs of stopping. Figure 18 compares the situation for men's world records in 1921 and 1979 with women's world records in 1979. Women long distance runners now perform better relative to women sprinters than did men long distance runners relative to men sprinters in the 1950s. If these changes continue, running will become the same as swimming, that is women will run closer to their maximal velocity at longer distances than do men. These are hazardous statistical projections but they reinforce those from world records and yearly best performances. Well before the end of the century there could be women medal winners in the Olympic marathon and 10,000 metres. The only thing likely to stop them is that men probably will not let them run.

4. COMPARISONS OF STRENGTH AND AGILITY

Women compete in the high jump and the long jump; men compete in these plus the triple jump and pole vault. With only two events to compare, differing in techniques and athletic requirements, comparisons are difficult. Some general points are nonetheless obvious from a study of figure 19 where the differences between the world records over the years are presented and table 20 where a sample of the figures are given. (The actual women's records are all presented in appendix B). The performance differential between the sexes has declined continuously since women started competing regularly, but the rate of decline is slower than in any of the track events. The differences between the sexes are greater than all (long jump) or most (high jump) of the track events and to make any predictions about equality between the sexes seems completely misplaced. If a date is calculated in the same way as for the track events, equality is predicted in the twenty-second century! Advances in achievement have been much more episodic than in the track events. In the high jump advances have followed the development of new techniques such as the "Fosbury Flop" or

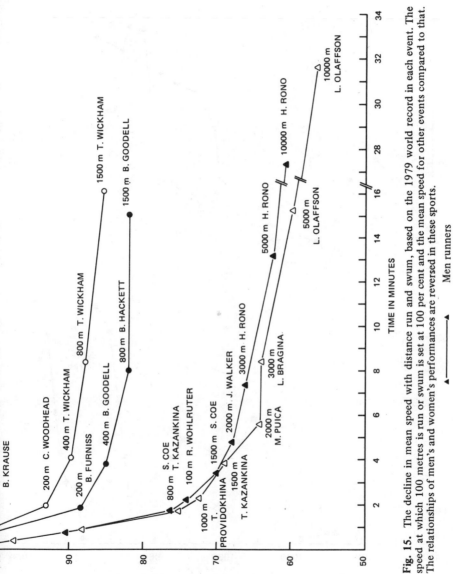

Fig. 15. The decline in mean speed with distance run and swum, based on the 1979 world record in each event. The speed at which 100 metres is run or swum is set at 100 per cent and the mean speed for other events compared to that. The relationships of men's and women's performances are reversed in these sports.

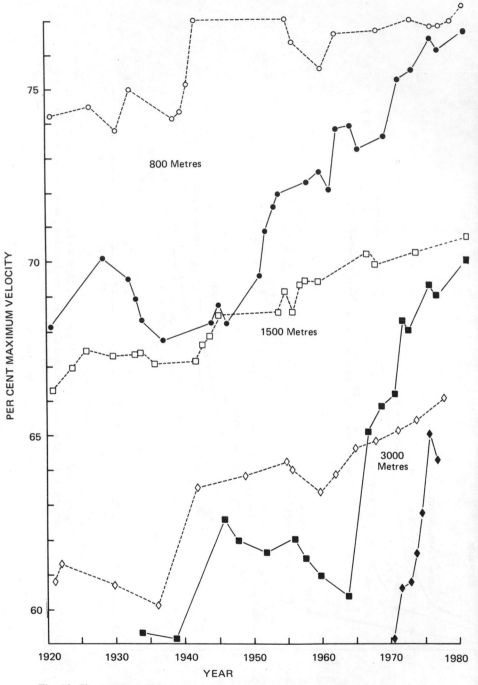

Fig. 16. Changes since 1920 in the relative speed at which men and women run three middle distance events, expressed as a percentage of their respective 100 metre speeds. The points represent improvements in the 100 metre and distance events world records. Women have cleary shown much more rapid change.

o------o Men's 800m world records   •——• Women's 800m world records

□------□ Men's 1,500m world records   ■——■ Women's 1,500m world records

◇------◇ Men's 3,000m world records   ◆——◆ Women's 3,000m world records

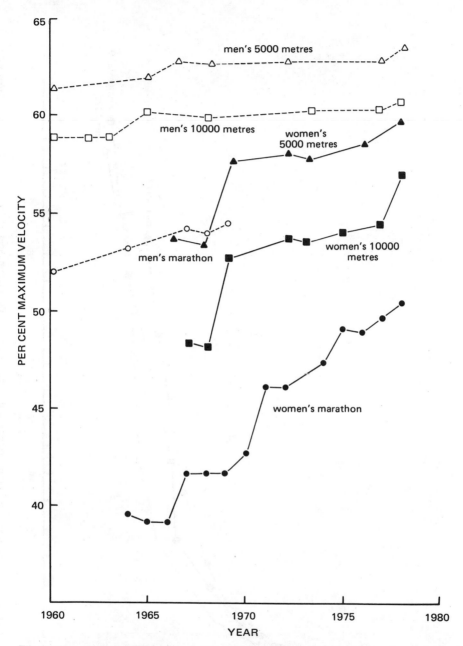

Fig. 17. Changes since 1960 in the relative speed at which men and women run long distance events expressed as a percentage of their respective 100 metres records. Women have shown and are still showing massive improvements. There had been no change in the men's 100 metres record since 1968 and no change in the marathon record since 1969 until the men's marathon record was finally broken by Alberto Salazar in the New York marathon 1981 with a time of 2:08:13. In the same race Alison Roe broke the women's record with a time of 2:25:28

◇------◇ Men's 5,000 metres   ▲——▲ Women's 5,000 metres

◻------◻ Men's 10,000 metres   ■——■ Women's 10,000 metres

○------○ Men's marathon   ●——● Women's martahon

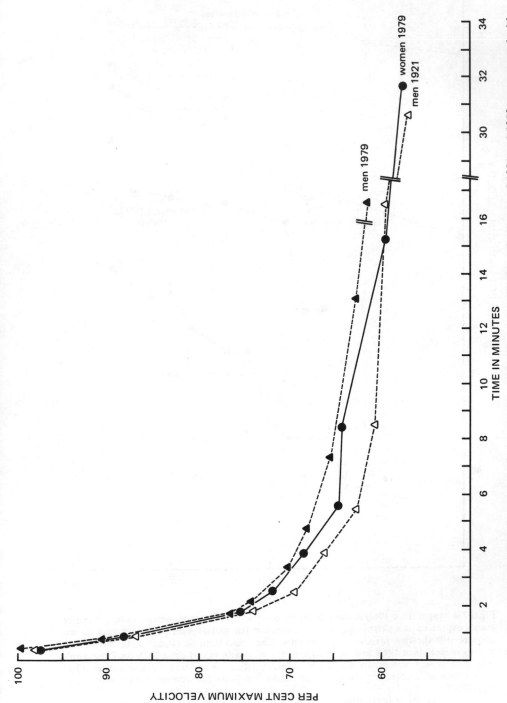

Fig. 18. A comparison of the decline of mean velocity with distance run. Men's performances of 1921 and 1979 are compared with women's performances in 1979 at the standard track distances. The full details for 1979 are given in figure 15.

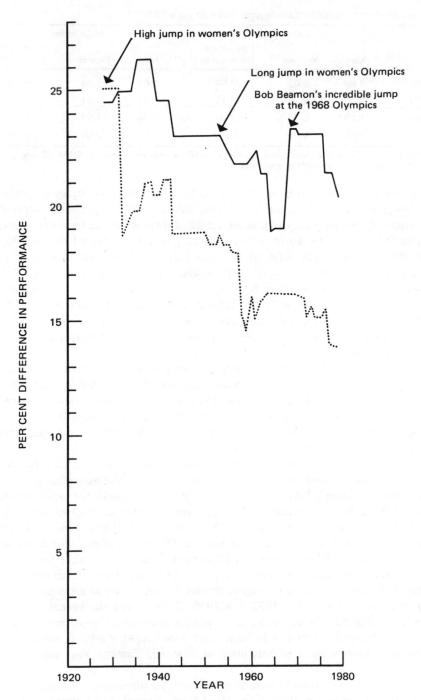

Fig. 19. The difference in performance in high jump and long jump represented by the men's and women's world records. Although erratic, the downward trend is evident in both.

Table 20. World records in the long jump and high jump 1927-77.

	Long Jump			High Jump		
	Men	Women	Percentage Difference	Men	Women	Percentage Difference
1927	7.89	5.62	24.59	2.04	1.52	25.22
1947	8.13	6.25	23.12	2.71	1.71	18.96
1967	8.35	6.76	19.04	2.28	1.91	16.23
1977	8.90	6.99	21.46	2.33	2.00	14.16

The full details of the men's and women's 1980 records are given in Table 25 and the women's progressive records in appendix B.

the straddle. In the long jump it seems to have been the very occasional juxta-position of optimum physical conditions, with a performer perfectly prepared emotionally and physically to take advantage of them which has been important. Jesse Owens held the world record for twenty-five years from 1936. In 1968 at Mexico, taking advantage of the rarefied atmosphere and consequently reduced air resistance, coupled with a just allowable following wind, Bob Beamon jumped an incredible 8.90 metres (or 29 feet 2½ inches) whereas the previous record had been 8.35 metres (or 27 feet 4¾ inches). This record looked destined to stand for many years since no-one else had managed to reach 8.53 metres or 28 feet until American Carl Lewis jumped 8.62 metres at the US Championships 1981.

Up to about 1931 women were about equally far behind men in both the high jump and long jump. Were biological factors responsible for this same-ness of performance and if so to what do we now ascribe the difference between the events? Perhaps some of the current difference is because the women's high jump was introduced into the Olympic Games in 1928 but the long jump was not on the programme until 1948.

Until 1951 the women's high jump record was set using a scissors jump which men abandoned before the 1920s. Iolanda Balas, the Romanian girl who dominated women's high jumping for many years and held the world record until 1971, used an outmoded Eastern cutoff technique. But women fairly rapidly took up the new Fosbury Flop and in 1972 West German Ulrike Meyfarth became the youngest ever athletics Olympic gold medallist when she used it to clear 1.92 metres (6 feet 3½ inches) equalling the world record at the time. The 1980 women's world record was 2.01 metres which was only 14.8 per cent below the men's. A jump of this height would have won the gold medal in the men's event in the 1932 and 1948 Olympics and the bronze medal as recently as 1952! The enormous improvement in efficiency which modern high jump techniques confer can be seen from photographs 9 and 10, which show Dorothy Tyler using a scissors jump in 1948 and Tamami Yagi using a flop in 1978.

There are no systematic records of women's performances in the triple jump or the pole vault. In 1959 Mary Rand triple jumped 12.22 metres (40 feet

1 inch) which represented 73.17 per cent of the then men's world record. Mary Rand was the 1964 Olympic long jump winner and holder of the world long jump record between 1964 and 1968. The triple jump is one of those events which authorities have been reluctant to introduce for supposed medical reasons. The jars on landing will damage the pelvis and the internal reproductive organs, so it is said. In fact the reverse is true. Exercise undertaken by women preparing for jumps strengthens the floor of the pelvis and surrounding tissues and improves tone in the muscles. Similar comments apply to the pole-vault.

There seems no reason why women should not compete and improve in these events if they were given sufficient competitive opportunity, just as they have improved in the other field events. The introduction of these other two jumps into national and international competition would probably increase the interest, the number of competitors and the performances of women for all the jumps, particularly in schools and universities where early attitudes are fostered. Long jumping and triple jumping in particular are closely related, and men, even at the international level, often compete in both.

Women compete in three throwing events: shot, discus and javelin. Men compete in these and in throwing the hammer. The weights and sizes of the implements thrown by men and women are different, comparisons are therefore not exact.

The weights for the implements and the performance ratios as at 1980 are shown in table 21. It is obviously not the weights which are the most important influences on relative performance. There is currently little difference between the sexes in performance with discus and shot but a very marked difference in javelin throwing ability. This is partly due to the skeletal differences in arms and shoulder between the sexes. These confer a disadvantage on women in the

Table 21. Weight of implements and performance ratios for discus, shot and javelin, 1980.

	Weight Thrown by Men (kg)	Weight Thrown by Women (kg)	Weight Ratio of Implements	Performance Ratio
Discus	2	1	0.500	1.009
Shot	7.25	4	0.552	1.014
Javelin	0.8	0.6	0.750	.741

throwing action required for the javelin but probably do not in the shot and discus where speed of movement, flexibility and sheer muscular power are more important.

As can be seen from table 22 and figure 20, women today throw their 4 kilogram shot as far as men throw their 7.25 kilogram shot. Yet only thirty or so years ago men were throwing more than seventeen per cent further than women. Women today throw their one kilogram discus as far as men throw their two kilogram discus. And yet only a decade ago the women's discus record was

Table 22. World records and performance differentials in the throwing events 1937-77. (The full details of the 1980 men's and women's records are shown in table 25.)

	Shot			Discus			Javelin			Mean Difference
	Male	Female	Difference (per cent)	Male	Female	Difference (per cent)	Male	Female	Difference (per cent)	
1937	17.40	14.38	17.36	53.10	48.31	9.02	77.23	46.74	39.48	21.95
1957	19.25	16.76	12.94	59.28	57.04	3.78	85.71	55.48	35.27	17.23
1977	22.00	22.32	+0.01	70.86	68.92	0.51	94.58	69.32	26.92	9.16

nearly eight per cent worse than the men's record. In these two events "equality" has been reached between the sexes as a consequence of extremely rapid improvement by women throwers over the last few years. Who would have predicted today's "equality" in the immediate post-war years? And who, in the light of it, would make any firm prediction for the future?

There has also been a marked relative improvement in women's javelin throwing over recent years, a trend which shows no signs of stopping, although the differences between the sexes remains large. The amount by which women are disadvantaged by skeletal differences in the arm and shoulder girdle is therefore quite uncertain.

No attempt has been made to make any sort of prediction for this group of events because they are so different. But figure 20, showing the decline of the three performance differentials, tells its own story. It seems that even in these throwing events, our ideas must be revised on the relative potential of women compared to men.

5. A PERSPECTIVE ON THE CHANGES

This chapter, so far, has been concerned mainly with the statistics of athletic improvement. But athletics is as much about human competition as it is about stopwatches. Progress in the sport is measured as much by the appearance of great champions as by new entries in the record books. Furthermore, the objective of athletics, whether it is winning one special event, that is, beating particular people in a particular situation, or breaking a record, that is, competing against the clock, has always to be attained in a particular set of environmental circumstances and social situations. Women's sporting performances must be assessed on a human basis as well as simply a statistical one.

The 1980 women's 100 metre world record holder was Maria Gohr (nee Oelsner). If she had produced her 10.88 in an Olympic event, she would have won the gold medal in 1896, 1900 or 1904. The world record for the 4 x 100 metres sprint relay is held by the East German women's team with 41.60. This time would have won the Olympic gold medal the first two occasions the event was contested by men in 1912 and 1920. But today's times are the result of electronic timing which is at least one tenth of a second slower for 100 metres than hand-timing which prevailed prior to 1968. Today's women sprinters are closer to the great men of the past than is apparent from simple comparisons of recorded times.

The 1980 400 metre women's record was 48.60 held by Marita Koch of East Germany, a time first achieved by men in 1895. Nevertheless, it would have been good enough to win a gold medal in the 1900, 1908 and 1920 Olympic Games, and even allowing for the rather aberrant 1920 result which was a consequence of interruption to competition during the First World War,

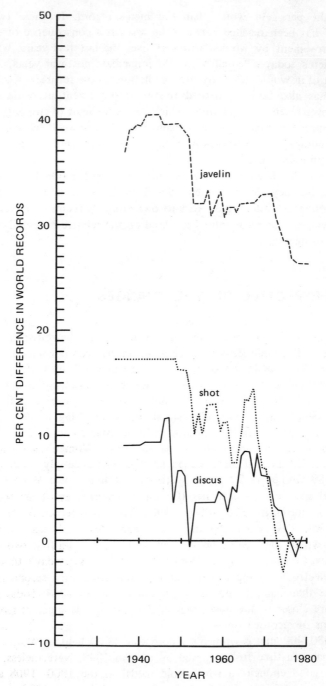

Fig. 20. The difference in men's and women's performances in javelin, shot and discus. The relative improvement of women, especially over the last ten years, is very obvious.

women's performance in this event is, in practical terms, a little closer to that of men than the shorter sprints. Again, today's women's records are electronically timed and are slower than the earlier hand-timed men's records.

Women were running 800 metres, 1000 metres and occasional 1500 metres events in the 1920s. The time achieved by the winner of their 1928 Olympic 800 metres was 2:16.8. This was about 18.3 per cent slower than the winner of the men's 800 metres and represented a distance of about 150 metres. In 1980, the difference between the world records was 11.1 seconds, about 10 per cent, representing a distance of 70 or 80 metres! The current women's 1500 metres world record would have been good enough to win an Olympic final up to 1920. The first man to run a faster time was the legendary flying Finn, Paavo Nurmi in 1924.

The event at which women have been increasing their performance fastest in recent years is the 3000 metres. Their current record of 8:27.1 represents a time achieved only in 1925 by men, again by Paavo Nurmi. Although women's 5000 and 10,000 metre track events are still rare, their performances over the last two or three seasons also show rapid improvement and their best performances are equivalent to those run by men in 1908 and 1904 respectively. Nevertheless, Loa Olaffson's 1980 10,000 metres record is marginally faster than Paavo Nurmi achieved in winning the Olympic 10,000 metres in 1920. Her 5000 metres record is faster than the 1920 bronze medal winner in that event. The astonishing Greta Waitz, though, shows that women's performances at 10,000 metres will improve a long way in the near future. In 1978 she ran a cross-country race in Sweden where she covered sixteen kilometres in 51:50. She passed the ten kilometre mark in under 32 minutes on what was said to be a very hard course. In a ten kilometre road race, she has recorded 30:59.8. Loa Olaffson's record on a flat track is 31:45.04.

The longest regular event of all, the marathon, is run on the road over a distance standardized in 1908 at 42,195 metres (26 miles 385 yards). Because of the differences in the courses, no official world record is recognized, although unofficial best performances can be compared. Most marathons now are open to both men and women, so competition and comparisons are direct.

The current best time by a woman was 2 hours 25 minutes 42 seconds run by Greta Waitz in 1980 until the 1981 New York marathon when New Zealander Alison Roe improved this to 2:25.28. The first man to run a time faster than this was Emil Zatopek in the 1952 Helsinki marathon. Waitz's performance is obviously faster than Olympic marathons prior to 1952, but also faster than the silver medal winner in 1956. Performances at this level are good enough to secure places in the top five or ten per cent of all but the strongest events. Such performances by women are in fact becoming almost commonplace; we have already mentioned Chantal Langlace's 14th place in the 1977 Spanish Marathon, Adrienne Beames's 69th out of 1700 in the Phoenix Marathon in 1977, Cindy Dalrymple's 59th out of 3050 in Honolulu in 1978 and Greta Waitz's 104th out of some 8000 finishers in the New York City Marathon in 1978, and her 74th out of 12, 262 finishers in 1980. In marathon running, then, women have achieved approximate parity with men; they can compete respectably even if they cannot, at present, beat the best men.

The IAAF have, at last, shown some signs of recognizing this. In the inaugural World Championships to be held in 1983 and every four years thereafter, there will be a women's marathon. It will be held concurrently with the men's event. A women's marathon may also be held in the 1984 Los Angeles Olympics.

The history of women's marathon and distance running is a very short one. A book concerned with distance running records 20,000 metres and over, published in 1962,[2] does not mention women nor does a book published as recently as 1966 concerned solely with the marathon.[3] Women only began running the marathon in the early 1960s and not until 1972 did a national athletic body, the AAU, sanction the practice and recognize the first national women's marathon championship.

Marathon runners need long periods of time for training and must run long distances to prepare themselves satisfactorily. Jim Peters, for example, covered nearly 4500 miles of races and training in the ten months between September 1953 and July 1954 preparing for his fateful Commonwealth Games Marathon at Vancouver in 1954. Few athletes begin a serious career in the marathon without a lengthy preparation which may well take two years or more. Many of the most successful marathon runners in the past have been successful 5000 and 10,000 metre runners who turned to longer distances in the later stages of their careers. The world records for one hour, 20,000 metres, 30,000 metres and so on have more often than not been held by successful marathon runners. Zatopek, for example, was the first man to run 20,000 metres in less than an hour and to go on and run more than 20,000 metres (20,052 to be precise) in an exact hour. He achieved these feats in 1951 and went on to win the 5000 and 10,000 metres on the track and the marathon at the 1952 Helsinki Olympics.

But until very recently there has been little in the way of a long distance track or road programme for women to allow the discovery and development of ability in this direction. Women have only been running 5000 and 10,000 metres for ten or fifteen years, and most longer distances are still very rare. A few brave women have now run ultra long distances, 50 and 100 mile events in America, an unusual enough activity for men and a surprising one for women, and they have done well at it too (see page 81–82). The 1980 men's and women's distance records are shown in table 23.

The women's marathon performance is relatively closer to the men's than their one-hour effort and almost as good as their performances at the much shorter 5000 and 10,000 metres. This obviously reflects the more frequent competition women have over the marathon. How much closer will all performances come when there is a greater depth of talent and a sufficiency of opportunities to sharpen up training and competitive ability at 5000 and 10,000 metres? As Greta Waitz said immediately after her record-breaking New York run, "Once some of the European women track runners take up marathoning

Table 23. A comparison of men's and women's long distance records as at the end of 1980.

Distance	Women's Record	Men's Record	Percentage Difference
3,000 metres	L. Bragina 8:27.2	H. Rono 7:32.1	10.8
5,000 metres	L. Olaffson 15:08.8	H. Rono 13:08.4	13.2
10,000 metres	G. Waitz[a] 31:00	H. Rono 27:22.5	11.7
10 miles	A. Sullivan 55:34	B. Rodgers 47:09	18.1
1 hour	M. Gargano 16,916 metres	J. Hermens 20,944 metres	19.2
20,000 metres	P. Lyons 1:08.36	J. Hermens 57:24.2	19.2
25,000 metres	N. Conz 1:30.26	B. Rodgers 1:14.12	21.6
30,000 metres	M. Cooksey 1:52.06	J. Alder 1:31.31	23.1
Marathon	G. Waitz 2:25.42	D. Clayton 2:08.34	11.37
50,000 metres	S. Kiddy 3:26.47	J. Norman 2:48.06	22.6
50 miles	S. Trapp 6.12.12	D. Ritchie 4:53.28	26.9
100,000 metres	C. Langlace 7:27.22	D. Ritchie 6:10.20	20.8
100 miles	N. Cullimore 16:11.00	D. Ritchie 11:30.51	40.1
24 hours	S. Trapp 198,480 metres (123 miles 675 yds)	S. Cottrell 269,160 metres (167 miles 440 yds)	26.3

a. A time recorded in a road race. The women's track record is 31:45.4.

the record is bound to go even lower". Their performances at the ultra long distances are even more staggering. They are no further behind men in these events than they were in the mile and other middle distance events two decades ago.

There is one further interesting comparison, that between the best women performers at 3000 metres and the marathon. The lists of the top ten performers for 1973 and 1979 are given in table 24. The highly successful women's athletic countries, East Germany, USSR and Poland, were not represented among the top marathoners. The magazine *Runner's World* published a list in March 1979 of the top fifty women marathon runners of all time. No less than thirty-four

Table 24. The ten best women performers over 3,000 metres and the marathon 1973 and 1979.

1973

3,000 m			Marathon		
P. Cacchi	Italy	8:56.6	M. Gorman	U.S.A.	2:46.3(
L. Bragina	U.S.S.R.	8:57.4	T. Anderson	U.S.A.	2:53.4(
I. Knoltsson	Sweden	8:58.36	N. Kucsik	U.S.A.	2:57.0
N. Holmen	Finland	9:00.48	M. Norem	U.S.A.	2:59.1
P. Vihonen	Finland	9:02.94	C. Koffenschlager	F.D.R.	2:59.2
T. Pangelova	U.S.S.R.	9:07.02	J. Ikenberry	U.S.A.	3:00.0
J. Smith	G.B.	9:08.2	K. Pagaard	Denmark	3:02.4
M. Istomina	U.S.S.R.	9:09.6	M. Preuss	F.D.R.	3:03.0(
S. Volgyi	Hungary	9:12.2	K. Piper	U.S.A.	3:03.1
N. Dobrynina	U.S.S.R.	9:13.0	L. Ledbetter	U.S.A.	3:03.3

Mean Speed		5.509 m/sec.	Mean Speed		3.640 m/sec.
Proportion of men's top ten speed		0.858	Proportion of men's top ten speed		0.743

1979

3,000 m			Marathon		
G. Waitz	Norway	8:31.8	G. Waitz	Norway	2:27.3
S. Ulmassova	U.S.S.R.	8:36.4	J. Benoit	U.S.A.	2:35.1
F. Krasnova	U.S.S.R.	8:41.3	J. Smith	U.K.	2:36.2
L. Smolka	U.S.S.R.	8:41.3	L. Moller	N.Z.	2:37.3
Y. Chernysheva	U.S.S.R.	8:44.1	G. Olinek	Canada	2:38.1
R. Beloussova	U.S.S.R.	8:44.7	P. Lyons	U.S.A.	2:38.2
R. Smechnova	U.S.S.R.	8:46.5	G. Adams	U.K.	2:38.3
V. Ilynikh	U.S.S.R.	8:46.5	S. Krenn	U.S.A.	2:38.5
T. Mechanaschina	U.S.S.R.	8:46.5	J. Gareau	Canada	3:39.0
S. Guskova	U.S.S.R.	8:46.8	S. Grottenberg	Norway	2:39.3

Mean Speed		5.743 m/sec.	Mean Speed		4.482 m/sec.
Improvement 1973-79		4.25 per cent	Improvement 1973-79		18.79 per ce
Proportion of men's top ten speed		0.889	Proportion of men's top ten speed		0.861

of these were Americans, four were West Germans and there were two each from Norway, New Zealand and Australia. Hungary's Sarolta Monspart was the only East European woman on the list. Since there is little international competition for women in the marathon at the present time, it presumably does not serve the ends which these countries require from sport, nor does it contribute much to standards in the 3000 metres (although Greta Waitz does top both lists in 1978 and 1979). Women, therefore, get few opportunities to run the marathon in these countries, whatever their feelings on the matter. Compare this with the situation in the 800 metres reported on page 46 where 87 per cent of the fastest 112 women performers of all time were from Eastern Europe. In the 3000 metres, as shown in table 24, both East and West Europeans were represented in 1973. In 1972 the 3000 metres for women was introduced into the European Championships and in 1974 an official IAAF record was recognized. The result has been an almost total domination of the event by

Eastern European women. At present, marathon and long distance track and road running is almost totally confined to North America and Western Europe. The magnitude of improvement, however, has been considerable — more so than in the 3000 metres. When gold medals, world records and international recognition are associated with these long distance events, Eastern European countries are likely to encourage their women to participate. And what will happen to standards and records then?

The claim that women are "catching up the men" can now be put into perspective. It is true in at least one sense: during the last decade, for the first time in athletic history, women runners have been able to compete in all running events open to men from the 100 metres to the marathon, with the single exception of the 3000 metres steeplechase. What they still have to achieve is an acceptance by athletics administrators that their endeavours should be officially recognized in terms of national and international competitions and of national and world records. There is little doubt that this will come. At the current rate of progress, it will certainly have arrived by the end of the century and will probably have been established within a decade or so.

One of the most striking developments in modern athletics, which increases the likelihood that this prediction will be borne out, is the development in junior athletics. Junior girls, those under fifteen on 1 September of the year of competition, now run 800, 1500 and occasional 3000 metre races, 100 and 400 metre hurdles, and compete in 2500 metre walks, high and long jumps, shot, discus, javelin and pentathlon events. In other words they have a wider choice of events than did adult women at the Olympics a few years ago. The times they are recording (around 2.00 for the 800 metres, 4.20 for the 1500 metres, 9.40 for the 3000 metres and 63 for 400 metres hurdles) indicate that continued rapid progress in these events is assured. Mary Boitano was placed fourth in the 1974 USA Women's AAU Marathon in a time of 3 hours 1 minute and 15 seconds. It was Mary's fifth year of marathon running — she was just ten years old! Women are catching up on the track itself — nowhere faster than among the juniors, the Olympic stars of tomorrow.

A combined team of Russian, East German, and American women runners at all distances from 100 metres to the marathon, lacking only steeplechasers, would offer at least the beginnings of competition to men from some countries which are reasonably well represented at the Olympic Games. Serious and effective competition between the sexes may well be a reality within a few years, were that thought to be a desirable objective.

In the whole history of track athletics it is just those events at which women are biologically most suited from which they have been banned or discouraged from participating. The survey in chapter six, of the biological differences between the sexes and of the advantages and disadvantages which they confer, predicted that women would be most effective at the longer distance running events, given suitable training. They have greater reserves of energy, more efficient aerobic energy systems and better temperature control mechanisms.

One cannot lean too heavily on biological explanations for sporting differences, but this is one which offers at least a little support. It is ironic that although biology has often been invoked by athletics administrators to prevent women competing or to explain their inferiority, this particular biological argument for female superiority has been little used. Perhaps it will get more mention in future.

The decline in performance differential between men and women in field events over the last fifty years has been even more striking than on the track (see table 25), having declined by well over a half in that time. Nevertheless, there is not the same expectation that they will be able to offer serious competition to men in the future. There are still two jumps, the pole vault and triple jump, and one throw, the hammer, closed to women, and although they occasionally practise them, there is not the same general ferment to be allowed to participate in these forbidden events as in the once forbidden long distance track events. This may be because the stimulus of possible competition with men is not there, or it may be because the field events are that much more specialized. The pole vault and hammer are not similar to any other events and do not provide training for other events. On the track, in contrast, 5000 and 10,000 metre races are commonly run by athletes who consider themselves primarily milers or marathoners and vice versa. Among field events there are similarities in long jumping and sprinting, discus and shot throwing, and long jumping and triple jumping. Only the latter combination is not already catered for in women's field athletics. There are therefore strong arguments for introducing women's triple jumping and no arguments against introducing the other field events.

Much of the thrust of this book is towards comparing male and female performances in the same events and predicting if or when equality might eventuate. Notional competitions between men and women are mentioned several times but, with the exception of the longer road races such as the marathon and occasionally the longer track races, women do not now nor have they ever run against men. In the United States there have been several court cases concerning the rights or otherwise of young women to run in men's high school or university athletics teams. In a number of cases the courts have ruled in their favour, on the grounds that if the women did not run in the men's teams they would not compete at all in track events and that the denial of the right to participate solely on the basis of sex is unconstitutional.

These developments have been viewed with mixed feelings by women athletes. In some respects they may be an advance, but as an editorial in *Runner's World* said:

A competitive runner must have races. Mixed races are the only opportunity open to hundreds of women. But as a runner advances, he or she needs a test against equals. Mixed competition is inherently unequal and should only be a step leading to the time when women's programmes can stand on their own apart from men's. Mixed racing is a noble beginning but a dead end. For no

Table 25. Comparisons of field events records as at the end of 1980.

	Women's Record		Men's Record		1980 Percentage Difference	1930 Percentage Difference
High jump	S. Simeoni (Italy)	2.01	G. Wessig (GDR)	2.36	14.83	20.69
Long jump	V. Bardauskiene (USSR)	7.09	B. Beamon (USA)	8.90	20.34	28.50
Shot	L. Slupianek (GDR)	22.45	U. Beyer (GDR)	22.15	+1.4	19.89
Discus	M. Vegova-Petkova (Bul.)	71.80	W. Schmidt (GDR)	71.16	+0.9	23.41
Javelin	T. Biryulina (USSR)	70.08	M. Nemeth (Hun.)	94.58	25.90	42.03
			Mean difference		11.75	26.90

matter how well a woman runs she'll never get the attention she deserves if she's back in a pack of men.[4]

6. EXPLANATIONS AND PREDICTIONS

There are many reasons for the continued improvements in athletic performance. There are the strict biological causes, including improvements to physique through better diet, training and technique: there are psychological factors including a greater willingness to train, understanding of the demands of competition and so forth: and there are the external environmental factors such as the improvements in facilities, changes in social attitudes, financial incentives and so on.

This book has emphasized the interrelated nature of all of these and has used simple statistical analysis of performances past to suggest what might happen in performances future. Astonishing as some of these predictions are, it can be argued that they are still underestimates because of the increasing social changes of sport in general and women's sport in particular.

The statistical data on which the predictions of this book are based come to a large extent from years when discrimination against women in sport was profound and their opportunities very circumscribed. To make the same sort of statistical extrapolation from their performances as is made from men's performances may seriously *underestimate* their future improvement.

In his 1980 presidential address to section X of the British Association for the Advancement of Science, Dr Brian Lloyd described a formula incorporating entirely biological variables which he has used to predict world record running performances for the year 2000. This formula in his own words is "an energy-balance equation describing the motion of a non-stop runner, male or female, covering any distance up to 167 miles. It includes acceleration, air drag, curvature (of the track), altitude and the short and long-term energy stores and supplies of the body".[5]

Computer analysis suggests that only two of the parameters have changed much since 1870: the first, a rate constant governing the use of the short term energy store and the one largely controlling the initial dash of a sprinter, has not changed much since 1939; the second, representing the rate at which indefinitely available energy from oxygen is supplied, has increased fairly steadily since 1874 and linearly since 1939. It is likely that the first is biochemical and intracellular in nature, and possibly not amenable to training; the second is dominated by the carriage of oxygen by respiration and circulation, both of which are amenable to training. Lloyd then makes some predictions of changes in world records by the end of the century using this formula. His predictions are set out in table 26. In all cases except the 100 metres it is predicted on this purely biological basis, that women will be considerably closer

Table 26. Some predictions for women's achievements by the year 2000.

	Actual Situation		Lloyd's Analytic Predictions[a]		Dyer's Empirical/Predictions[b]	
	1980 Women's World Record	Percentage Sex Difference	2000 Women's World Record	Percentage Sex Difference	2000 Women's World Record	Percentage Sex Difference
100 metres	10.88	8.56	10.77	8.82	10.00	1.06
200 metres	21.71	9.17	21.35	8.05	20.80	1.72
400 metres	48.60	9.76	45.49	6.36	44.00	3.94
800 metres	1:53.50	9.77	1:44.42	5.38	1:43.04	3.65
1,500 metres	3:52.47	9.08	3:42.13	7.30	3:22.2	0
5,000 metres	15:08.8	13.24	13:52.84	9.11	12:43.0	1.24
10,000 metres	31:45.40	13.79	28:46.31	9.41	26:37.0	0
Marathon	2:25:42.00	11.37	2:14:36.80	9.37	2:05:00.0	0

a. Using a formula incorporating only biological variables.
b. Using the data of section 3, pp. 133-44 and presented partly in figure 13 and tables 15-17.

to men in performance in 2000 than they were in 1980. Predictions based on data presented earlier in this chapter are for much lower sex differences. These are entirely statistical predictions.

The last few pages of this chapter summarize some of those social changes which neither Lloyd's biological predictions nor my statistical predictions fully take into account. It is my belief that when the social changes described and predicted in this book begin to have their full effect, the relative changes in women's sporting performances will be even faster than biologists or statisticians alone predict.

The present century has seen, irregularly and unevenly it is true, enormous improvements in living conditions, levels of health, hygiene and nutrition and marked reductions in hours of work for the majority of the peoples of the developed world. When the average male working week was fifty-six, fifty-two or even forty-eight hours, little time was left over for training or competition in any sport. The same was true for women bringing up large families without today's labour-saving devices. There was also, often enough, little money left over from housekeeping for buying equipment, travelling to competitions, buying special foods, or paying the doctor to treat sporting injuries. Job security was not then what it is today and in times of depression few people were allowed or could take lengthy periods of time from work to take trips overseas or even a few days here and there to attend local meetings. Ten years of the first forty-five of this century were almost completely removed from the sporting calendar because of war, whereas there has now been more than thirty years of relative peace. The continuity of training and competition which this has allowed has been of inestimable value.

Today the average working week in developed countries is forty hours or less and employers are much more willing, indeed often anxious, to release sports stars for national and international competitions.[6] A much greater proportion of the population attends universities and colleges where sports opportunities and facilities are readily available. Subsidies by the state, by sports organizations and, often unofficially from commercial sponsors, have considerably lightened the financial burden. But they have not, for most competitors in western countries, removed it completely. Improvements in health, hygiene and nutrition are still continuing for most western people and these, as well as being of importance in themselves, have undoubtedly contributed to the increases in average height, weight and speed and level of muscular development seen in most populations over the last hundred years or so.

European men and women are on average about six per cent taller and about five per cent heavier than they were, for example, in 1927. An increase in bodily dimensions of this magnitude means an increase in muscular strength of about thirteen per cent. The physiques of the athletes have changed over the years. This is partly because everybody's physique has changed, partly because there has been more specialization among athletes, with individuals increasingly choosing the sport, and the events within the chosen sport, which are most appropriate to their particular body build. It is also partly because athletes are starting their sport earlier in life and undertaking longer, more intensive and more effective preparation and training.

Between 1928 and 1964, men Olympic shotputters became eight centimetres taller and twenty-eight kilograms heavier. The 5000 and 10,000 metre runners became five and six centimetres taller and seven and five kilograms heavier over the period. The maximum work which muscles of a decathlon competitor can yield today is about twenty per cent higher than thirty years ago. Similar improvements have occurred in the respiratory and circulatory systems, maximum oxygen uptake levels, for example, having increased by about thirteen per cent over the last half century.

There is today a much greater understanding of how the body provides for and reacts to extremes of effort. This has led to marked improvements in the efficiency of training, and recognition of different types of training required to develop the energy systems important in different events. With greater knowledge has come a greater willingness to punish the body in training and a greater ease in overcoming psychological barriers, such as the four-minute mile, the seven-foot high jump and so forth.

Other biomedical advances include the drugs now available to athletes, although these are a somewhat mixed blessing. Some are undoubtedly beneficial such as antibiotics, decongestants, pain-killers, asthma suppressors and so on. But the anabolic steroids and the artificial stimulants are not so welcome.

Then there are the material and social changes. The material changes include such things as light-weight running shoes, special jumping shoes, all weather synthetic tracks, portable extra-soft landing pits, fibreglass poles and many, many others. Even starting blocks only came into general use late in the 1930s; previous to that holes were dug in the cinder tracks by the sprinters before the start of every race. Related to these are the training aids such as video film units, computer analyses of mechanical stresses, and the whole range of biomedical equipment available to coaches and sports scientists.

The social changes include the vastly increased amount of international competition and the considerably greater prestige to be gained from winning. There is also now the possibility of rich financial rewards from journalism, advertising, or professional sport at the end of an amateur career or even, for top performers, during their careers. Perhaps above all, international sport, athletics included, has now a much greater political dimension than before. Athletics may now be a largely classless sport in most countries but it has become an essentially nationalistic one, very much involved in the ideological struggles of today's world. One need only recall the events and controversies surrounding South Africa, Rhodesia, Israel, Taiwan, New Zealand, black Americans, Afghanistan and various black African countries at Mexico, Munich, Montreal and Moscow to realize that.

But there are also less obvious political perspectives to today's sport. In Russia and the Eastern European countries sport has become very much part of the foreign policy initiatives, designed to demonstrate the values and successes of their way of life. Athletes are given government employment, teams and team visits are government supported and foreign tours are carefully chosen for their likely successes and political impact. And, of course, these attitudes and values transfer themselves to western countries, many of which have established sports development plans and whose governments are beginning to fund international sport more generously in an attempt to compete.

But the most profound changes in recent years have been in community attitudes, and it is probably here that the greatest potential for future change lies. The first woman officially to run in the famous Boston marathon in the USA was Kathy Switzer in 1967 although, as mentioned in the introduction, she was nearly prevented from competing "for her own safety" by a zealous official at the starting line-up. In 1970 the national chairwoman of women's track in the USA dismissed long distance running as a "lark". Sufficiently a lark was it regarded, though, that women were forbidden to run in the long distance races held in America at that time. But so strong had women's distance running become that by 1972 there was a women's division in the Boston marathon (even though they were supposed to start ten minutes before the men). By 1974 there was a national championship in the marathon and other long distances and in September 1974 the USA could send a team of six to the first International Women's Marathon held in West Germany. Since then the popularity of running among women has soared. The consequences for numbers competing in major races and their performances were documented in pages 153–58.

Attitudes among both men and women have certainly changed rapidly. And with changing attitudes have come improving performances. The questions that must ultimately be asked about these trends are: Where will they end? Can we really see any limits to women's performances? Do we really expect to see women taking up the hammer throw, the steeplechase or the other "missing" events in the future? Will women really catch up the men?

The best statistical predictions suggest that in *all* events women will one day equal men in performance. For some events, the year in which it is predicted that this will occur is so far in the future as to be really meaningless. But in some events equality is predicted within twenty-five or thirty years' time, and although all statistical predictions are fraught with uncertainties, changes in women's performances are occurring faster in some events at present than the long term statistics predict. In the past all predictions of women's equality were rejected on what seemed to be self-evident biological grounds; we now know that such biological grounds are suspect. In the past those who urged that women be allowed to run 1500 metre races or 400 metres hurdles or whatever, were constantly faced with assertions that women could not safely or satisfactorily compete in such events; it is now known that they can. More recently when women wanted to compete in 3000, 5000, 10,000 metres and marathon races they were again told that they could not safely or satisfactorily compete. Again it is now known that they can. Why, therefore, should assertions be accepted today that women cannot compete in the steeplechase, triple jump, pole vault or whatever? They are likely to be no more valid than were the similar assertions of the past concerning all those other events which are now a firm part of women's athletics programmes.

Thirty or forty years ago it was "self-evidently" true that women would never run long distance races, let alone that they could approach within measurable distance of men's performances. Today it is said knowingly, "Yes, but women never will run 100 metres as fast as men", or "of course they will never jump as high as men". But on what basis are these assertions made? The biological differences which were used to explain, for example, the 25 per cent performance differential in the high jump in 1927 or the 18 per cent performance differential in 1957 were clearly not sufficient explanation for these differences. Why, then, should they be regarded as sufficient for today's 14 per cent difference? Clearly they are not. But for what level of performance differential are biological differences responsible? The truth is that we just do not know. To say that women will never equal men in the high jump, or long jump or marathon or whatever, is shown up to be what it is — an assertion with precious little scientific justification.

Unfortunately in this field of sporting endeavour, science has been mobilized as a conservative defender of the social status quo. And yet the science was and is riddled with absurdities and ideological underpinnings. Perhaps the science used in other socially sensitive areas has been similarly suspect and applied to essentially conservative ends?

Top left. Miss Godbold USA shown putting the shot at the Women's World Games, Pershing Stadium, Paris 1922, one of the earliest of all women's international meetings. The best women's achievements at this time were a modest nine metres. (Credit: Central Press Agency.) **Top right.** Ilona Slupanick of East Germany, winner of the Women's Shot Put at Moscow, and world record holder in 1980 with a distance of 22.45 metres, more than twice that achieved by Miss Godbold. Over the same period the men's record has increased by a more modest 40 per cent. The throwers of today are stronger and more muscular than those of fifty years ago (as well as having a vastly improved technique), but much press coverage has overemphasized this aspect of their development and failed to mention the doubling of world records in this time. (Credit: Allsport/Tony Duffy.) **Bottom left.** American speed skater Sheila Young, winner of several world championships and Olympic events and holder of the world 500 metres record. Women roller skaters approach equality with men at long distances but their longest event on ice is 3000 metres. The men's longest event is 10,000 metres! (Credit: Allsport/Tony Duffy.) **Bottom right.** Beryl Burton OBE, foremost British cyclist from the late 1950s to the early 1980s. Her twelve hour time trial record was superior to that of the men's record for a couple of years in the late 1960s. She is here seen winning the 3000 metres pursuit at the British championships in 1974. Beryl Burton has also been very successful in massed start road races. Although there is a slightly restricted programme of events in the World Championships there are no women's events at all in the Olympics. (Credit: Allsport/Tony Duffy.)

CHAPTER NINE

Swimming

1. BIOLOGICAL AND SOCIAL FACTORS IN SWIMMING SUCCESS

In no sport have women's achievements been as dramatic as in swimming. If today's top women swimmers had been swimming in the 1968 men's Olympic finals they would have had a rich medal haul. And yet women have had to fight as hard for competitive opportunities in swimming as in athletics. Swimming is a more widespread and popular leisure activity than athletics and is in some ways a better sport in which to compare the ability of men and women. It is of more equal popularity among men and women than athletics, and it has been a competitive sport for both sexes longer. Men and women swim mostly the same events and have done so since women started international swimming at the turn of the century. Tactics are less important in swimming than running, most swimming races being swum at nearly uniform maximum sustainable speed. Finally, the environment in which the events take place is more uniform than for most other speed sports: the water temperature is controlled; wind, rain and air pressure effects are virtually non-existent; and interference with one competitor by another is largely eliminated.

There have been some important social and economic factors in the development of swimming which are still major influences on its activities. International swimming requires heated indoor pools preferably fifty metres long, although twenty-five metre pools are useful for training purposes. In the initial stages of discovering and fostering young talent the availability of backyard, school and community pools is important, indeed quite crucial. The USA has more pools per head of the population than any other country in the world. In many parts of the USA outdoor pools can be used a good deal of the year too. These are important reasons why the USA has been the top swimming nation in modern times. But not one of the National Swimming Champions of the USA, nor those who have represented it in international competition, has been black. Although biology may have something to do with this, the lack of swimming pools in black ghettoes is probably more important, together with blacks being barred from many of the public and most of the private pools to which they might have sought access in learning to swim or for training.

In contrast, although Russia has been among the most successful nations since its re-entry into the Olympics in 1952, Russians had, prior to 1980, won no gold and only a handful of silver and bronze medals for swimming. In 1952 there were only three indoor swimming pools in the whole of Russia or about one pool per 60 million people and by 1980 the USSR had still only about one pool per 100,000 people, although the situation was rapidly improving. (In contrast Britain, in 1970, had one indoor pool for 37,000 people.) But in 1980 Russia did win gold medals at the Olympics and her swimmers held four world records; her facilities were now equal to the best in the world.

Swimmers are, on average, taller, heavier and less fat than non-swimmers. The maximum oxygen uptake of highly trained swimmers is, on average, as high as that of trained runners. However, at this same maximum oxygen uptake, pulmonary ventilation is lower, oxygen extraction is higher, the respiratory exchange rate is lower and the heart rate is lower. The respiratory rate is lower (normally forty-five to forty-nine breaths per minute) because swimmers never take more than one breath per stroke cycle. All of this suggests that physiological differences between the sexes are not so important in swimming as in other sports.

Swimming is a highly inefficient means of movement for humans. Careful studies on the mechanics of swimming have put the efficiency of the arm stroke at no higher than 6.9 per cent and of the leg kick at no higher than 1.2 per cent. These figures explain the emphasis on arm action and the relative unimportance of leg movements in competitive swimming. They also explain one highly characteristic feature of swimmers; their very great arm strength. Because of this low efficiency, about 5 or 6 per cent overall, even small improvements are of relatively great importance in achieved performance. Many swimmers of similar physique and high maximum oxygen uptakes have very different best times for various events because of their differences in efficiency.

2. THE HISTORY OF WOMEN'S SWIMMING

Although swimming is an ancient pastime it was not until the nineteenth century that there is any reference to it as a competitive sport. It was certainly not on the programme of the ancient Olympic Games or any other great sporting occasions of the classical world. Britain was one of the first countries to build indoor swimming pools. By 1837 there were six pools in London and a National Swimming Society was formed in England in that year. The Amateur Swimming Association was formed in 1886 and is today the governing body of the sport in Britain.

A German swimming federation was founded in 1882, a Hungarian association in 1896 and a French organization in 1899. Other early swimming organizations were the New Zealand ASA founded in 1890, the New South Wales ASA in 1891 and the United States Amateur Athletic Union, which included control of swimming, formed in 1880. Representatives of these national bodies met in London in 1908 during the Olympic Games and founded the Federation Internationale de Natation Amateur (FINA) on which initially eight countries were represented. There are now more than one hundred countries affiliated. One of the first activities of FINA was to recognize world records, mostly the best performances of 1908, but including some earlier authenticated times. Twenty records were recognized for men and one for women (the 100 metres freestyle), although curiously FINA did not recognize women's competitions until 1921.

The first modern swimming championships were organized in 1846 in Australia and various national championships followed, mostly at about the time of the formation of the national association. Women's championships were usually started long after the men's. The first country to hold women's national championships appears to be Scotland in 1892, followed by England in 1901, the USA in 1916 and Russia in 1922 (although men's events in that country were not held until 1921). In these and most other early national championships, there were only one or two women's events, usually the 100 and/or 200 metres freestyle, compared to a full programme for men. Nevertheless photograph 11 shows that by the turn of the century in England at least women's swimming was well established.

But it was the Olympic Games more than anything else which accelerated the technical advancement and popularity of swimming as a competitive sport throughout the world. The men's Olympic programme started in 1896 and the women's programme, with only two events, the 100 metres and the 4 x 100 metres relay, in 1912. The women's programme is now almost as large as the men's, although, as in athletics, their events were usually introduced well after those of men. The details are set out in table 27. The dates of recognition of women's world records are also almost always well after the comparable men's

Table 27. The dates of introduction of men's and women's swimming events into the Olympic Games.

		Men	Women
Freestyle	100 metres	1896	1912
	200 metres	1968	1968
	400 metres	1900	1924
	800 metres	—	1968
	1,500 metres	1908	—
	4 x 100 metres relay	1964	1912
	4 x 200 metres relay	1908	—
Backstroke	100 metres	1904	1924
	200 metres	1964	1968
Breaststroke	100 metres	1968	1968
	200 metres	1908	1924
Butterfly	100 metres	1968	1956
	200 metres	1956	1972
Medley	200 metres	1968	1968
	400 metres	1964	1964
	4 x 100 metres relay	1964	1964

records. As well as the Olympics there are World Championships every four years which began with a full programme of both men's and women's events in 1973. European men's championships were first held in 1926 and the following year women's events were added. The Commonwealth Games started in 1930, and although a women's swimming programme was included in the first meeting it was a very restricted one.

One astonishing thing about world swimming in the 1970s was its domination by two nations, the USA and East Germany. In particular it was American men and East German women who dominated Olympic and World Championship swimming. In the men's events at the Montreal Olympics, USA won twenty-nine medals and East Germany only one. In the women's events, however, East Germany dominated by winning nineteen medals to the USA's ten and the USSR's six. Australia was important in the late 1950s and early 1960s but by 1980 had only two or three swimmers of world class; by the 1980s the USSR had become a force to be reckoned with.

Since 1920, with the exceptions of only 1932 and 1956, and of course 1980 when they were not present, United States swimmers have won the largest number of medals at each Olympiad. One of the most important reasons for this is probably the age group swimming programme which has been sponsored by the AAU for many years and which in the 1970s involved more than one million swimmers. In this boys and girls compete on local, sectional and national levels in all competitive strokes at specific age levels: <10;11–12; 13–14; and 15–17. East Germany, of course, has its sports plans, its coaching and superb facilities. Australia has none of these and its performances are suffering accordingly by world standards.

3. CURRENT WORLD RECORD PERFORMANCES

Women's performances are much closer to those of men in swimming than running. The mean difference for all freestyle events, 100 metres to 1500 metres, including the relay, was 7.72 per cent in 1978 compared to 10.17 per cent for track events of the same distances. The world records as they stood at the end of 1980 are shown in table 28. Comparing this with table 15 shows that women are closer to men in the long distance swimming events but are closest to men in the shortest track events.

There is another important difference between the two sports. The decline of speed with distance is much less in swimming than in running (see figure 15). The 1500 metre track and 400 metre swimming events each last between 3½ and 4 minutes, but the 1500 metres is run at a speed which averages only about 70 per cent of the maximal speed as attained in the 100 metres on the track, while the 400 metres is swum at a speed about 90 per cent of that attained in the 100 metre swim. The 3000 metres, taking about 8 minutes, is run at a speed

Table 28. World swimming records as they were at the end of 1980.

		Men				Women				Percentage Difference
Freestyle	100 metres	J. Skinner	SA	49.44	1976	GDR	B. Krause	1980	54.79	9.79
	200 metres	R. Gains	USA	1:49.16	1980	USA	C. Woodhead	1979	1:58.23	7.70
	400 metres	P. Szmidt	Canada	3:50.49	1980	Aust.	T. Wickham	1978	4:06.28	6.40
	800 metres	V. Salnikov	USSR	7:56.49	1979	USA	C. Woodhead	1980	8:18.77	4.48
	1,500 metres	V. Salnikov	USSR	14:58.27	1980	USA	K. Lineham	1979	16:04.49	6.84
	4 x 100 metres		USA	3:19.74	1976	GDR		1980	3:42.71	10.33
						Mean difference				7.59
Breaststroke	100 metres	G. Morken	W. Germany	1:02.86	1977	GDR	U. Gewiniger	1980	1:10.11	10.36
	200 metres	D. Wilkie	UK	2:15.11	1976	USSR	L. Kachushite	1979	2:28.36	8.92
Backstroke	100 metres	J. Naber	USA	55.49	1976	GDR	R. Reinisch	1980	1:00.86	8.83
	200 metres	J. Naber	USA	1:59.19	1976	GDR	R. Reinisch	1980	2:11.77	9.52
Butterfly	100 metres	P. Arvidsson	Sweden	54.15	1980	USA	M. Meagher	1980	59.26	8.65
	200 metres	C. Beardsley	USA	1:58.21	1980	USA	M. Meagher	1980	2:06.37	6.39
Medley	200 metres	W. Barrett	USA	2:03.24	1980	GDR	P. Schneider	1980	2:13.00	7.33
	400 metres	J. Vassallo	USA	4:20.05	1978	GDR	P. Schneider	1980	4:36.29	5.86
	4 x 100 metres		USA	3:42.22	1978	GDR		1980	4:06.67	9.89
						Mean difference at all events				8.09

about 65 per cent of maximum, whereas the 800 metres in the pool, taking about the same time, is swum at more than 80 per cent of maximum speed. The difference in loss of speed becomes greater with increasing distance. Overall, runners lose speed at a rate almost three times greater than swimmers.

There are a number of reasons for this. When the body is horizontal, rather than vertical, the heart expands. When the body is immersed in water the state of weightlessness is simulated and the heart expands a good deal more. The heart volume of one man measured from X-ray pictures was 698 millilitres when standing, 771 when lying down and 992 after immersion. The swimmer's heart can therefore pump more blood at each stroke than can the runner's. The heart's ability to pump blood forward is further enhanced by the horizontal swimming position and the cool environment causes blood to be diverted from the skin to the central circulation which is an additional help in oxygen distribution.

At present, as shown in figure 15, women lost a little more of their maximal speed on the track than do men, whereas they lose rather less of their maximum speed in the pool. (In this respect swimming is similar to cycling and skating and therefore it is athletics which is different. As figures 16 and 17 suggested, athletics may soon come to be like the others). Another point of interest is that in 1980 the men's 1500 metre record represented almost exactly the same swimming speed as the 800 metre record (1.670 metres/second and 1.678 metres/second respectively). If women could swim 1500 metres as fast as they swim 800 metres, their record at the longer distance would be 15:57.24, compared to the men's record of 14:58.27. This would be a difference of only 6.17 per cent, not the 6.84 per cent it was in 1980.

Recent performances of Australian girl Tracy Wickham in breaking the 1500 metre world record is a portent of things to come. In February 1978 she returned a time of 16 minutes 14.9 seconds, breaking the previous record by no less than 9.7 seconds or 0.98 per cent. Conditions during her swim were not ideal, however; the water temperature was twenty-seven degrees, three degrees warmer than the Olympic temperature, which is probably about optimum; Tracy had only just recovered from a strained arm muscle; she had trained about fifteen kilometres already that day; and the swim was a solo one in front of a small crowd. She nevertheless believed after the race that she could break 16 minutes and her coach said of her new record that "In six months she will knock 25 to 30 seconds off that". In fact it took her twelve months to lower the record by 8 seconds or so under equally adverse conditions in Perth in February 1979.

Among other interesting things about her 1978 swim was that she swam the first 800 metres in 8:40.14, only 10 seconds outside the world record, at a mean speed of 1.538 metres/second, and the second 700 metres slightly faster in 7:34.79, a mean speed of 1.539 metres/second. The last 100 metres she swam in 63.85 seconds which was 0.05 seconds faster than the first 100 metres and represented a speed of 1.566 metres/second. Jenny Turral, an earlier Australian holder of the 1500 metres world record, also had this ability to cover the last half of a race faster than the first, an ability which many female marathon and ultra-long distance runners also have.

In athletics women are now running the sprints in times achieved by men in the 1880s. Current women's middle distance events track records were achieved by men early in this century and women's long distance times were achieved by men in the second and third decades of this century. Table 29 shows how different is swimming. At distances greater than 100 metres women are now swimming at speeds which men did not attain until the middle or late 1960s. At both 400 and 1500 metres, for instance, the present women's world record would have won a gold medal in the men's event up to and including 1968. (And yet a women's 1500 metres is still not on the Olympic programme.)

Table 29. Women's world freestyle swimming records in 1972 and 1980 and the men's records which first exceeded them.

	1972 Women's World Record[a]	First Men to Achieve Better Times		1980 Women's World Record[a]	First Men to Achieve Better Times
100 metres	58.5	Johnny Weismuller	1924	54.79	Dick Cleveland
200 metres	2:03.56	John Konrads	1958	1:58.23	Don Schollander
400 metres	4:19.04	John Konrads	1959	4:06.28	Hans Fassnacht
800 metres	8:53.68	Murray Rose	1962	8:18.77	Steve Holland
1,500 metres	16:56.9	Mike Burton	1966	16:04.49	John Kinsella
4 × 100 metres	3:58.11	Yale University	1940	3:42.71	France

a. The full details of the holders of these records are given in Appendix C.

The early 1978 women's world 1500 metre record represented a mean speed of 1.539 metres/second. That speed was not attained until 1959 by a man in a 400 metres race and not until 1967 in an 800 metres race. To put this into perspective it means that famous men long distance swimmers such as Australians Murray Rose and John Konrads, and Americans Don Schollander and George Breen, in setting their world records and winning their Olympic medals at 400 and 800 metres in the late 1950s and early 1960s would, at the end of their races, still have been behind today's top women swimmers. The women, however, would be only halfway through their 800 and 1500 metre races!

If a race could be staged over 1500 metres between Tracy Wickham and some of the famous men world record holders of the past, Boy Charlton (20:06.6, 1924) would be more than three lengths behind, Murray Rose (17:59.5, 1956) would be more than two lengths behind and John Konrads (17:11.0, 1960) would be more than one length behind. In a race over 800 metres Tracy Wickham would be more than a length ahead of John Konrads, 1958 men's world record holder, at 9:14.6.

Johnny Weismuller won the Olympic 100 metres title in 1924 and 1928 and the 400 metres in 1924. Matched against today's women he might just stay ahead of the women's 200 metre swimmers in his 100 metres race, but in his 400 metres race he would fall steadily behind today's women 800 metre and 1500 metre swimmers. He would be some way behind them when he finished his distance while they, of course, would be only part way through theirs. Weismuller's predecessor as Olympic 100 metre champion, the famous Hawaiian, Duke Kahanamuku, would have fallen behind today's women 400 metre swimmers and would barely have beaten the 800 metre swimmers in his 1912 victory in the 100 metres!

Complete comparisons of the changing speeds at which freestyle races are won can be had from figure 21 which shows the evolution of the world record speeds for all freestyle events from the time the records were recognized for both sexes.

4. THE IMPROVEMENT OF WOMEN'S PERFORMANCES

One of the difficulties in studying the evolution of swimming records is that the events themselves, the length of the pool in which they are swum and the strokes and techniques have changed over the years. For these reasons it is better to restrict comparisons prior to 1956 to freestyle events only. Comparisons can be extended back to 1908 for the 100 metres, 1918 for the 200 metres, 1919 for 400 and 800 metres and 1922 for 1500 metres. (The full details of all recent women's records are given in appendix C. The details of the earlier evolution of swimming events and their records are given in Pat Besford's *Encyclopaedia of Swimming*.)

The method of comparison is as in athletics, calculating the speed in metres per second which a record represents. Although the distances are very different the speeds at which they are swum are similar and allow comparison in one composite figure (figure 21), in which the declining difference between the sexes for all events is obvious. The records themselves and the sex differences they represented in 1936, 1956 and 1976 are given in table 30 so that the numerical basis of the conclusions set out below can be seen. The difference between the sexes over the last forty years or so has declined by more than a quarter for all events and by about 40 per cent for the longer events. Improvements in the swimming records over the last fifty years or so are between two and four times greater than in athletics, as shown in table 31. It is surprising that this is so since the history of competitive swimming and hence of record-breaking is at least as long as in athletics, and for women's swimming is in fact rather longer. We are not therefore seeing the early rash of records in new events as is arguably the case in some of the women's track events.

There have been some technical improvements which undoubtedly aid performance — wave killing gutters in the pools, race lane markers reducing surface turbulence, underwater cameras to aid training, large face electric stopclocks to aid swimmers in pacing, briefer and better designed swimwear, and so forth — but their importance is probably less than similar technical improvements in athletics. The amount of improvement is generally greater in the longer events

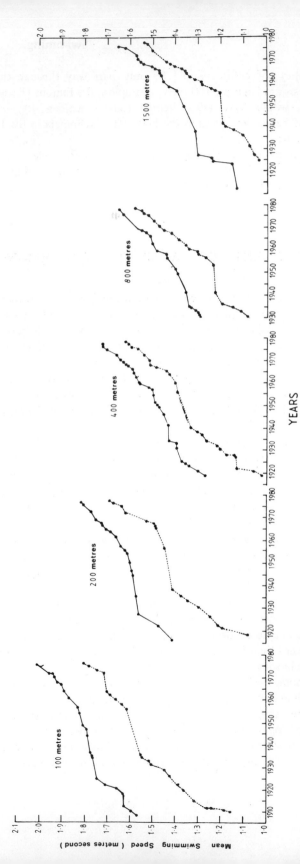

Fig. 21. The changes in mean swimming speed in individual freestyle events represented by men's and women's world records. The astonishing improvement in both sexes is obvious, but women are still creeping closer.

Men's world records

Women's world records

	1936			1956			1976		
	Male	Female	Percentage Difference	Male	Female	Percentage Difference	Male	Female	Percentage Difference
100m freestyle	56.4	64.6	12.69	55.4	62.0	11.05	49.44	55.65	11.16
100m butterfly				62.3	76.6	13.64	54.27	60.13	9.77
100m backstroke	64.8	73.6	11.92	62.2	72.9	14.66	55.49	61.51	9.77
100m breaststroke	70.0	80.2	12.74	68.2	76.9	11.32	63.11	70.80	10.86
200m freestyle	127.2	145.3	12.47	123.2	134.7	8.54	110.29	119.29	7.52
200m butterfly				136.7	160.5	14.83	119.23	131.22	9.15
200m backstroke	144.0	168.7	14.61	138.4	157.4	12.07	119.19	132.47	10.01
200m breaststroke	157.2	180.4	12.81	156.5	171.3	8.64	135.13	153.35	11.90
200m medley							126.08	137.14	8.07
400m freestyle	278.7	316.0	11.78	267.0	287.2	7.01	231.90	249.89	7.19
400m medley				312.9	343.7	8.96	263.68	282.77	6.72
800m freestyle	595.8	671.7	11.32	555.7	630.9	9.54	482.91	517.44	6.64
1,500m freestyle	1,147.2	1,356.7	15.44	1,072.9	1,222.8	13.95	906.6	993.94	9.37
4 x 100 freestyle	250.2[a]	272.8	8.32	226.8	257.1	11.79	201.11	224.82	10.56
4 x 100 medley				254.8	293.1	13.06	222.22	247.95	10.39
Mean Difference			12.41			11.36			9.27
Freestyle Events Only			12.00			10.31			8.74

a. 1937

Table 31. Percentage improvement in world records 1928-77.

Distance	100m		200m		400m		800m		1,500m	
	Men	Women	Men	Women	Men	Women	Men	Women	Men	Women
Athletics	4.33	9.34	6.60	12.22	6.68	18.75	6.48	15.98	8.13	24.60
Swimming	15.60	22.93	13.78	25.76	20.23	26.63	22.30	30.89	25.09	31.55

Table 32. The decline of the sex differential in swimming events 1976-80.

| | Freestyle | | | | | | | Backstroke | | Breaststroke | | Butterfly | | Medley | | | Overall Mean |
	100m	200m	400m	800m	1,500m	4 × 100	Mean[a]	100m	200m	100m	200m	100m	200m	200m	400m	4 × 100	
1976	11.16	7.52	7.19	6.64	9.37	10.56	8.74	9.77	10.01	10.86	11.90	9.77	9.15	8.07	6.72	10.39	9.27
1977	11.37	7.52	6.97	6.52	8.38	10.51	8.54	10.11	10.01	11.30	11.90	9.41	9.15	7.77	6.72	10.39	9.20
1978	10.78	6.95	5.96	4.60	7.42	10.63	7.72	9.77	9.65	10.62	10.80	8.87	9.09	7.82	7.42	10.39	8.72
1979	10.78	7.08	6.07	5.60	6.44	10.63	7.77	9.77	9.65	10.62	8.92	8.87	6.26	8.01	7.42	10.39	8.43
1980	9.79	7.70	6.40	4.48	6.84	10.33	7.59	8.83	9.52	10.36	8.92	8.65	6.39	7.33	5.86	9.89	8.09

a. The average decline in sex differential for these freestyle events over this five year period was 0.24 per cent. The average decline in sex differential for the corresponding 6 track events was 0.33 per cent.

but even the longest track events, 5000 and 10,000 metres which are primarily aerobic events of similar duration to the longer swimming events, have been improved by men less than 15 and 20 per cent respectively in the last fifty years, whereas men and women have improved their long distance swimming records by more than 30 per cent in forty years. The rate of improvement of records in both men's and women's swimming is also greater now than it has ever been. (This can be seen from appendix C and from figure 21 in which the evolution of all freestyle records is shown.) Since 1976 the rate of improvement of women's records compared to men's has become faster than before. Table 32 shows that the overall mean difference has declined from 9.27 per cent in 1976 to 8.09 per cent in 1980, that is, the difference declined by an average of 0.25 per cent per annum over this five-year period compared to declines of 0.05 per cent 1936–56 and 0.10 per cent 1956–76. It seems inevitable, therefore, that women's swimming performances will get even closer to those of men than they are at present.

Statistical analysis suggests in fact that equality will be reached in all events eventually. Current trends may not be maintained, of course, and the predictions to which they give rise represent only a plausible possibility. They are, nevertheless, more plausible than most other predictions. Women's performances are expected to equal men's in the freestyle events in the following years:

100 m	200 m	400 m	800 m	1500 m	Mean
2018	2019	2020	2009	2011	2018

Figure 22, showing the decline of the mean difference between the sexes for all the swimming events and the statistical prediction based on these annual figures, indicates that the mean difference is declining at present just about as fast as expected. But this is a mean difference and hides some important variation between the events. The events which in 1978 had the highest and lowest sex differences in performance were the 100 and 800 metres. Figure 23 shows that women have not got much closer to men in the 100 metres over the last ten or twenty years (although records have been broken as frequently as ever by both men and women). The actual performance difference is at present well above that predicted and the same is true for the 4 x 100 metres relay. The difference in both events seems to be settling down at or a little below 10 per cent and further narrowing of this gap may be very slow. On the other hand women are catching men in the 800 metres faster than ever and the 1978 difference is well below that predicted. Equality seems highly probably by 2009 at the latest.

There is some other evidence, though, that women are catching the men in the shorter swimming events as well as the longer. A study of data from the 1971–75 National Indoor Championships in the USA showed that women were gaining on their male counterparts at the rate of .45 per cent a year in the 100 yards freestyle but only at about .155 per cent in the 1650 yards. In 1971 the differences were 14.4 per cent and 8.6 per cent respectively. At

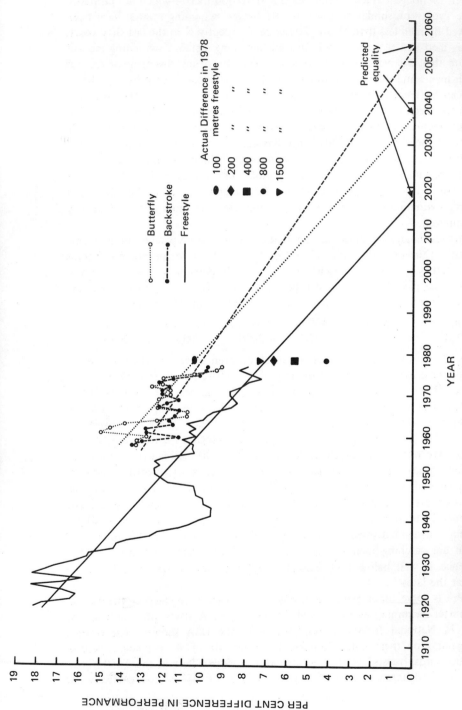

Fig. 22. The average difference in performance for the different swimming strokes over various periods of time and the regression lines calculated from these figures. The actual differences for the freestyle events at the end of 1978 are also shown.

— — — Actual differences and calculated regression line for freestyle events
● — — ● Actual differences and calculated regression for backstroke events
○ .... ○ Actual differences and calculated regression for butterfly events

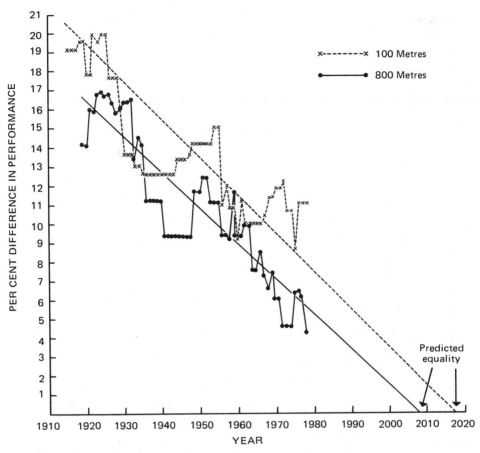

Fig. 23. Actual and predicted differences in performance of men and women at 100 metres and 800 metres freestyle, together with regression lines calculated from these. The actual difference at 800 metres in 1978 was well below that predicted.

this rate women would catch the men in 2003 in the 100 yards but not till 2021 in the 1650 yards.

As already pointed out women swim longer distances at speeds closer to their top speed than do men and are still rapidly improving in this respect. This improvement shows little signs of stopping, although there is presumably some limit to the performances of distance swimmers. It is hardly likely that men or women will ever swim 800 or 1500 metres in times merely eight and fifteen times longer than those in which they cover 100 metres. The achievements in this direction, though, have been quite astonishing, as shown in figure 24. The women's 100 metres world record was broken in February 1956 by the great Dawn Fraser of Australia with a time of 1:04.5. If Dawn Fraser had managed to keep up this speed for a further 700 metres, her time at 800 metres

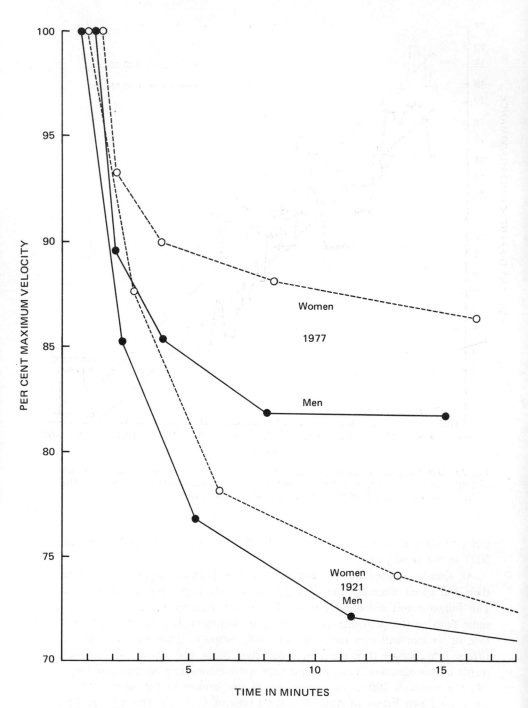

Fig. 24. The proportion of their maximal velocity at 100 metres with which men and women swam the freestyle events during world record performances in 1921 and 1978. The differences between men and women became much greater over this period.

would have been 8 minutes 36 seconds. In February 1978 another Australian, Tracy Wickham, returned a time for 800 metres of 8 minutes 30.53 seconds, comfortably inside eight times Dawn Fraser's 100 metre record. If Dawn Fraser had kept up her 100 metres world record speed over 1500 metres she would have recorded 16 minutes 7.5 seconds. Tracy Wickham's 1500 metre record set in early 1979 was just over one second outside this!

The conclusions arrived at in discussing biological sex differences and re-affirmed in examining track and roadrunning records are further reinforced: at the aerobic longer distances, women have fewer biological disadvantages and perhaps even some advantages over men. In such events women are clearly catching up the men.

There are now no events longer than 1500 metres regularly swum in the pool. Longer events are usually swum in lakes or the sea, and are subject to variations of course, tides, weather and other variables; comparisons between different events are less exact than with FINA controlled pool races.

The English Channel is probably the best known long distance swim. Although the straight line distance is about thirty-five kilometres (or twenty-one miles), swimmers may cover between forty and even eighty kilometres through being carried by currents and tides. Women started Channel swimming later than men. Captain Webb managed the feat in 1875 but it was not until 1926 that Gertrude Ederle became the first woman to accomplish the crossing. Nevertheless, by 1977, the fastest time, indeed the three fastest times, for swimming from England to France, were held by women, the fastest being twenty-year old Wendy Brooks, who took 8 hours 56 minutes, beating the old record by 7 minutes. The fastest time by a man in this direction before 1977 was 10 hours 21 minutes. In 1977 Nasserel Shazley of Egypt broke the record with a time of 8 hours 45 minutes, but in 1978 United States student Penny Dean recorded 7 hours 42 minutes to reassert female supremacy. In what is allegedly the easier direction from France to England the record is held by a man, Syrian Marawan Saleh, at 9 hours 27 minutes, with a woman holding the third fastest time at 9 hours 46 minutes. In 1977 a nineteen year old Canadian girl, Cindy Nicholas, swam the English Channel both ways without stopping and knocked two hours off the previous best time which was held by a man. In 1979 she recorded 19 hours 12 minutes for the two way swim which still stands as the best performance.

Wendy Brooks set her Channel swimming record in 1976. Four days after doing so she beat forty-three opponents, including thirty-three men, over a distance of 10½ miles in the annual long distance championships at Lake Windermere, with a time of 4 hours 25 minutes 47 seconds. This was thirty-five minutes ahead of her nearest rival. The following weekend she won the women's three-mile race in Trentham Lake in 1 hour 3 minutes 42 seconds, which was four minutes faster than the winner of the men's event.

The equivalent in America of swimming the English Channel is swimming the twenty-eight kilometre Catalina Channel in California. The record from the mainland to Catalina is held by Penny Dean who in 1976 swam the distance in 7 hours 15 minutes 50 seconds. In 1977 she shattered Greta Anderson's two way non-stop swim record by recording 20 hours 3 minutes 17 seconds. On the way she set a new record from Catalina to the mainland of 8 hours 33 minutes and 15 seconds.

To all intents and purposes, therefore, equality between the sexes has already been attained in long distance swimming, as evidenced by the following: the winners and place getters in any event cannot be predicted on the basis of sex alone; it is no longer the case that the fastest performers for any course or distance are invariably men; two of the four fastest times in Lake Windermere are held by women, eight of the ten fastest English Channel swims in either direction and the non-stop record each way are held by women; and the each way and both way records for Catalina Channel swims are all held by women.

CHAPTER TEN

Other Speed Sports

1. CYCLING

Following Queen Victoria's purchase of tricycles for her daughters in the 1880s, cycling for women became acceptable. When Amelia Bloomer showed women what to wear while cycling in the 1890s, it became practical. Not surprisingly, therefore, cycling led the way in the emancipation of European and American women at the turn of the century. But it was taken up by sportswomen as well as cyclists and it is one of the few sports in which a major women's world record for a regular event has been superior to the corresponding men's world record. And yet women cyclists are still denied entry to the Olympic Games and cannot take part in many of the other major events of the sport.

There are several different types of competitive cycling. In Europe massed start road racing is very popular. This is a male dominated, largely professional sport, in which races are held over distances of more than a hundred kilometres or over several daily stages of this length. The most famous one is the *Tour de France* which involves nearly a month's gruelling racing, although there are several others almost as long. There are few massed start or multi-stage races for women and hardly any of the rich prizes and commercial sponsorship which dominate men's cycling. This much reduces women's opportunities as a whole, since although the various types of cycling are quite different, there are opportunities to cross the divides which separate them. Eddie Merckx, for example, several times winner of the *Tour de France*, also holds several track records, and Beryl Burton who dominated English time trial cycling in the 1960s and 1970s has taken part in track races and massed start road races in the women's world championships with considerable success.

Racing on the track, over distances from one kilometre to ten kilometres, is also very popular in Europe and to a lesser extent in other parts of the world. The shorter distances are raced as desperate sprints over the last two or three hundred metres, as individual "flat out all the way" time trials or as pursuit races in which individuals or teams start from opposite sides of the track and endeavour to catch each other. There are both amateur and professional races on the track and world championships for both men and women, but the distances are usually different for the sexes and the distances over which world records are recognized are not usually the same as those raced on the track. For example, in the World Championships, women's distances are always shorter than men's. In the individual pursuit, amateur men ride over 4000 metres, women over 3000 metres and professional men over 5000 metres.

In 1978 all the men's track cycling records, other than the one kilometre, were held by two professionals, namely de Ritter of Denmark (five kilometre and one hundred kilometre) and Eddie Merckx of Belgium (ten kilometre, twenty kilometre and one hour). Women's performances have been falling further behind those of men in most of these track events. This is mainly due to the increasing professionalism of men's cycling and the importance of the men's road-racing programme in providing record breakers. There are no real parallel opportunities in women's sport. Furthermore, the one-hour unpaced track record has been set on the last two occasions (by de Ritter in 1968 and Merckx in 1972) on the track at Mexico City in special sponsored attempts. Such financial backing is just not available to women.

Men's track world championships were started in 1893 with amateur and professional sprints and a hundred kilometres motor paced event. In 1946 men's amateur and professional pursuit races were introduced. Men's cycling was introduced into the Olympic Games in 1896 with a road race, and the programme now comprises, in addition, a 1000 metres sprint, 1000 metres time trial and 4000 metres individual and team pursuits. Women's cycling was first recognized by the Union Cycliste Internationale, the body responsible for world cycle sport, in 1955 and women's world records were first recognized in this year. Women's world championships, which included a massed start road race, were first held in 1958. There is no women's Olympic cycling programme, nor is it on any of the other major games' programmes.

For all these reasons, comparisons of men's and women's records on the road and track are either impossible or are seriously misleading. But they are possible in time trialling, the other important type of competitive cycling, where competitors race essentially against the clock on road courses which are as flat as possible and on an out-and-back route to minimize the effects of wind and gradient. Competitors are started singly at one minute intervals and pacing of other entrants is forbidden. Time trialling over distances of ten, twenty-five, thirty, fifty and one hundred miles or for periods of twelve or twenty-four hours is particularly popular in Britain. The records for all events as they stood at the end of 1980 are shown in table 33. With the exception of the thirty mile and twenty-four hour events which are infrequent, especially for women, the differences between the sexes are lower than other speed sports. The smallest difference, furthermore, is in the longest event regularly competed in, the twelve hour event. It was in this event for two years or so during the late 1960s, that the women's record was superior to men's, 277.25 miles (446.19 kilometres) covered compared to 276.55 (445.06 kilometres).

As well as races over each distance, there is a British Best All Rounder (BBAR) Championship each year based on riders' results in three different time trials. The men's competition is decided on the average speed of the rider's best performances over fifty miles, one hundred miles and twelve hours. The

Table 33. British road time trial cycling records (as recognized by the Road Time Trials Council at the end of 1980).

Event	Men's Record	Women's Record	Percentage Difference
10 miles	19.44	21.25	9.30
25 miles	49.24	53.21	7.89
30 miles	1:02:07	1:09.16	11.42
50 miles	1:43.46	1:51:30	7.21
100 miles	3:41.43	3:55.05	6.15
12 hours	288.51 miles	277.25 miles	3.90
	459.48 km	446.19 km	
24 hours	507.00 miles	427.86 miles	15.88
	815.93 km	688.57 km	
		Mean Difference:	8.82

women's competition is decided by their average speed over twenty-five miles, fifty miles and one hundred miles. The men's BBAR competition was started by the magazine *Cycling* in 1936 and taken over by the National Road Time Trials Council in 1948, from which year a full women's competition was organized.

Although men's time trialling had been popular throughout the century, 1938 was the first year that any significant number of events for women were organized. There were no fifty mile open events promoted however, and only one twelve hour event. As an article in *Cycling* at the time said: "Women's time trials have obviously come to stay and I hope there will soon be a woman representative on the National Council of the controlling body".[1] Even after the women's BAR competition started in 1948, the number of events for women remained much lower than for men. A plea in the 26 November 1953 issue of *Cycling* was for more events at one hundred miles, and the writer of that plea went on to point out the considerable paucity of opportunities for women to compete at longer distances.

In fact the number of women who compete at the longer distances is still very small, although it is not clear whether this is because such events are infrequent or whether they are infrequent because few women want to take part. An estimate from the National Competition Secretary of the Road Time Trials Council is that there were between 4000 and 5000 men competing in the 1978 season but no more than 350 women. Women are allowed to enter men's events and this is sometimes done by some of the more able women. In the earlier years of the women's BAR competition, however, their performances in men's events were recognized neither for record purposes nor for the BAR competition itself. Some comparisons of male and female performances in time trial cycling from 1938 to 1978 are shown in table 34.

Table 34. Some comparisons of men's and women's performance in time trial cycling 1948-78.

	Mean Difference in Speed of RTTC Records[a]		Mean Difference in Speed of BBAR Competition Winners
	Those in BBAR Competition	All Records	
1938	14.66		
1948	11.37	11.08	3.67
1958	11.18	11.51	3.47
1968	3.72	6.97	0.86
1978	4.83	7.57	1.07
Year Equality Predicted	1996	2017	1968

a. The Women's BBAR Competition was not started until 1948; nor, before that, were women's records at all distances recognized.

The evolution of the national records since their establishment is shown in figure 25. This shows how close women's performances now are to men's and the superiority of their twelve hour record for those two years 1967–69. The whole situation is quite a remarkable one but is not widely known, partly because it is not a spectator sport which gets a wide media coverage.

As mentioned the BAR competitions are not the same for men and women: women competing over twenty-five, fifty and one hundred miles, men over fifty and one hundred miles and twelve hours. Figure 26 shows the performance differential for these four events over the years and the statistical prediction to which they give rise. It emphasizes the rapid and until recently the almost uniform decline in performance differential between the sexes. Women's achievements represent those attained by men only within the last ten or fifteen years as shown in table 35.

Cycling, other than the one kilometre events, is primarily an aerobic activity and over the longer distances accessible energy reserves are very important. In both of these sex differences are small. The power used in cycling comes primarily from the leg muscles and here too the differences between the sexes are minimal. Air resistance is one of the most important limiting factors in attaining and maintaining speed. Hence the universal adoption of the crouch position and the frequency with which riders will tuck in close behind a rider in front in road racing. The smaller body frame and more rounded contours of women are therefore important advantages.

For all these reasons women's performances are expected to be closer to those of men in cycling than in many other sports. Women's performances at longer distances should also show less of a decline compared to short distance

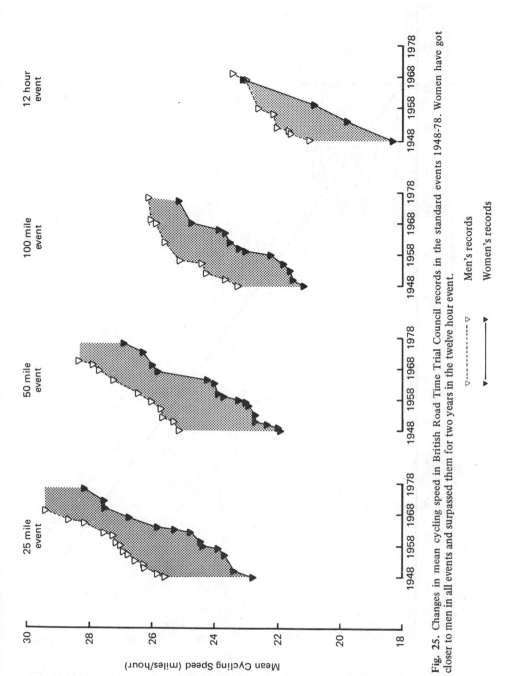

Fig. 25. Changes in mean cycling speed in British Road Time Trial Council records in the standard events 1948-78. Women have got closer to men in all events and surpassed them for two years in the twelve hour event.

Men's records ▽ --------- ▽

Women's records ▼———▼

Mean Cycling Speed (miles/hour)

25 mile event

50 mile event

100 mile event

12 hour event

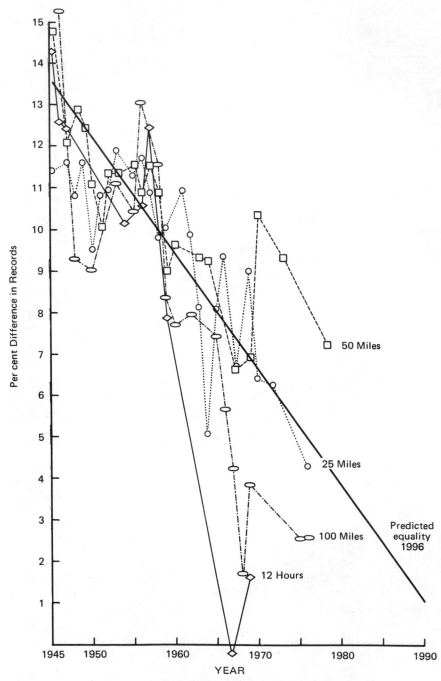

Fig. 26. The difference in men's and women's performance in the standard British cycling time trials, together with the regression based on the mean of all four events. The improvement of women's performance is obvious.

Table 35. Women's cycling records at the end of 1980 compared to men's performance.

Event	Women's Record	Year Men Achieved a Better Performance
25 miles	53 minutes 21 seconds	1965
50 miles	1 hour 51 minutes 30 seconds	1964
100 miles	3 hours 55 minutes 5 seconds	1968
12 hours	277.25 miles	1969

performances. Both of these expectations are indeed fulfilled. Women, for example, can cycle for twelve hours at 77 per cent of their speed over one kilometre; men can manage no better than 65 per cent of their top speed for twelve hours.

In some types of cycling, then, women are indeed catching up the men. In others where it is possible to judge, such as track events, this is not the case, largely because of the very restricted opportunities for women, and in the professional and largely commercialized world of massed start racing, women hardly ever compete. On the basis of the evidence here presented, it seems that were women to be admitted to these events, they would be able to perform quite satisfactorily. The problem, of course, is to develop an initial programme with enough events and enough sponsorship to render it a viable proposition. There is a women's world road championship race and a few other women's events, so a start has been made. It is quite astonishing that women's cycling is still not an Olympic sport. Even allowing for the desire not to enlarge the Games it seems that women's cycling has a greater claim than almost any other sport. It can hardly be doubted that were this eminently justifiable decision taken, then the standards of women's cycling in all areas would improve still further.

2. SKATING

Ice skating is a sport of grace and skill, agility and balance, of beauty and finesse. Much of the sport's popularity comes from figure skating and ice dancing in which women are fully the equal of men in participation and performance. There is sufficient carry-over of public acceptance of women in this branch of the sport to smooth the path of would-be women speed skaters.

Roller skating is derived from ice skating and is very similar in its physical and physiological demands, being organized along similar lines – figure skating, dancing, speed skating and hockey. There are some important differences between ice and roller skating: ice skating is an Olympic sport while roller skating is not, and they are popular in different countries. But in both sports, racing is essentially against the clock, with pairs of skaters skating together round 400 metre circuits keeping to their own lanes throughout and not inter-fering in any way with each other.

In ice skating, world and Olympic championships for men are held over distances between 500 metres and 10,000 metres, whereas women race over distances between 500 and 3000 metres only (up until 1955 women raced over 5000 metres, but in 1956, the 1500 metre event replaced it). In roller skating, world championship races for men are held over 1000, 5000, 10,000 and 20,000 metres, whereas women race over 500, 3000 and 5000 metres, although here too the distances have varied in the past. The fact that women race over shorter distances than men is highly significant, because at all distances over 25,000 metres, women roller skate faster than men. Ice skating events over this distance are quite unknown.

One of the most important prerequisites for would-be competitors in either sport is a satisfactory circuit for training and competition. Although basic training can be carried out on any circuit, a full 400 metre track is essential for the full development of technique. Such circuits are a very expensive invest-ment, especially an ice skating rink which requires a good deal of equipment to establish and maintain a very large surface area of ice. Competitors from countries without 400 metre circuits have to travel to a country which has one and take up at least temporary residence in order to train. This period of training should be at least two months in the year preceding and coinciding with the time of the main competition. Competitors who can afford to do that will, in most countries, be an affluent male minority. Ice skating may be a mass participation sport in the Netherlands and Scandinavia, it certainly is not in most other countries.

Ice speed skating began on the frozen canals of Holland during the thirteenth century and competitions are known to have started there in 1676. An early women's competition was organized in 1805 at Leeuwarden in Holland which attracted an entry of 130. The sport spread from Holland and competitions are recorded in Norway in 1863, in Sweden in 1882, Finland in 1883 and Russia in 1885. The first United States championships were staged in 1879, the year in which the National Skating Association of Great Britain was formed.

Despite the fairly early participation of women in the sport, competitions and championships for men were officially recognized long before those for women. World championships for men were officially recognized in 1893, the year after the International Skating Union was formed. Separate European men's championships were also started in 1893. Men's speed skating gained Olympic status in 1924 when the first winter Olympics were held. The first women's world championships were not held until 1936, however, and women's speed skating was not added to the Olympic programme until the 1960 Olympics at Squaw Valley, USA.

The world ice skating records are given in table 36, together with the mean differences in performance which they represent. The performances of women skaters are, overall, slightly closer to men skaters than women runners are to

Table 36. The world ice speed skating records as at the end of 1980.

	Men				Women				
	Holder	Time	Speed m/s	Percentage Maximum speed	Holder	Time	Speed m/s	Percentage Maximum speed	Percentage Difference in speed
500 m	E. Kulikov (USSR)	37.00	13.514	100	S. Young (USA)	40.68	12.291	100	9.05
1,000 m	E. Heiden (USA)	1:13.60	13.59	100.59	N. Petruseva (USSR)	1:23.01	12.05	98.05	11.33
1,500 m	E. Heiden (USA)	1:54.79	13.07	96.74	K. Vorobyeva (USSR)	2:07.18	11.794	95.96	9.74
3,000 m	D. Oglobin (USSR)	4:04.06	12.29	90.97	G. Stepanskaya (USSR)	4:31.00	11.070	90.07	9.95
5,000 m	K. Stenshjenmet (Nor.)	6:56.90	11.993	88.75					
10,000 m	V. Leskvin (USSR)	14:34.33	11.437	84.63					
							Mean difference		10.01[a]

a. The mean difference for the same track events in 1980 was 10.28.

men runners (compare table 15). The performance of women compared to men is proportionately best at the longest distance at which they participate, again a situation different to that found in athletics.

Both ice and roller skaters achieve much higher speeds than runners. The current skating records for men and women over 500 metres are more than six and nine seconds respectively faster than the corresponding 400 metres records on the track. Ice skaters cover a mile or 1500 metres nearly one minute faster than runners, they are about six minutes faster over 5000 metres and more than twelve minutes faster over 10,000 metres. In other words they can maintain their high speeds for much longer times than can runners. It is altogether a much more efficient activity than running.

Men should have an advantage at the start where muscular power is important, but this advantage should be of progressively less importance over longer distances as anaerobic energy sources give way to aerobic in importance. It has already been seen that this transition occurs gradually, starting after about two minutes of effort and being essentially complete at about ten minutes. It is therefore quite astonishing that women should have discontinued their competition over 5000 metres which takes about seven minutes to cover. Their biological advantages are by then just beginning to tell.

World and Olympic championships are normally held over two consecutive days with two events on the first and two on the second. All competitors normally participate in all four events and in the case of the world championships, as well as individual winners at each distance, there is proclaimed an overall world champion.

Women's world championships have been held since 1936, although until 1955, 500 metres was the only distance skated by both sexes. From 1956 the 500 and 1500 metres have been skated by both sexes and direct comparison is therefore more meaningful. Figure 27 shows the mean speeds and the difference between the mean speeds for the overall world champions since 1956. The statistical prediction from this decreasing difference between the sexes is "equality" by the year 2020, although because of the differences in the events in the competition, the equality is not exact. Men are still improving their performances as fast as they have ever done since their championships started in 1896. It is not, therefore, just a case of women seeming to improve because men's performances are stationary.

Roller skating, like ice skating, probably originated in Holland, perhaps as a warm weather substitute for ice skating. The modern type of ball-bearing roller skate was introduced by an American in 1884 and the modern sport dates from this. Speed roller skating is essentially confined to Europe, being especially popular in Britain and Italy.

The men's world speed skating championships were inaugurated in 1937 but women had to wait until 1953 for their world championships to be introduced. In addition to official world records there are also world best performances at distances up to twenty miles and 30,000 metres. The changing

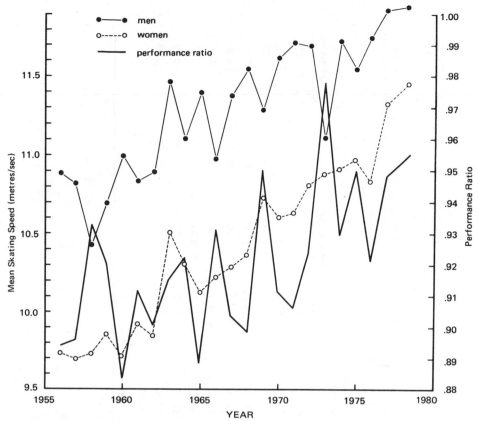

Fig. 27. The mean skating speed for men and women world champions 1956-78 based on the four distances skated by each sex. The performance ratio of women to men is also shown. This shows a large if somewhat erratic improvement by women.

relationship between the men's and women's records at these longer distances over recent years is especially significant. Until the 1960s world records at all distances represented distinctly superior performances by men, although the actual margins of superiority were always smaller than those in running. Since then women have much improved their performances relative to men. Their performances for distances up to 15,000 metres are still inferior to those of men. But, at all distances above this, women's records become progressively better than men's. Recent improvements in the shorter events suggest that in many of them too, women's performances will be better than men's in the not too distant future! Furthermore at all distances greater than 5000 metres, which is skated in about nine minutes, women skate at a faster average speed than that which they achieve over 5000 metres. The world records and the performance differences they represent are shown in table 37. Notice, too,

Table 37. World roller skating records for men and women, the sex differences they represent and the retention of maximal skating velocity.

	Men			Women			Difference
	Time	Speed (m/sec)	Percentage Maximum Velocity	Time	Speed (m/sec)	Percentage Maximum Velocity	
500 m	43.7	11.44	100	49.6	10.08	100	11.89
1,000 m	1:30.0	11.11	97.12	1:42.7	9.74	96.63	12.33
1,500 m	2:12.4	11.33	97.04	2:28.3	9.48	94.05	16.33
5,000 m	7:44.9	10.76	94.06	9: 2.3	9.22	91.47	14.31
10,000 m	16:54.5	9.86	86.19	17:55.3	9.30	92.26	5.68
15,000 m	26:16.7	9.51	83.13	26:47.4	9.33	92.56	1.89
20,000 m	33:30.0	9.95	86.98	35:32.0	9.38	93.06	5.73
25,000 m	44:40.1	9.33	81.56	44:28.3	9.37	92.96	−0.43
30,000 m	54:10.8	9.23	80.68	53:35.8	9.33	92.56	−1.08
50,000 m	1:41: 0.1	8.25	72.12				
100,000 m	3:23:42.0	8.20	71.68				

that women retain a greater proportion of their maximum velocity than men at all distances above 10,000 metres. Moreover, they retain more of their maximal roller skating speed over 30,000 metres than they retain of their maximal ice skating speed over 3000 metres.

Here, then, is a sport where women have indubitably caught up the men in performance. It is significant in this respect that more women take part in speed roller skating than ice speed skating. The sport as a whole does not get so much publicity as ice skating which accounts, perhaps, for the fact that this astonishing situation is not very well known. The British National Skating Association first applied for admission to the 1908 Olympics. The sport's world governing body, the International Roller Skating Federation, formed in 1924, has since the Second World War pressed hard for Olympic admission, but in vain.

Women can obviously roller skate over the longer distances at speeds closer to their best possible than can men. Can they do the same on ice? Table 38

Table 38. Percentage of average maximum speed maintained by men and women in ice speed skating for 1937 and 1977.

	1937		1977	
	Male	Female	Male	Female
500 metres	100.00	100.00	100.00	100.00
1,000 metres	95.00	93.92	97.75	97.48
1,500 metres	94.07	88.05	96.01	93.95
3,000 metres	87.64	84.47	89.40	90.07

shows the percentage of their average maximum speed (that is, of that at 500 metres) at which men and women skated longer events in 1937 and 1977. In 1937 women skated at speeds further below their maximal velocity than did men at all distances. In 1977 the position was very different. Both sexes skated much closer to their maximal velocity, but at every distance women had improved their relative performance much more, and at 3000 metres they were closer to their maximum velocity than men. Both sexes were skating closer to their maximal velocity in 1977 at 1500 metres than in 1937 they were at 1000 metres, and women were skating 3000 metres at closer to their maximal velocity (which itself of course, had been markedly increased) than previously they were skating 1500 metres. This is truly an astonishing change. It re-emphasizes yet again just where many of the women's marked improvements have been taking place in all sports — at the longer distances. Table 39 gives the 1977 women's world record and the year in which that time was first beaten by men and shows how close women are to men's achievements. In this respect women are as close in skating as they are in cycling and swimming to catching up the men.

Table 39. Women's world ice skating records for 1977 and the year in which men beat that time.

	Women's Record	Year in which men beat that time	
500 metres	40.68	E. Grishin	1956
1,000 metres	1:23.46	E. Grishin	1955
1,500 metres	2:09.90	E. Grishin	1955
3,000 metres	4:31.00	J. Nilsson	1963

There are three crucial factors important for success in skating: the amount of muscular force that can accelerate the body: the oxygen transport that can maintain its speed against the resistance of the wind; and sheer technique. Muscular power is mainly important at the start of races. Thereafter technique is of more importance and since surface friction is less than in running, muscular power is less important. The disadvantage of women in this respect is therefore less than in running.

Women gain a small advantage from their more rounded contours and the smaller body surface presented to the wind. Since the speeds are so much greater in skating than running this factor is that much more important. It is not known whether women have a better skating technique than men − the problem has never been investigated. It is interesting, though, that in swimming, which is a highly inefficient activity, and skating, which is a highly efficient one, women are closer to men in performance than in other speed sports and are getting closer in both.

Skating, then, is a sport in which many of the biological differences between the sexes appear in some respects to favour women, especially in events of medium and long duration. Women's performances are quite close to or surpass men's, again especially in the longer events. How long will it be before this situation gets as much publicity as the biological differences allegedly causing inferior performances in other sports?

3. ROWING AND CANOEING

Rowing as a sport can be traced back to ancient times. In modern form it dates from the early eighteenth century, particularly in England. As in so many sports there are fairly obvious military connections, although it is also highly functional in many places. The first rowing regatta on the Thames was held in 1775, the Oxford and Cambridge Boat Race dates from 1829, and the Henley Royal Regatta from 1839. The sport spread to other countries, notably the United States and Australia in the nineteenth century, with such early landmarks as the Harvard–Yale race in 1852 and the Royal Hobart Regatta in 1838.

Rowing has been an Olympic sport for men since 1900 and now has eight events; but only since 1970 for women, and then with only six events. That women's rowing only became an Olympic sport so recently is very surprising even in this story which is so full of surprises. Women's canoeing, which makes similar demands on stamina and skill to rowing, has been on the Olympic programme since 1948. And women's rowing dates back in some instances to the early years of the twentieth century.

In England the Cecil Ladies Boat Club on the Lea in London was in existence prior to 1914. There was also women's rowing at Reading and London Universities before the Women's Amateur Rowing Association (WARA) was formed in 1923. At about this time women could also row at Oxford University and although they could not race they could take part in time tests. One restriction was that they had to wear long black stockings in the boat — bare legs were not allowed.

After the WARA was formed they organized regattas. Long distance rowing by women's eights began in 1927 over the Putney-Mortlake course of 6.779 kilometres and a best time of 19 minutes 25 seconds was recorded. For comparison the Oxford and Cambridge Boat Race over this course was first rowed in a faster time in 1892 and the current record is 17 minutes 35 seconds set in 1974. Women's rowing on the Thames is now over a two mile course.

Women's rowing reached sufficient international support and standards by 1954 for women's European championships to be held in Amsterdam. At these championships Russian women swept the board and they have remained prominent in women's rowing ever since, although often sharing honours with other East European countries including the ubiquitous East Germans. Annual World Championships superseded these European championships in 1974 and in the 1978 championships, East Germany won three golds and a silver, Russia one gold, two silvers and a bronze and Bulgaria two golds.

Men's and women's performances are not directly comparable because men's races are held over 2000 metres, whereas women's races are held over only 1000 metres. Furthermore, course conditions often vary, since races may be held on lakes or rivers where currents, tides, waves, winds and so forth may vary. It is clear, though, that the differences between men and women are considerable. The average speed for men rowing over 2000 metres is faster than women rowing over 1000 metres, this being so for all events from the single sculls to the eights.

Rowing requires a greater degree of all round muscular strength and endurance than most other speed sports, the muscles of the arms, shoulders and back being crucially important. Since these are the muscular groups where women are at the greatest disadvantage in terms of pure strength, this actual difference in performance should not be surprising. The inevitability of the difference is another matter altogether.

The first national canoeing championships seem to have taken place in Germany in 1919. Only two years later regattas with mixed crews were organized and in 1925 the German Federation arranged the first regatta exclusively for women. But it was only in 1937 after the Olympic Games in Berlin that women's national championships were established in Germany, initially in Kyak single and double seaters (K1 and K2 events), while in 1939 a K4 event was introduced. In 1920 Czechoslovakia had K2 events for mixed teams and in 1933 separate races for women were introduced. Poland had women's national championships in 1933 and Austria, Denmark, Finland and Sweden also introduced them before the war. In 1924 four national federations had founded the International Federation, and at the first European Championships held in 1933 in Prague there was a Kyak race for women over 600 metres. At the first world championships in 1938 at Waxholm in Sweden there were K1 and K2 races for women over 600 metres, a distance reduced to 500 metres in 1948. A K4 race for women was introduced in the 1961 European championships at Poznan, Poland and in the 1966 Berlin World Championships.

The first official Olympic race for women was the K1 500 metres at London in 1948. The K2 women's event was added in Rome in 1960. The K4 event for women has not yet been accepted by the International Olympic Committee, although men have had a K4 event since 1964 and in the 1979 World Championships in Duisberg, West Germany, eleven nations took part in the women's K4 event.

It is commonly the case that crew in the K4 event are also the competitors in K1 and K2 events. The refusal to have K4 events is therefore a refusal to have one more female competitor from a dozen or so countries. This is hardly a rational reason for excluding the event, but unfortunately it is a typical one.

Men have K1 and K2 events over 500 metres and 1000 metres in the Olympics. They also have C1 and C2 events (Canadian canoes) over 500 metres and 1000 metres for which there are no corresponding women's events.

4. SKIING

There are three important types of skiing: Alpine skiing which is basically a timed descent down mountain slopes either with or without pairs of poles known as gates between which the skiers must pass (an event known as a slalom); Nordic skiing which is basically long distance cross-country ski-running; and ski-jumping in which only men compete.

Men and women compete in Alpine skiing, but the women's courses are usually shorter, less steep and the slaloms have fewer and more easily negotiated gates. Men's downhill courses are usually more than 3000 metres long whereas women's are usually between 2500 and 3000 metres long. Men's and women's world championships were established in 1931 and it has been an Olympic event for both sexes since 1936. The format of the events is that each contestant races downhill by him or herself and the contestant with the fastest time is the winner. In the case of men's events this time has always been the sum of two runs. It was only in the 1978 world championships that a similar arrangement was introduced for women. Prior to that their events comprised only one run.

Because each course is unique and because the men's and women's courses are not identical, precise comparisons of men's and women's performances are not possible. Nevertheless the comparison of the winners' average speeds in the Olympic downhill races 1936–80 given in table 40 shows how much closer women now are to men in attainment in this sport than hitherto. From skiing at less than 82 per cent of the speed of men in 1936, the top women stars are now skiing downhill at speeds of about 97 per cent those of men; both sexes have more than doubled their average speeds of descent. Perhaps the time will soon come when men and women will compete directly against one another over the same course. The courses are designed as tests of daring and skill and it is not clear that men have any intrinsic advantage over women in either of these respects. Women's very successes in recent years suggest not.

Both men and women also compete in Nordic skiing but sex comparisons are not possible because the courses are cross country and are always different. Men ski over fifteen, thirty and fifty kilometres and have a four by ten kilometre relay. Women ski over five and ten kilometres only and have a three by five kilometre relay, although this was increased to four stages in the 1976 Olympics. The improvements in performance by both men and women in this event have been quite astonishing although much of this is due to improved design of skis, boots and clothing.

Women's ten kilometre cross country skiing was introduced in 1952. The average winning speed of the three place getters then was 3.93 metres per second. By 1976 this had increased to 5.49 metres per second, an increase of 39.7 per cent. During the same period the men's fifteen kilometre medal winners increased their mean speed from 4.03 metres per second to 5.67, an increase of almost the same magnitude, 40.07 per cent. During this period, too, men increased their average speed over fifty kilometres by about 35 per cent.

The five kilometre event for women was only introduced in 1964 and the four by five kilometre relay in 1976 so changes are still occurring in women's skiing.[2] Women take about forty minutes to ski their ten kilometres. This is the longest lasting of all speed events in which women regularly compete. If they can ski competitively for forty minutes over ten kilometres in the winter Olympics there seems no reason why they could not run for thirty minutes over the same distance in the summer Olympics. But the logic of such comparisons seems always to escape the male members of the International Olympic Committee.

Table 40. Average speeds in Olympic downhill races 1936-80.

	Men		Women		
	Length of course in metres	Winner's average speed km/hr	Length of course in metres	Winner's average speed km/hr	Women's speed as percentage of men's
1936 Garmisch	3,800	47.599	3,300	39.031	82.00
1948 St Moritz	3,210	66.034	1,800	43.695	66.17
1952 Oslo	2,414	57.629	1,500	50.420	87.44
1956 Cortina	3,461	72.356	1,552	55.484	76.68
1960 Squaw Valley	3,095	88.429	1,828	67.426	76.25
1964 Innsbrook	3,120	81.297	2,450	76.496	94.09
1968 Grenoble	2,890	86.808[a]	2,160	77.080	88.79
1972 Sapporo	2,640	85.291	2,110	78.568	92.11
1976 Innsbrook	3,020	102.828	2,515	85.286	82.94
1980 Lake Placid	3,009	102.677	2,698	99.598	97.00

a. The winner of this event was one of the most famous and successful of all Olympians, Jean-Claude Killy of France. Anne-Marie Moser-Proell the winner of the women's 1980 downhill attained an average speed considerably faster than his.

CHAPTER ELEVEN

Catching up the Men?

1. COMPETITION AND OPPORTUNITIES

There are two ways for women to catch men in sport. They can swim, run, cycle, skate, ski or whatever as fast, throw as far, jump as well or otherwise perform at a level not inferior to that of men. And they can have opportunities to compete in the same range of sports as men, under the same rules and conditions and in the same events, be invited to the same number of sports meetings, to compete for the same material rewards, have the same number of representatives teams to be selected for, and so on and so forth.

Much of the statistical evidence analyzed in the preceding chapters shows that, in general, women are catching up in most of the speed sports. In the second area, women are doing less well. Many ball games, including golf, tennis, handball, volleyball and others are as popular among women as among men, but their facilities are still inferior. Although the more strenuous and body contact team sports such as football, ice hockey and polo are or have been forbidden to women, women already play in some sports of this type such as lacrosse and field hockey, and are now taking up many of the others. Women's soccer, for example, is claimed to be the fastest growing sport in the world and a women's World Soccer Championship was held in 1978 in which a number of nations took part. Nevertheless, in these sports, they have a long way to go. The combat sports such as boxing and wrestling are almost totally restricted to men. But here too some, including judo and fencing, are popular with women and the current emphasis by many women's groups on learning the martial arts for self defence may lead to their increased participation in the sporting versions.

In some sports such as motor racing, horse racing, speedway and others, women have traditionally been barred, although there are no convincing reasons why. They are now demanding the right to take part in these and here and there have been given jockey's licences, been admitted as racing drivers and so forth. Women's participation in these sports may remain largely token, or fully integrated sports or parallel women's sports may develop alongside men's.

In a very few sports including show-jumping, shooting and yachting, the rules of many competitions including, most importantly, the Olympics, do not distinguish or specify sex of competitor and women can compete on conditions of absolute equality. Rather few women have in fact competed in major events of these sports; equality may exist in the rules but seems somehow to be wanting in reality.

Women came later to the speed sports than did men and their participation is still restricted. The same is true for most other sports. In the Olympics, for example, most women's sports were introduced well after they were introduced for men. Table 41 shows the development of the Olympic programme for men and women. The extent to which women now lag and have always lagged behind men is very evident (see also table 13 which shows women's increasing participation in the summer Olympics). The same is true of their programme in the Commonwealth Games. Similarly, women's national championships were started after those of men's in most sports in most countries in the world. In almost

Table 41. The introduction of men's and women's sports into the Olympic programme.

	Men		Women	
	Date Introduced	No. of Events[c]	Date Introduced	No. of Events[c]
Archery[a]	1972	1	1972	1
Athletics (Track & Field)	1896	23	1928	14
Basketball	1936	1	1976	1
Boxing	1904	11	–	0
Canoeing	1936	9	1948	2
Cycling	1896	6	–	0
Equestrian Sports[b]	1900			
Fencing	1896	6	1924	2
Field Hockey	1908	1	1980	1
Football (Association)	1900	1	–	0
Gymnastics	1896	8	1952	6
Handball	1972	1	1976	1
Judo	1964	6	–	0
Modern Pentathlon	1912	1	–	0
Rowing	1900	8	1976	6
Shooting[b]	1896			
Swimming & Diving	1896	15	1912	15
Volleyball	1964	1	1964	1
Water Polo	1900	1	–	0
Weightlifting	1928	9	–	0
Wrestling	1896	20	–	0
Yachting[b]	1972			
Nordic Skiing	1924	9	1952	3
Alpine Skiing	1948	3	1948	3
Figure Skating	1908	1	1908	1
Speed Skating	1924	5	1960	4
Bobsleigh	1924	2	–	0
Tobogganing	1964	2	1964	1
Ice Hockey	1920	1	–	0
		152		62

a. Previously introduced in 1900 but dropped in 1920

b. Open Event

c. In 1980

every country there are still gaps in women's sport, just as there are gaps in international competition.

These anomalies are quite glaring. For example, there is no women's cycling in the Olympics or any other games despite its being a very popular women's sport in which world championships have been organized since 1958. Worldwide, field hockey is as popular among women as it is among men. It has been a men's Olympic sport since 1908 but was not on the women's programme until Moscow 1980. There is no example of what is primarily a women's sport, such as netball, being on any major games programme. It is not that the sports missing from women's international programmes are just the vigorous or in any sense the deviant ones. Lawn bowls, for example, is an immensely popular sport in Britain, Australia, South Africa and elsewhere. Ladies Bowling Associations date from 1907 in Australia and 1910 in Britain, and there are more than fifty-three thousand bowlers in clubs affiliated to the English Women's Bowling Association alone. But mixed events are not allowed and although Lawn Bowls has been a popular men's sport in the Commonwealth Games since the start of these Games in 1930, there are no women's events.

One way in which the difference in both participation and achievement has been justified and explained in the past has been to consider women as immature or truncated men. As such they can be permitted, very reluctantly, to engage in some of the same sports as men but in restricted and watered-down versions. The performances of men are treated as a norm with women being given less demanding, less difficult and what are stated to be less dangerous tasks. By this means, their supposed inherent weaknesses can be catered for and their femininity and feminine sensibilities preserved.

Women's field hockey is played over two thirty-minute halves, whereas men play two thirty-five minute halves. In men's basketball, there are five players in each team, whereas women, until recently, had six who were not permitted to run up and down the court. Men fence with three swords, foil, epee and sabre; women fence only with foils and their target is much smaller, the lower limit being the hip-bones whereas men's target is the entire torso, ending with the groin lines. The winners of fencing bouts are those who score five hits (men) or four (women) in the target area in the prescribed six minutes (men) or five minutes (women). The 1968 Olympic Fencing champion, Helena Novokova of Russia, entered a men's tournament in 1970 and won half her matches, so women can hardly be considered totally incapable. Men's tennis matches are decided over five sets, women's and mixed doubles over only three sets. In diving, women are allowed fewer voluntary dives, four in high diving while men have six, and five in springboard while men have six. And so it goes on.

All this is curious. The logical procedure would be to extend the sort of divisions used in boxing, weightlifting and judo into all sports and thus allow, for example, all persons under 150 centimetres, between 151-60, 161-70, 171-80 centimetres, and so on, to high jump against one another, irrespective of sex; or persons of similar weight to throw the discus, javelin or whatever. Alternatively, the isolation of the sexes might be maintained, but divisions based on height and weight might be used for both sexes in a number of sports. So far as women have some advantage in endurance events, their restriction to shorter playing times, shorter events, fewer trials, and so on, is just the reverse of what should be the situation if they are to use their abilities to the best advantage.

The story of the open events at the Olympic Games is particularly interesting. The IOC forbade open Olympic competitions in 1930 and specifically rejected an appeal to open the equestrian events for women in 1936. Nevertheless, the IOC office permitted women to participate in equestrian events in 1948, and in 1952 Denmark's Lis Hartel, a polio victim at the age of twenty, and Germany's Ida von Nagel, became the first women Olympic medal winners in equestrian events. The IOC statutes were changed after this to make women's participation legal. Since then, some of the equestrian events have become almost dominated by women. In the dressage final in Munich in 1972, there were twelve women among the sixteen participants and four years later in Montreal there were seven women among the twelve finalists. But women have not excelled in dressage alone. In 1956 in Stockholm, Pat Smythe of Great Britain won a bronze medal in the team's Nation's Cup. In 1964, Lana Dupone of the USA became the first woman to win an individual Olympic medal in jumping when she came second. Women won nine medals, including four gold medals, in the equestrian events in Munich and eight in Montreal four years later. The USA team, which won the dressage bronze medals in Montreal, was all women, as were the German silver medallists in the event in 1956.

The first women shooters in the Olympics appeared in 1968, when Mexico, Peru and Poland had women in their teams. In 1976 the USA's Margaret Murdock became the first woman shooter to win an Olympic medal, missing the gold medal only because of a weaker last series than her male opponent.

The question immediately arises as to why the similar sport of archery is not also an open sport. Archery is a sport with a long history and rather obvious military, functional and recreational origins. It also has a fairly long history of women's participation, being one of the very few approved sports for women — upper class women, of course — in the nineteenth century. Archery for both men and women was on the Olympic programme between 1900 and 1920 but was then dropped and not reintroduced until 1972.

A competition round consists of thirty-six arrows at each of four different distances: for the men, at ninety, seventy, fifty and thirty metres, and for women, at seventy, sixty, fifty and thirty metres. A match comprises two such rounds.

Although there is a difference in the weights of the bows used by men and women (that is, in the effort required to draw back an arrow to its fullest extent), there is an overlap in weights used and that is therefore hardly an explanation for the distance difference.

Archery targets are divided into ten zones, the scoring values ranging from ten for the central gold, down to one for the outermost ring. Thirty-six arrows at each distance can therefore score a maximum of 360. The 1979 world records for each distance are shown in table 42.

Table 42. World archery records as at the end of 1979.

	Men		Women		Percentage Percentage
90 metres	R. McKinney (USA)	318			
70 metres	S. Spigarelli (Italy)	338	N. Butuzova (U.S.S.R.)	328	2.96
60 metres			V. Kovpan (U.S.S.R.)	334	
50 metres	S. Spigarelli (Italy)	340	N. Butuzova (U.S.S.R.)	330	2.94
30 metres	D. Pace (USA)	354	J. Wilejto (Poland)	349	1.43
Single Round	D. Pace (USA)	1,341	N. Butuzova (U.S.S.R.)	1,321	1.49
Team	USA	3,812	U.S.S.R.	3,772	1.05

In the last two decades the difference between men's and women's performance over single and double rounds have decreased significantly, as shown by table 43. The justification for having women shoot at sixty metres rather than ninety metres seems remarkably flimsy. The separation of the sport into men's and women's seems equally unjustified.

Table 43. Men's and women's performances in single and double rounds in archery, 1959 and 1979.

	Single Round			Double Round		
	Men	Women	Percentage Difference	Men	Women	Percentage Difference
1959	1,148	1,120	2.44	2,247	2,120	5.66
1979	1,341	1,321	1.49	2,571	2,538	1,28

If there is any important conclusion to be drawn from the immediately preceding pages, it is how irrational are most of the differences between men's and women's sport and the reasons for maintaining them.

Some examples of women's achievements in what are generally thought of as men only sports make the point. In June 1978, twenty-nine year old Naomi James completed a single-handed around-the-world yacht voyage. She was the first woman to sail alone around the world by the Cape Horn route and she did it in 272 days, two days fewer than the late Sir Francis Chichester's fastest solo voyage. Only damage to her steering gear, which forced her to make repairs at Cape Town, cost her the chance of being even faster and the first woman to make a non-stop trip. Women have competed in the single-handed North Atlantic Races and all-women crews have competed in major ocean yacht races. Gone are the days when women crew-members were occasionally tolerated, provided they stayed in the galley.

Horse racing is still largely male dominated, but in the United States the number and quality of women jockeys have been rising impressively since Diane Crump became the first female jockey to race in the Kentucky Derby.

In Britain, records of the Lady Jockeys Association of Great Britain show that between 1972, when they were first allowed to race on the flat, and 1978, nearly four hundred women have managed to get themselves mounts. They became entitled to compete in certain races over obstacles four seasons later. Amateur members of the Lady Jockeys Association rode in more than forty flat races in 1978, including thirty in which men amateurs also took part. In New Zealand in August 1978, after a very long campaign, a small number of women were given jockey's permits by the racing authorities. By November, twenty-six year old Linda Jones had climbed to second place in the Jockey's Championship table, having twenty-five wins compared to the leading man's thirty-six wins. In January 1979, Linda Jones won the Wellington Derby — the first woman to win a major Derby anywhere in the world, although women have twice won the trotting Derby in the USSR. In Australia a number of women have qualified as reinswomen in trotting. Prior to 1978, there were separate reinsmen's and reinswomen's championships. In 1978, this arrangement was scrapped and a single open reinsperson championship was instituted. Australian women have also been permitted to ride as jockeys in horse racing for a few years and from April 1979 were given permission to ride in all metropolitan race meetings. One of the first to take advantage of this ruling was New Zealand's Linda Jones, who finished third on her first mount in Sydney on 31 March 1979. Yet, despite all this, one still hears arguments that women should not be allowed to ride because they have not the strength in the arms to control a galloping racehorse, nor the stamina to last an event right through.

The whole area of women's participation in sports hitherto closed to them is in a state of turmoil. Organizations in Britain such as the Jockey Club, the Football Association, the MCC and County Cricket Associations and other sporting bodies have in the past exercised a de facto and often enough a de jure policy of sex discrimination, based on the belief that women are incapable of participating in the sports in question and that they will never want to. Similar bodies in other countries have done the same thing. But women are now saying that they do want to take part and, where it is possible and seems fruitful to do so, are moving into the courts as well as on to the playing fields to make their point. In Britain, in 1978, an eleven year old girl took the Football Association to court over their refusal to let her participate in mixed soccer matches. She was supported by Britain's Equal Opportunity Commission. In Australia there was a similar challenge from a twelve year old who wished to play Australian Rules League Football. At present, women's aspirations in this direction are being vigorously resisted, but major changes cannot be far away.

In 1971, in New York State in the USA, a law was passed which empowered the New York State Education Department to permit mixed competitions in archery, badminton, bowling, fencing, golf, gymnastics, riflery, shuffleboard, skiing, swimming and diving, table tennis, tennis, track and field, and rowing (but only as coxswain because it was said rowing was too strenuous for girls).

In 1973 the Californian Interscholastic Federation allowed all high school sports teams to be coeducational and stated that "coaches will still make the decisions on who is most skilled and who will play". The Eastern College Athletic Conference ruled in the autumn of 1972, that women could play on men's teams and many women are now members of swimming and tennis teams. Yale University has had a woman in its junior varsity polo team and Cornell has fielded a women's ice hockey team. In various parts of the USA women have played in college baseball and basketball teams but, because these are more popular men's sports, controversy still surrounds their participation and it is always very rare.

In a recent editorial, *The Sportswoman* suggested that neither insistence on not distinguishing between the sexes nor commitment to total separation of the sexes was appropriate.

> By basing our demands for women to compete on men's teams as a temporary reparation until women's programmes are comparable, we will not run the risk of men taking over women's teams. We will also give those schools where the men's athletic director blanches at the thought of women on his team a good incentive to make sure that school's women's programme is built up quickly. Most important, we will be building up our women's programmes to the quality they need and deserve without sacrificing our top female athletes.[1]

Women have made some small progress in the USA and elsewhere in these male-dominated sports as administrators. Several baseball and basketball teams and even the occasional football team have had women presidents, managers, administrators and statisticians – positions with real meaning, not just cheer leaders as has hitherto mostly been the case.

The other important area of improvement, almost the world over, is in levels of participation at junior and local level. At present in the United States, 33 per cent of the high school athletes and 30 per cent of the intercollegiate athletes are women, reflecting 600 and 250 per cent increases respectively during the 1970s. At this rate of increase, female participation will equal male participation by the end of the 1980s.

It is estimated that more than 50 per cent of the nation's fitness enthusiasts are women. Women buy nearly half of all the sportswear sold in the United States, and activities such as hiking, biking and swimming attract more women than men. Of the 17 million joggers, 6.5 million are women; of the 14 million tennis players, 6.5 million are women and of the 20 million bowlers, more than 9 million are women.

2. PREPARATION AND PERFORMANCES

Sport, like so many human activities, has undergone changes of quite staggering dimensions this century. It has changed from being a minority, largely upper class activity, restricted to a few countries in the world, to being a mass movement world-wide in extent and almost universal in appeal. Achievements have been revolutionized as much as if not more than organization.

On the running track, for example, the men's 5000 metres record holder between 1922 and 1932, the great Paavo Nurmi no less, whose record was 14:28.2, would be convincingly lapped by the 1978 record holder Henry Rono, who covered the distance in 13:08.4. In the pool, the 1902 220 yard record holder, Freddy Lane of Great Britain, who swam the event in 2:28.6, would be over a length of the pool (50 metres) behind the 1978 200 metre freestyle record holder, Brian Furniss of the USA, who swam 1:50.32. Lane would also be about a length behind the 1978 women's 200 metre record holder Cynthia Woodhead of the USA whose time was 1:58.53.

The important point is that even after a hundred years or more of reasonably standardized competition in running, swimming, skating and cycling, men are improving their records and overall performances as fast now as ever they were in all but a handful of events. Women are doing the same in all their sports, those in which they have been competing for seven decades as much as those in which they have been competing for just one.

Part of the reason for these continued improvements is the greater number of men and women competing, so that the likelihood of discovering supreme talent is that much greater. But, as we saw in chapter five, numbers are not everything. Most of the vast improvement is due to the enormous amount and the greater efficiency of training which today's sportsmen and women carry out. The intensities of training described in chapter five would have been unthinkable twenty or thirty years ago. Training schedules as hard as these were ushered in by long distance runners such as Emil Zatopek and Jim Peters in the 1940s and early 1950s and made the norm by runners such as Kuts and Pirie in the mid-1950s. They replaced the amateur, almost offhand, approach to training typified by English runners such as Chataway and Bannister who, as true part-timers, could not train so lengthily or rigorously, nor would they, for fear of becoming stale and overtrained. Today, these extra kilometres of running or swimming and the extra hours in the gym are part of scientifically prepared training schedules, individually tailored to the athlete and his or her event by an ever-increasing army of coaches and sports scientists.

As in so much else East Germany leads the way in this. One of the major sports training institutions in East Germany is the Deutsche Hochschule für Korperkultur (DHfK) or German University for Physical Culture at Leipzig. It was set up in 1950 with ninety-six students and fourteen full time staff and by 1975 had more than two thousand students and three hundred staff members including medical personnel, physiologists, biochemists, anatomists, psychologists and dietitians, all lavishly funded and provided with a wide range of apparatus and a powerful computer. In the DHfK Library Documentation Centre there are fifty researchers employed in monitoring every magazine on sport published throughout the world. They are looking for new research on training and coaching which is summarized and made available to the coaches. Sport science is also taught as a separate discipline at the universities of Berlin, Greifswald, Halle, Jena and Rostock, as well as at several university-level teacher training establishments.

There are twenty-one major sports clubs in East Germany and they heavily support the athletes who belong to them. These clubs are funded by local industry and business (by law 6–8 per cent of their profits must go to local sport, although how meaningful this is in the East German socialist economy is not easy to say). They employ full time coaches, managers, cooks and sports medicine doctors. Single athletes can live in club dormitories and are given specially prescribed diets cooked in the club kitchens. Athletes have free use of all equipment and facilities including a weight training room. The club doctors treat any injuries and masseurs provide a daily rub down. The clubs arrange educational opportunities and jobs are provided from which time off with pay is allowed before major competitions. All expenses incurred in attending competitions are met.

The degree of specialization and efficiency of the East German coaching system can be shown by describing just one sport — long distance running. The competitive performances and some of the training sessions of their top runners are filmed so that biomechanists can analyze their running action from head to toe. The runners undergo regular muscle exercise tests to look for imbalances and weaknesses which, if discovered, can be corrected by systematic programmes involving weight training and flexibility prescribed by coaches and sports scientists. World class runners from other countries are also filmed in order to analyze their movements and pinpoint their strengths. All these data are recorded, indexed and computerized.

Medical centres are established close to the track in major national meets to which competitors report for blood tests immediately before and after their events. If an athlete runs a personal best time in a particular race, then the sports scientists have an exact profile of his/her blood at the time. Doctors and coaches try to ensure that this profile is replicated by diet or additives so that the excellent performance might be repeated. All of the physiological data collected are processed and made available to coaches the very next day through the computer. These blood profiles are correlated with the athlete's performance, training programme and diet, and compared with data obtained after previous performances.

Using these data it is possible to assess on any occasion the physical condition of the runners, their state of exhaustion, whether they are recuperating, their biorhythms, metabolic efficiency, training capacity and performance capability. The computer storing these data is programmed to print out graphs and charts indicating desirable speeds and distances for the next training sessions, right down to length of warm-up, number of repetitions, the number of calories required over the next few days and a performance goal. All of the data collected accumulate in a master data bank, enabling sports scientists to assess the effectiveness of distance training programmes generally.

This approach to support for sport is unique and revolutionary. Only in a few other Eastern European countries is there anything like it. But most important, everything is as available to women as to men. Women are being trained scientifically and to something like the limit of their potentialities for the first time anywhere. And far from women being looked on as deviant or aberrant in some way, sportswomen are encouraged as much as sportsmen and are rewarded as much (or so it is claimed; but see pages 214–16). The results, many of which have been documented in preceding chapters, speak for themselves.

There are at present nineteen track and field events for women in which official world records are recognized by the IAAF, and there are fifteen women's swimming records recognized by FINA. At the end of 1978 East German women held six of them in each sport. Of the world junior records in athletics, they held at the end of 1980 no less than nine. At the 1978 world rowing championships, East German women won three of the six gold medals and a silver. East German women won the 1978 women's world handball championship. At the 1978 world canoe championships, East German women won all three of the races at 500 metres. In the 1976 Winter Olympics East German women won one gold, two silver and two bronze medals from twelve events. By 1980 they had improved to four gold, two silver and two bronze.

Competition may be fiercer among men but by any token East German men are remarkably successful. At the end of 1980, they held two field event records and three junior world records in athletics. They won two golds, two silvers and a bronze at the 1976 Olympics in track and field events and in 1980 were the second most successful nation of all in the absence of the Americans. They won five golds, a silver and a bronze from eight events in the 1978 world rowing championships; they won two out of five races at 500 metres and two out of five at 1000 metres in the 1978 world canoeing championships. In swimming, between 1968 and 1976, East German men won five gold, two silver and one bronze medal, not as striking a record as the women but important nevertheless. In the 1976 Winter Olympics, from twenty-three events, East German men won six gold, two silver and three bronze medals; in 1980 they improved to five gold, five silver and four bronze. And in many other sports, they are also prominent and successful.

If there is any country in the world in which women are reaching anything like their sporting potential, it is East Germany. Since East German men are obviously no slouches, a comparison of men's and women's performances in East Germany should give an indication of what women can really do. The mean difference between the sexes in East Germany for all swimming events based on 1978 national records was 6.91 per cent. As Table 28 showed, the mean difference for all world records was 9.38 per cent. For the freestyle events alone the mean sex difference was 5.38 per cent, compared with 7.72 per cent for world records. On the track the mean difference between the sexes based on the latest national records for the regular ten women's events is 6.97 per cent, compared to 9.91 per cent difference between the world records for these same events. In both cases, this difference is much smaller than any other country. They represent levels of performance to which women in other countries can aspire.

There are three reasons why women will probably get closer to men even than they are in East Germany. First, scientific understanding of sport and its requirements, despite considerable recent progress, is still very imperfect and has far from exhausted the potential for improvement in performance. This is particularly true for women's sport. Second, women and women's sports are in fact some way from equality of treatment even in those countries of Eastern Europe which claim to have removed inequality. Third, many women's events are still very new and reservoirs of specialists in them have yet to be established. And because there are still gaps in the range of events for women in world and Olympic championships, there are still areas where women of talent are denied opportunities to compete and have to restrict their activities to events at which they have lesser abilities.

First, consider the point about science in sport being still relatively undeveloped. For all their scientific sophistication, East German men, although a major force in world athletics, are not a dominant one; also mistakes are still made in their programmes of talent search and training. Waldemar Cierpinski spent seven years as a rather moderate steeplechaser and only decided to run in the Kosice Marathon on his own initiative while on holiday in Czechoslovakia. He subsequently went on to win the Montreal Olympic marathon. The list of world record holders and Olympic title holders over the last two decades for all track events shows the dominance of Africans or Afro-Americans first and foremost, with New Zealanders, Australians, Britons and other Europeans represented. None of these have been through the same selective processes, had the technical back-up or had the same material support as the East Germans or the Russians. Certainly, most of the Africans have benefited from varying periods of residence and competition in the United States, but nothing like the East German facilities have been available to them. Not even the all-conquering American sprinters have had these. Furthermore, simply in terms of scientific and technical equipment, the East Germans are not all that advanced. Dr Alois Mader was Chief of Sports Medicine for four years at the elite sports club in Halle, East Germany, from which came Olympic champion Kornelia Ender. He was removed from his post in 1973, however, accused of having too much contact with westerners and since 1974 has worked as a research associate at the West German Sports College in Cologne. As quoted in a recent article in *Women's Sports*, he claimed that the scientific equipment available to him in East Germany "was largely very primitive, certainly more primitive than what is available here".[2]

However, to whatever extent governmental support for and scientific investigation into sport have become the norm for men's sport, women's sport and scientific investigation of it has been grossly neglected in most countries. There are still many more men participating in sport today than women and most coaches and sports scientists are men. Only a fraction of physical education research deals with women's performance or compares men and women under conditions of maximum effort. "It's almost as if there were a cultural or professional taboo against designing a research study involving women", comments Dr Clayton L. Thomas, Vice-President of medical affairs for Tampax, a member of the United States Olympic Team's medical staff and one of the relatively few experts on female physiology in the male-dominated medical field. (In the USA, only 7 per cent of doctors are women, and of 250 or so exercise physiologists in the country, fewer than 10 are women. In the USSR, on the other hand, a majority of doctors, at least among general practitioners, are women.)

There are very few studies of the long-term effects of strenuous training and fitness programmes on women. There is almost no information on the physical capabilities of older women and little is known about the physical advantage that girls aged twelve to fourteen have over boys the same age. The influence of sexual activity on women's performance has never been studied (Masters and Johnson found it had no effect on the muscular performance of men). Nor has anyone studied the influence of menstrual cramps (dysmenorrhea), although Thomas suggests that "If men had cramps, we'd have had a National Institute of Dysmenorrhea for years". Worst of all, the effects of birth-control pills on a woman's strength, co-ordination, timing, endurance and emotional stability are still a mystery, although one 1969 experiment indicated that the additional oestrogen in most pills might cause women to be less physically active. "All in all what we know, compared to what we don't know is a drop in the bucket", according to Dr Dorothy Harris, whose new Centre for Women in Sport at Penn State University, Pennsylvania, is attempting to dispel some of the uncertainties.

In a recent authoritative review, one of the foremost experts on women's physiology, Dr Barbara L. Drinkwater, could say:

> Regardless of the unpopularity of the notion that physiological differences between the sexes affect job performance, there is little scientific evidence to support any position on this controversial subject. For example, do the standards set for the safety of men who work in a hot environment apply equally to women? How does age affect the ability of women to perform physical tasks? Does the menstrual cycle affect the physical work capacity of women? Formerly the answers to questions such as these were largely a matter of theoretical interest and were too frequently based on the subjective impression of the observer. Today answers are needed to resolve questions of immediate and practical significance.[3]

When this sort of research *is* carried out and answers *are* available then women's performances will probably show further and perhaps more rapid improvements.

Second, consider the continuing inequality of women's sport. One of the aspects of their society about which Eastern European countries are most proud is the emancipation of women. This emancipation is claimed on the basis of written guarantees in their various constitutions (see page 45) and on the levels of participation of women in the workforce. The 1959 Soviet census, for example, showed that only 18 per cent of Soviet women of working age were housewives, compared with 52 per cent of such women in the USA. Above all, they claim, it is seen in the participation of women in sport.

The USSR has "won" all but one of the summer and winter Olympiads which they have entered and it is women who have given it the margin of victory. Similarly it is Soviet women who have given the USSR victory in most of the annual USA versus USSR athletics matches. Western writers have usually taken this as evidence of the extent of women's emancipation in the Soviet Union. American W. M. Mandel writing in *Soviet Women* in 1975 said that: "There can be only one explanation for the pre-eminence of Soviet women among female athletes worldwide: it reflects a degree of equality for women that none of the non-communist countries has yet attained".[4] Or as B. L. Bennett and associates wrote in another 1975 book: "Some people have attributed this success to the masculine qualities of their women athletes. However it is quite apparent that the communist superiority has been due to giving their female athletes the same access as the men to excellent facilities, first class coaching and extensive competition."[5]

The reality, however, seems to be somewhat different. In the Soviet Union women continue to bear their traditionally unequal share of responsibility for domestic work, despite their prominence in the industrial workforce. In one survey published in 1972 it was shown that men had between 1.5 and 2 times more free time than women (thirty-five hours compared to twenty hours a week), although both men and women were employed for roughly the same number of hours. The same survey showed that women working a five or six day week spent 2 per cent of their total spare time on regular sporting activities and 9 per cent on casual sporting activities. Men on a five day week devoted 7 per cent of their total free time to regular sport and 22 per cent to casual sport; men on a six day week spent 5 per cent and 21 per cent respectively. Although in 1972 more than fifteen million Soviet women claimed to participate regularly in sport this was only one third of the total for the two sexes.

It appears, therefore, that Soviet women have little time available for sport and certainly less than men. In 1969 only 14.1 per cent of the female population regularly pursued an organized sport, whereas 37 per cent of the male population were so involved. This was certainly an improvement on ten years earlier when only 5.6 per cent of the female population participated in sport on an organized and regular basis, but there is still a long way to go before anything like equality is reached.

In many republics in the USSR where Muslim culture is important, the disparity between men's and women's opportunities is even greater. In Tadhikistan, for example, in 1969 only 9.5 per cent of women were involved in sport, in Uzbekistan only 10.8 per cent and Azerbaidzhan only 11.4 per cent. The Chairmen of the Uzbek Supreme Soviet Commission on Youth Affairs has admitted that "In Uzbekistan, as in other central Asian republics, women's path to sport has been linked with a struggle against religious prejudices and for equal status in society. I would call our first sportswomen real heroines. They accomplished real feats of valour in liberating women from the age-old yoke of religion and the feudal-boy order".[6]

East Germany does not have these major problems with Muslim minorities, but in other respects its society is similar to that of Russia. In East Germany, Poland and some of the other Eastern European countries, the Catholic church has had and still has important influence. This body, as we saw in chapter six, has hardly been the most enlightened and progressive with respect to women's sporting participation. In East Germany women make up only 25 per cent of total membership of clubs affiliated with the Gymnastic and Sport Federation. It is clearly a mistake to think that equality in the sporting sphere or really anything like it has been achieved in Russia or other East European countries. If and when social equality is achieved, then one might expect sporting performances of men and women to be more nearly equal than is currently the case.

The third major reason why women's performances should improve markedly in the future is that there are still very many gaps in the sports and range of events within sports which are open to them. The lack of women's long distance running events has already been discussed. How much better would women 1500 and 3000 metres runners be if they had available regular 5000 metres events to train for and compete in? Notable men 1500/5000 metres runners have included Nurmi, Chataway, Ibbotson, Keino, Dixon and many others. Even when new events are gradually included in the women's programme it takes time before all meets include them and a core of specialists in them have become established. Such is the case, for example, in the 400 metres hurdles.

In the last fifty years, the differential between the men's 400 metres hurdles and the flat 400 metres has declined from about 6.8 seconds in 1920 to 3.27 in 1980. Women hurdlers, on the other hand, were no better in 1980, when the difference was 5.68 seconds than in 1973 when it was 5.7 seconds. Women's hurdles are lower than men's and women's clearance/fatigue factor should be about the same as men. In which case, since Marita Koch had run 48.60 for 400 metres on the flat by 1980, somebody should have run about 52.00 over hurdles, although the 1980 world record was only 54.28. And if women had run 52.00, the differential between men's and women's 400 metres hurdles performances would have been about 10 per cent, compared to the 13.17 per cent that it actually was in 1980.

Since the 400 metres hurdles event is not yet on the Olympic programme, it is infrequently run in East Germany, their sights being firmly set on Olympic medals.[7] Nor do East German women often run in events longer than 1500 metres, for the same reason. There is no national East German women's 1500 metres freestyle swimming record since it is not a universally recognized distance and it does not appear on the Olympic programme. The worldwide level of women's performance in these events must inevitably be less than it would otherwise be because of restricted participation.

The final points in this book take up another theme touched on at several places earlier: the very limited participation by women in sport considered on a worldwide basis and the conservative nature of sports organizations even in societies where women's sport does thrive.

There were more than 120 countries represented at both the Munich and Montreal Olympics, but in each case only about half of them had women in their teams. Since 1896 women athletes from only thirty-two countries have gained Olympic medals in the summer Games, while more than double that number of countries have had men medal winners. Among these thirty-two countries, nineteen are European, two North American, two from Central America (Mexico and Cuba), two from Oceania, four from Asia (Japan, North Korea, South Korea and Taiwan), two from South America (Argentina and Chile), while Africa is represented on this list only by South Africa (see appendix D). In spite of the expanded women's programme in Montreal, women from only seventeen countries won medals.

This concentration is definitely focused in Eastern Europe. Prior to 1980, American women had still won the largest number of medals in the summer Games (210, mostly from swimming), but the USSR had won far more (180) since 1952 when it rejoined the Games and East Germany had won more than both (83) since its first independent appearance in 1968. Since the war, Hungary, Romania, Czechoslovakia and Poland have been prominent in a wide range of sports including, variously, swimming, gymnastics, fencing, track and field, rowing, canoeing, volleyball and others. In the winter Games, the USSR is already way ahead in the list of medal winners and most of the other East European countries are represented among the medal winners. When the communist countries made their debut at the 1952 Olympics, they won 29 per cent of the medals, in 1972 they won 47 per cent and in 1976 57 per cent. Their domination of European Championships and World Cups has been even more complete.

The vast majority of women are, at present, either quite unrepresented or markedly under-represented in the Olympic movement and other major sporting bodies. India, for example, with a population in excess of five hundred million, despite the fact that it has had a woman prime minister and although it has sent more than six hundred men athletes to post-war Olympiads, has sent fewer than a dozen women in that time. Women from Islamic countries are almost unknown at the Olympics. The African boycott of the Montreal Games had practically no effect on the women's competitions. Fewer than thirty athletes from ten countries stayed away from the track and field competitions as a result of it.

Since African, Latin American, Asian and Arab countries form a powerful voting block at meetings of the IOC and other international bodies, they are a powerful conservative force. The Moroccans, for example, when voting against the introduction of longer distance races at the Olympics, said that women running distances was blasphemous, ruining their femininity. Women's judo will find it difficult to get Brazil's vote for inclusion, since it is illegal in that country, although men's judo is not.

In international competition generally, women usually get fewer opportunities than their performances warrant. There are fewer international meets for women, fewer international marches, fewer athletics scholarships and so on. They are usually less likely to be chosen for overseas teams compared with their numbers in home matches or home meets. For example, in Rome, the Italian team was thirty-four; in 1964, in Tokyo, it was reduced to eleven. At the 1964 Tokyo Games, Japan was represented by sixty-one women athletes. To the following two Olympic Games, Japan sent a total of only sixty-eight women athletes. In these and many similar cases, the reduction of the men's teams sent to overseas venues was much less than women's.

Not even the Eastern European countries are immune from this sort of thing. The Hungarian Athletic Federation refused Sarolta Monspart a visa to visit Atlanta in Georgia USA for the Avon International Woman's marathon in 1978, even though she had run 2:48:53 in a Budapest marathon. She managed to obtain a visa from the Hungarian Orienteering Association (at which sport she is also most able) and duly competed. She finished second in 2:51:40 in a race which attracted 186 runners.

There is one other major area where women are still seriously under-represented: the whole area of organization including coaching, team managing and administration is almost exclusively a male preserve in all countries of the world. The small advances made by women in the USA recently, mentioned on page 209 are rather few and far between and restricted to that country. Prior to 1980 more than three hundred men were members of the International Olympic Committee, but no women. The first attempts to obtain women's representatives on the IOC were made in 1960 by prominent women representatives from Australia, the USA and USSR, but were unsuccessful, as have been all subsequent attempts.

In 1975, International Women's Year, only 25 countries out of 132 with National Olympic Committees had any women members and only 55 of the countries had any top women sports officials. Characteristically, the countries with the most women members on their National Olympic Committees were Eastern European — Czechoslovakia (six), Hungary (five), Bulgaria (five), Albania (four) and Romania (four) — though the USSR and GDR had only two women members each on their NOCs. Many western countries, including Austria, Canada, Italy, Japan, Netherlands, Norway and Switzerland had no women members at all on their NOCs.

The exclusion of women from team management and coaching positions is equally complete. Women held these positions in the early days of separate women's sports meetings, of course, but with the development of joint organizations and joint meetings the number of women in positions of importance in this field declined into insignificance. Women coaches are few and far between today, far fewer than the number of serious women athletes deserves. Even in the Eastern European countries where women's sport is so strongly encouraged, coaches are almost entirely men. The composition of the parties of officials at the Montreal Olympics tells its own story.

There were ninety officials in the Great Britain party in Montreal (administering a total team of 259 in all sports). Twenty-one of these officials, or 23 per cent, were women. But ten of these were grooms (and one was a vet) concerned only with the equestrian team (there was also one male groom), one was the pianist (for the women's gymnastics) and three were designated female officials who, according to Olympic rules, have to be present on the floor during women's gymnastics. This left just five women occupying positions of substance or in positions of direct relationship to the women competing. There were 70 women actually in the team or 27 per cent. In 1972 there were forty-seven men athletes in the team and twenty-six women athletes. To administer and coach these athletes there were eight men and one woman. Other countries' officials were similarly structured. East Germany had eighty-nine officials of whom six were women, two masseurs and four designated female officials (East Germany did not enter the equestrian events). West Germany had 106 officials of whom eleven were women (including six grooms). The USA had 129 officials of whom seventeen were women (including nine grooms).

The conclusion is clear. Women get neither the same opportunity to travel and attend these major events as do men, nor do they get much chance to occupy the same sort of positions of authority, prestige or influence as do men. The effect that this has on the morale and hence on the levels of performance of women competitors is unknown. It must surely be disadvantageous, though, in view of the incentive effects of overseas trips and the dominating influence of some sports coaches discussed in chapter five.

The ferment over women's opportunities in sport has led several major United States universities to appoint women Directors of Coaching. But a recent survey of AIAW institutions in the USA during the years 1974–79 showed that the increase in the number of male head and assistant coaches was 182 per cent, while female coaches showed only a 3 per cent increase. At the assistant coach level, the men's positions rose 368 per cent and the women's positions 174 per cent, but at the head-coach level, the men's positions were up 132 per cent, while women's positions actually decreased 20 per cent.

Funds are currently being sought from the United States Department of Health, Education and Welfare to provide training in practical and theoretical course work for female coaches so that they have the skills, knowledge and experience needed to compete for these jobs. The Australian Athletic Union in 1979 appointed an American-trained woman as national Director of Coaching, so at least some are already available. When women have a significant proportion of positions as coaches and administrators, this will surely give a further impetus to women's sporting performance, although by how much of course is quite unknown.

All of this leads to the following conclusions: our knowledge of women's physiology and psychology relevant to sporting endeavour is still very imperfect, being much less than that for men, however imperfect that is.

Women are still significantly under-represented in most sports and, by virtue of the social and domestic pressures on them, find it much harder to continue in top level sport than do men. If they do continue, they find it much less easy than men do to devote the time required for rigorous training and systematic participation.

There are very few women coaches to train and support women, very few women doctors specializing in sports medicine and very few women officials at such meetings as the Olympic, European and Commonwealth Games.

Women are still overtly discriminated against in almost all countries, although to very different levels, having fewer opportunities to take decisions on their own behalf and to administer their own chosen sports.

Many of the sports and events in which women do now participate are relatively new, have low levels of participation and have few people able to offer coaching or plan training schedules. The standards in these new events are therefore rather low.

These reinforce the prediction that women now entering sport will come much closer to equalling men's performances than women have hitherto done. Whether, in most events, they will actually catch the men rests in large measure on whether they believe they can, that is, on their attitudes and expectations.

3. ATTITUDES AND EXPECTATIONS

The attitudes of most societies are, to an overwhelming extent, either those of men or are strongly influenced by those of men. This is not to say that societal attitudes on such things as women's sport are necessarily uniform — they are not; there are differences between countries and differences between individuals within countries and however widely and strongly societal values are held there are always more or less deviant men and women who hold different views or do different things. But men's attitudes are undoubtedly of major importance.

We have already seen that much of organized sport among men in the nineteenth century grew up out of upper and middle class activities. Athletics, horse racing, polo, shooting, yachting, fencing and others had strong military origins and associations. Tennis, cricket, golf and others were very middle class leisure pursuits. Working class men could not afford the elaborate equipment required by these sports and in the ninteenth century certainly did not have the time to practise them.

There was a similar division among women. The lifestyle of middle and upper class women centred on leisure. Aside from purely domestic occupations, activities such as croquet, archery, lawn bowls, and a little golf and tennis were allowed. The lifestyle of working class women centred on work and home and they had neither time, money, nor opportunity for much else.

By the turn of the century many women had taken up bicycling in company with men. It is this which seems to have emancipated them from the cumbrous dress of the period and allowed them to wear bloomers and show their ankles. Much of the impetus for the participation of women in sport in the second and third decades of this century came from working class women. Perhaps this was a result of what they were asked to do and what they did during the first world war. From about 1920 on women played a large and significant part in international sport. They organized their own Women's World Games, started international competition and sought admittance to the Olympic Games in the central sport of athletics. Although attitudes of men to these developments were not uniform the opinions of those in authority in society and sport were largely opposed to these developments and were certainly opposed to extending women's participation in organized sport.

The man most closely associated with the birth of the modern Olympic movement, Baron Pierre de Coubertin, was throughout his life opposed to women in sport, particularly in the Olympics.[8] In 1902 Coubertin claimed that women's sports were against the "laws of nature". In 1908 he spoke out against women's tobogganing as "the most inaesthetic sight human eyes could contemplate". Four years later he simply claimed that the Olympic Games should be reserved for men. In 1920, twenty years after women had begun to take part in the Olympic Games, Coubertin suggested that the IOC expel them altogether from the 1924 Games. At the Olympic Congress in Prague in 1925 Coubertin claimed that women's participation in the Olympic Games was illegal and on the celebration of the fortieth anniversary of modern olympism in Lausanne in 1934 he warned the modern (male) athlete that "contact with feminine athletes is bad for him". Writing in 1935 on "The Philosophical Basis of Modern Olympism" he says: "I personally am against the participation of women in public competition . . . At the Olympic Games their primary role should be like in the ancient tournaments – the crowning of the victors with laurels". Coubertin's successor as president of the IOC was Belgian Count Henri de Baillet-Latour. He it was who suggested to the 1930 Olympic Congress in Berlin that women be allowed to compete only in "aesthetic events".

In 1936 Avery Brundage, then president of the United States Olympic Committee, and in 1952 to become president of the IOC said: "I am fed up to the ears with women as track and field competitors . . . her charms sink to something less than zero. As swimmers and divers girls are beautiful and adroit as they are ineffective and unpleasing on the track".[9]

Of course these men can be dismissed as merely espousing the general opinions of their time, but it is not quite so simple as that. Avery Brundage remained president of the IOC until 1972 and there is little reason to suppose his views mellowed much as he got older.

Perhaps as a result of this some of the IOC rules are still discriminatory against women. There is, for example, a rule governing the circumstance of a woman moving from the country of her birth to the country of her husband when she marries. The alternative possibility of a husband following his wife is not allowed for. Men and women are discriminated in team sports and the possibility that an international federation might wish to have only its female athletes compete in the Olympic Games is not allowed for. Furthermore, although the IOC rules do not allow discrimination on the basis of race, religion or political affiliation they fail to mention sex as a possible ground for discrimination. The IOC could hardly fail, of course, to be in contravention of any rule it might adopt on the subject.

Certainly things have changed in the last few decades, but equally certainly there is still a lot of room for further change. The latest rules of the IOC adopted in 1972 regarding new sports are symptomatic of new attitudes. These rules set much easier terms for new women's sports applying for future inclusion in the Olympic programme than they do for men's sports. Women's sports practised in twenty countries on two continents may apply for inclusion in both the summer and winter games. The respective figures for men's sports are forty countries on three continents for the summer games and twenty-five countries on two continents for the winter games. At least in theory this opens up the possibility that a new women's sport could be introduced without a corresponding men's version. Alternatively, this rule ensures that only sports widely practised by men and practised in a subsidiary way by women will ever be included in future in the Olympic programme.

The problem of how men's attitudes can be changed without changes in women's participation and performance to prompt them is the sort of chicken and egg problem already encountered in the major speed sports. Early practitioners of new sports have almost always been seen as socially deviant and have been held up to ridicule and reproof. As performances of the few have improved the amount of criticism has decreased and levels of participation have increased. There seems little reason to believe that the pattern will be much different for those sports into which women have yet to venture.

But while men's attitudes are very important in society, women's attitudes and beliefs about themselves are also important. For example, it took some courage on the part of women and considerable confidence in their own abilities, to believe that they could run a marathon when all the medical and sporting advice (from men) was to the effect that they could not and should not. It takes courage for women to train as hard as men in the pool, on the track and most of all in the gym, when they are frequently told that to do so will destroy their femininity and possibly do them physical harm as well. It will take courage and firm beliefs on the part of women to take up water polo, pole vaulting, hammer throwing, speedway, ski jumping or whatever. It will also take a change in attitudes on the part of men who at present largely control the facilities and set the conditions for these sports to allow women to participate in the first place.

It is curious that throughout much of the history of women's sport, many women and women's organizations have been at the forefront of efforts to restrict the growth of women's sport and restrict women's sporting participation. Some of these attitudes prevail even today. In 1970 Dr Nell Jackson, head of AAU Women's Track and Field Committee expressed her opposition to the marathon at a national convention. "I'm very concerned about the effect of these long distances on females", she remarked and went on to refer to women's long distance running as a "lark". As late as 1966 a woman physical educator and chairperson of the Women's Board of the United States Olympic Development Committee, S. S. Jernigan, wrote:

> To most of the women in the United States and to many women in other nations the shot put and discus throw are forms of competition that are generally unacceptable to the feminine image. They are men's sports requiring tremendous explosive strength and a large physique for a superior performance. Generally speaking women do these very badly, poor mimics of men and these sports have a limited appeal to the female sex. It is a known fact that chiefly the hefty masculine woman gains sufficient satisfaction from performances of these two athletic activities. There are very many men and women around who would be delighted if the IOC would eliminate the shot put and discus from the field events for women in the Olympic Games because often the feminine self-image is badly mutilated when women perform in these two sports.[10]

Needless to say there would also be many women (and men) who would be most upset if the IOC did any such thing. The media has often greatly overemphasized the physical development of women throwers. Photograph 14, of Ilona Slupianek of East Germany, 1980 gold medal winner and world record holder, shows a feminine image about which Ms Jernigan or anyone else would surely find it difficult to complain.

Rarely is such a negative attitude or failure to believe in female abilities so marked, but the effects of so much negative socialization and misinformation of the sort previously described can often be found in active sportswomen today. The magazine *Sportswoman* polled a large number of sportswomen in 1976 to determine whether they thought they were reaching their athletic potential. There was overwhelming agreement that women athletes are culturally conditioned to consider their athletic prowess inferior to men's, but there was sharp disagreement as to whether such conditioning hindered women in developing their maximum potential in sports and their desire to get to the top.

More than three quarters of the women athletes responding to the poll felt that women athletes train as intensively as men but only half of the women questioned trained with weights, even though they all said that the men in their sports did so. According to Shirley Babashoff almost 40 per cent of the American women swimmers at Montreal had never worked with weights. There is little doubt that all the East German team trained with weights and those women who do train with weights appreciate the benefits it gives them. American rowing silver medallist Joan Lind said, for example: "There isn't a decent woman rower in the world who doesn't treat weight training seriously".[11] Audrey McElumury, America's first woman to win a world cycling championship said: "I don't think I could have won without weights". In swimming and in track and field athletics weight training is still the exception rather than the rule outside the Eastern European countries.

Two thirds of the women athletes polled felt that women could not become as proficient as men athletes in their sport because of men's innate superior strength. Some believed that as their performances got closer to those of men so their performances would improve. American skier Suzy Chaffee claimed that: "As long as you have women competing only against women their standard of excellence will be lower than that set by male athletes". She went on to say that after competing against men she had to rethink her whole philosophy of competing. An American table tennis player said that: "I like to play the best men because of the high level of play — it's a challenge".

Distance swimmer Greta Anderson, holder of the world fifty mile record, has at one time or another beaten every male she has ever swum against. She believes that in distance swimming women can compete equally with men: "I think that women are tougher than men . . . we're more determined to win". She feels that this determination and long-term strength compensate for the males' better sprinting ability.

Excellence was the word that most women athletes emphasized more than strength. Most believed, or wanted to believe, that muscular strength is not needed. Yet the men, who are usually stronger than the women to start with, are building up their strength with weight training, whereas most women are not. Clearly there is some confusion and disagreement among women, probably associated with rapidly changing beliefs and attitudes at the present time.

4. BODY IMAGES

Ideas about what is beautiful and sexually attractive for each gender are very deeply ingrained and therefore very difficult to change. But two important phenomena of recent years, the women's movement and the physical fitness movement, are beginning to effect an enormous change in our attitudes to ourselves and to the opposite gender. For increasing numbers of men and women, the conventional media images of sexuality are rapidly becoming obsolete.

Women who begin to feel emotionally strong through the women's movement, but feel physically weak and incompetent, start training or learn self-defence so that their bodies and abilities match their self-images. On the other hand, women who are already athletic and who have strong athletic bodies are becoming more accepting of this and more confident of asserting their continuing femininity and sexuality. The magazine Womensports[12] recently interviewed a number of athletes on this point and their answers are illuminating. Long distance runner and artist Anna Thornhill had always wanted to be taller and more sensual in conventional terms. But now she says:

I don't worry about fitting into a fashion type image any more . . . After running a marathon and then a 7-mile race the following day and feeling no pains at all, I looked in the mirror and said "Body, you're okay. You're doing your job". My husband doesn't want me to become too thin but I no longer want to surrender to someone else's view of sexuality, because for me, at this point, functionalism and sexuality are fused. My sexuality isn't affected by the way I look any more but how I feel: healthy, confident and functional.

Another marathoner, Canadian Gail Olinek, recalls that:

I have always been strong, always been developed and I can remember when I was a kid growing up in Canada how the salesmen used to make me cry when they couldn't fit me with a pair of boots. "Why don't you try a man's shop?" they'd say. Or when I was running, the people on the sidelines — both men and women — would yell insults, call me a freak.

Unlike many women faced with these sorts of situations, Gail Olinek continued running and was the fifth fastest woman marathoner in the world in 1979. Her body is extremely developed with powerful well-defined muscles in arms and legs. But she is very pleased about the way she looks. She says:

It's very important to change the image of the developed woman. In Europe, my kind of body — we're called Sportsfrau — is much more developed than in America . . . I believe that strength is beauty and there can be no such thing as too strong. Attitudes here are changing, although it's been gradual. Last year I was asked to compete in a women's body-building contest in Florida — they're beginning to take place — and I said no. But I'm changing my mind. I think I'll enter this year.

Changes of attitude are apparent among mature athletes and, aided by some enlightened coaches, also among the young. This pressages further and more widespread changes for the future. American John McCravey, who has coached boys and girls for a number of years, says that:

The changes are coming; kids are different now. I grew up in the south where women athletes were ostracized and girls had a great fear of masculinization; but now even in the South, I found that the kids had really absorbed the social changes. The girls I've trained are intensely competitive. They're gaining all the secondary advantages of participating: feeling strong, competent and successful. And these things vastly outweigh whatever negative attitudes still exist.

But attitudes to men's bodies and their sexuality are also changing. The rugged he-man macho image — an image of dominance rather than actual sexuality — is no longer everything. Sexuality itself has hitherto been primarily a "feminine" trait and therefore unwelcome, especially to committed sportsmen. The outmoded idea that sex itself was to be avoided for two or three days before a big event and that wives or girlfriends should not accompany touring teams is part of that tradition. But men are now accepting their sexuality and, again, sporting and social changes are proceeding hand in hand, the one reinforcing the other.

The greater knowledge, permissiveness and openness of society today about anatomy, physiology and sex is one aspect. Women can now observe, evaluate and fantasize much more freely and openly than ever before about men's bodies. Men have always had the female nude as an art form to comment on and now have the female form thrust at them in almost any and every situation. Women have had little opportunity in the past to observe and less opportunity to comment on the male body. That they can do so now, and what is more, openly discuss men's sexuality, is having its effect.

Athletic coach John McCravey finds that: "The men I know who work out — and I include myself — are amazed and delighted by their new attractiveness to women."

American long-distance runner Marty Liquori (183 centimetres and seventy kilograms today) remembers that: "I was always the skinniest guy I knew when I was a kid, but I looked on it as an occupational factor, since I started running seriously when I was 14." Although Liquori says that he was not bothered by the disparity between his looks and the social norm, he believes that men like himself are being perceived differently now than they were a few years ago: "We're extreme cases and some women like it. We're thinner, less intimidating. Women aren't looking to be dominated any more."

What seems to be happening, at least in some of the sports subcultures, is that the differences between the body images and some of the gender characteristics are being reduced. This convergence of gender characteristics — androgyny — is an attractive ideal to many people. It is an attempt to combine the physical virtues of each gender — not for women to be "masculinized" or men to be "feminized" but for both to be humanized and enriched.

Currently androgynization mainly refers to the strengthening of women's bodies, not the weakening of men's bodies, primarily because many more women are discontent with societal views of their sexuality than are men. Furthermore, the lean, lithe, graceful fit men already have several acceptable models including Gene Kelly, Fred Astaire, Paul Newman and so forth. Outside sport, women have few androgynous strong and developed female bodies as models.

In Western European countries, change — as always, in the field of social attitudes — is slow. In many East European countries, the changes are being socially engineered. In East Germany promising young athletes are inducted into sports schools between the ages of eight and eleven, depending on a particular sport's requirements for physical size and maturity. This is largely before the age when boys and girls begin to differ in the kind and intensity of their athletic interest. As a culture within the larger East German culture, the environment of the sport school is so controlled that there is no chance for any external influence to indicate to the female athlete that her femininity is endangered by being an athlete. On the contrary, she receives special rewards, both material and psychological, for athletic accomplishment. East Germany thus provides a more congenial environment for promising sportswomen to train and perform. Not only are the opportunities and material resources for women athletes equal to those provided for male athletes but, just as important, no conflict between their femininity and athletic achievement is allowed to develop in the minds of the women athletes.

As has been extensively documented in this book, the success of East German sportswomen has been enormous. As this reduction of conflict, and change in body image spreads to other countries, together of course with the material provisions, women's sporting performances are likely to improve even more rapidly.

5. MYTHS AND REALITIES

Throughout the history of women's sporting participation there have been an incredible number of myths regarding possible hazards of vigorous sport to them. Many of these have already been mentioned and dismissed as illfounded and absurd, but the very fact that it is necessary still to consider and dismiss the following notions suggests how persuasive they must be amongst would-be sportswomen:

- Menstruation is no handicap to either training or performance for the vast majority of women.
- Neither internal nor external sex organs are especially vulnerable to injury or distortion.
- Vigorous training and competition is not harmful to subsequent pregnancies, nor is pregnancy deleterious to subsequent performance, quite the reverse in fact.
- Women do not reach physical peak earlier than men nor do they decline faster or earlier.
- Hard training, including weight training, will not lead to excessive muscle development or masculinize a woman's body.
- It is not true that women engaged in sport are more commonly or more seriously injured than men.

The general attitude which these and other myths suggest is one of fragility and feminine weakness. It is just such an attitude which is fostered by other social beliefs regarding the "fairer" or "weaker" or "gentler" sex. The fact that there is virtually no truth in any of them is well known amongst most practising women athletes and those who actively coach women. It is gradually becoming more well known amongst girls and young sportswomen setting out on their careers. They will be likely to train harder and compete harder, secure in the knowledge that it is doing them good, not harm.

In the last few years, indeed, there has been growing a belief among many coaches, including the renowned Dr Ernst Van Aaken, that women can in fact train *harder* than men with beneficial results; that for some sports, especially those of endurance, they are better suited than men; that in flexibility, buoyancy and contour, they are at an advantage in swimming and some other sports. Rudi Schramme, the head coach of swimming for East Germany at the 1976 Olympics, believes that: "We, earlier than other countries, realized that girls and boys can stand about the same stress in swimming. Our coaches have increasingly realized that the same demands can be made on girls as are being made on boys and that girls must be encouraged to the same extent that boys are."[13] All in all, it can be said that as women gradually move their sights on to the performances of men and come to believe that they can catch up, and realize that men will not think less or differently of them if they do, then they automatically bring the day nearer when they really do catch up.

Figure 29 summarizes more or less the whole area of women's sporting involvement. Although, in general, women are most successful with an aerobic workload, this figure shows that there are some major sports of this type in which women are at the moment largely unrepresented. This will probably change in the near future.

In aerobic events in which they compete, women have attained virtual equality with men. This assertion is based on the following facts, most of which have been mentioned earlier.

- Between 1967 and 1969 a woman held the twelve hour time trial cycling record in Britain, exceeding the men's performance by 0.2 per cent. At present the women's record is just 1.66 per cent inferior to the men's record.
- Women have completed a majority of the ten fastest swims across the English Channel and their dominance has been particularly marked in the last three years. They also hold all the records for swimming the Catalina Channel of California. These events involve eight or nine hours' swimming.
- Women have held the fastest times for the fifty mile swim (Greta Anderson) and fifty mile run (Natalie Cullimore) in the 1970s.
- Natalie Cullimore convincingly won the AAU hundred mile run in 1973.
- Marathon swimmer Diana Nyad became the first person to swim from the Bahamas to Florida on 20 August 1979. She swam the eighty-nine mile distance in 27 hours 38 minutes.
- Women are now consistently achieving times in the marathon (42,195 metres) of under 2 hours 40 minutes. With such times they can confidently expect a placing in the top 5 per cent or so of male finishers in even the strongest events.
- Women hold the fastest times for all roller skating events of 25,000 metres and over.
- Women are now swimming 800 metres, their longest Olympic distance, in times not achieved by men until the early 1970s.

Reference to figure 29 shows that there are whole areas of aerobic sports where women are totally unrepresented, notably the long distance and multi-stage massed start cycling races and biathlon skiing. In many other sports, on the track, in the pool, Nordic skiing, ice and roller skating, rowing and canoeing, women are not allowed to compete over the longer, and arguably their best distances, in most officially organized sports meetings. In the basically anaerobic

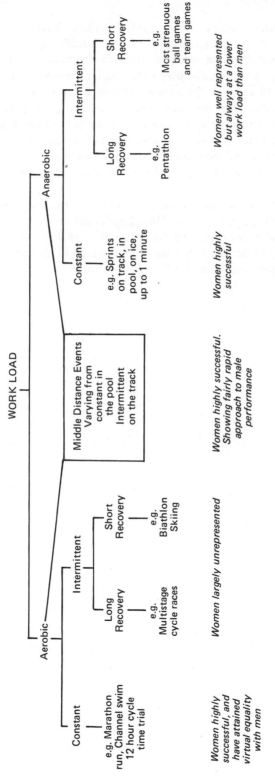

Fig. 28. A classification of sport according to the nature of the workload. The level of women's participation and their successes are indicated.

team sports, there must be a significant if variable aerobic component, since hockey players, football players and others are usually in some form of motion and cannot rely entirely on anaerobic sources of energy. But here too women, when they play at all, usually play over shorter periods or to modified rules which deny them some of the advantages they might have.

The whole pattern of women's participation in sport is clearly still quite irrational. It has developed in ignorance of many of the true biological differences between the sexes, it overemphasizes some of the differences which do exist and is based on quite unwarranted assumptions about some supposed and seemingly obvious biological sex differences which, in reality, are nothing of the kind.

I hope this book has made clear where some of the real differences lie and what their sporting significance is. More important, however, I hope that some of the myths have been exposed for what they are and that women will now have the chance to demonstrate their true potential in all sports in which they wish to participate and at all levels of performance.

NOTES

CHAPTER ONE

1. G. Kelly, *Mr. Controversial: The Story of Percy Wells Cerutty* (London: Stanley Paul, 1964), p. 139.

CHAPTER TWO

1. K. Pearson, *Surfing Subcultures of Australia and New Zealand* (St Lucia: University of Queensland Press, 1979), p. 7.

CHAPTER THREE

1. The Italian Pietro Mennea broke Tommy Smith's 200 metres record in 1979, but he did so on the same track in Mexico City as that on which the Olympic events were run.

CHAPTER FOUR

1. C. Sherif, in *Women in Sport: A National Research Conference* (University Park, Pa: Pennsylvania State University, 1972), pp. 115–33.
2. Quoted by C. Gillett in *Connexions: The Function and Meaning of Sport* (Harmondsworth: Penguin, 1971), pp. 16-17.
3. This and other quotations of Mary Peters come from *Mary P: An Autobiography* (London: Stanley Paul, 1974).

CHAPTER FIVE

1. For the source of these quotations and an analysis of the development of East German sport see G. Ehrbach and E. Buggel, "Sociological problems in the presentation of development tendencies of socialist physical culture in the German Democratic Republic", *International Review of Sports Sociology* 7 (1972): 103-10. For a more general description of East Germany's sport see J.O. Riordan, ed., *Sport under Communism* (London: C. Hurst and Co., 1978), pp. 67-102.
2. *Sport in the USSR* 8 (1977): 3-12.
3. For the source of these quotations from Gonzalez see A. Wohl, "Prognostic models of sport in socialist countries", *International Review of Sports Sociology* 6 (1971): 17-47. For a general description of modern sport in Cuba see Riordan, ed., *Sport under Communism. (loc. cit* footnote 1).
4. F. Stampfl, *Franz Stampfl on Running* (London: Herbert Jenkins, 1955), pp. 146 and 151.
5. M. Peters, *Mary P: An Autobiography* (London: Stanley Paul, 1974), p. 81
6. G. Kelly, *Mr. Controversial: The Story of Percy Wells Cerutty* (London: Stanley Paul, 1964), pp. 138-39.

CHAPTER SIX

1. I. Kostrubala, *The Joy of Running* (Philadelphia and New York: J.B. Lippincott, 1976), p. 123.

2. C.E. Klafs and D.D. Arnheim, *Modern Principles of Athletic Training*, 4th ed. (St Louis: C.V. Mosby, 1978), p. 146.
3. J.S. Mill, *The Subjection of Women* (London: Everyman Library, 1970).
4. S. Westermann, *Sport, Physical Training and Womanhood* (Philadelphia: Lea and Febiger, 1939), p. 76.
5. E. Hay, "Considerations on Women's Sport", *Olympic Review* 12 (1977): 684-87.
6. Some of the examples on the effects of pregnancy on athletic performance are quoted from James Fixx in *The Complete Book of Running* (New York: Random House, 1976), chapter 8, and some are from *The Female Runner* (Mountain View, Calif.: World Publications, 1973), chapter 3.
7. Miki Gorman became the first woman to win the Boston Marathon twice, in 1974 and 1977. Between these victories, at age forty, she had given birth to her first baby. She was quoted on the relative difficulties of the two achievements in *Athletics Weekly* 24 March 1979, p. 20.
8. In *Report of the Games of the XVIII Olympiad Tokyo 1964* (Tokyo: Japanese Olympic Committee, 1966), p. 78.
9. *Ibid.*, p. 96.
10. *Ibid.*, p. 117.
11. In his early autobiography *First Four Minutes* (London: Putnam, 1955), pp. 221-22.

CHAPTER SEVEN
1. S. Brownmiller, *Against our Will* (Harmondsworth: Penguin, 1977), pp. 401-2.
2. Quoted in *The Female Runner* (Mountain View, Calif.: World Publications, 1973), p. 10.
3. Quoted in M. Hart, "Sport: Women sit in the back of the bus", *Psychology Today* (October 1971): 64-66.
4. W.F. Connell et al., *Growing up in an Australian City* (Melbourne: Australian Council for Education Research, 1957), p. 132.
5. A study of the media in Australia by Helen Menzies, a member of the Women in Sport and Recreation Group, convened by the Women's Advisory Unit of the Premier's Department of South Australia. Some of the newspaper articles cited in this section are quoted in "Media Malpractice", in *Women and Sport*, VTU Elimination of Sexism in Education Project, (VTU Victoria n.d.), pp. 53-55.
6. B. Gilbert and N. Williamson, "Women in Sports: A progress report", *Sports Illustrated* 43 (1974): 25-31.
7. These examples are from a study issued by the project on the Status and Education of Women of the Association of American Colleges, Washington D.C., entitled *What Constitutes Equality for Women in Sport?* by M. Dunkle.
8. C.A. Oglesby, ed., *Women and Sport: From Myth to Reality* (Philadelphia: Lea and Febiger, 1978), p. 238.
9. T. Boslooper and M. Hayes, *The Femininity Game* (New York: Stein and Day, 1973), front cover.
10. Quoted in "Media Malpractice", in *Women in Sport.*
11. In D. Harris and R. Christina, eds., *Psychology of Sport and Motor Behaviour* (University Park, Pa.: Pennsylvania State University, 1975).
12. This information and much else on the situation in New South Wales quoted in this section, comes from a discussion paper produced by the Social Development Unit of the NSW Ministry of Education with sports sociologist Elizabeth Coles as consultant entitled *Sport in Schools: The Participation of Girls*. Hopefully, this government involvement and awareness will lead to governmental action to induce change.
13. Quoted in P. Huckle, "Back to the Starting Line: Title IX and Women's Intercollegiate Athletics", *American Behavioural Scientist* 21 (1978): 379-92. Some of the other examples mentioned later in this section are quoted by Boslooper and Hayes in *The Feminity Game*, chapter 5.
14. Dunkle, *What Constitutes Equality for Women in Sport?*
15. L. Huey, *A Running Start: An Athlete, A Woman* (New York: Quadrangle Books, 1976).

16. V. Parker and R. Kennedy, *Track and Field for Girls and Women* (Ph Saunders and Co., 1969).
17. B. Leroy, ed., *Dictionnaire Encylopedique Des Sports et Des Perf* Deuvel, 1973).
18. London: Stanley Paul, 1961.
19. Oxford: OUP, 1964.
20. Huckle, "Back to the Starting Line". Other responses to Title IX referred quoted here are given in C.L. Hogan "Title IX: Fair State or Shakedown", *Women-sports* 3 (1976): 50-54.

CHAPTER EIGHT

1. From an interview in *Athletics Weekly*, 18 January 1977, p. 26.
2. D. Roberts, *Distance Running Records* (London: The International Athlete, 1962).
3. J. Hopkins, *The Marathon* (London: Stanley Paul, 1966).
4. *Runners World* 7 (1974): 4.
5. B.B. Lloyd, "Athletic Achievement – Trends and Limits", British Association for the Advancement of Science Presidential Address to Section X 1980.
6. These words were written in 1978 before the tragic massive rises in unemployment had really begun in Britain, the USA, Australia and many other Western countries. It nevertheless remains true that time off for sporting participation is easier than it was.

CHAPTER TEN

1. *Cycling* (December 1938): 2.
2. A 20 kilometre cross country event for women has now been accepted for the 1984 Winter Olympics.

CHAPTER ELEVEN

1. *Sportswoman* 4 (Sept/Oct 1973): 6.
2. *Women's Sports* 2 (August 1980): 61.
3. B.C. Drinkwater, "Physiological responses of women to exercise", in *Exercise and Sports Sciences Reviews*, 1, ed. J.H. Wilmore (New York: Academic Press, 1973), pp. 125-53.
4. W.M. Mandel, *Soviet Women* (New York: Anchor Books, 1975), p. 156.
5. B.L. Bennett, *Comparative Physical Education and Sport*, (Philadelphia: Lea and Febiger, 1975), p. 183.
6. Quoted in J.O. Riordan, *Sport in Soviet Society* (Cambridge: Cambridge University Press, 1976), p. 320.
7. As already mentioned, it is on the programme for Los Angeles 1984 and East German interest in the event is increasing.
8. Baron de Coubertin's articles and speeches are collected and translated into English in *The Olympic Idea* (Cologne: Carl Diem Institute, 1966).
9. Quoted in U. Simri, *A Historical Analysis of the Role of Women in the Modern Olympic Games* (Netanya: Wingate Institute for Physical Education and Sport, 1977), p. 21.
10. Proceedings of the International Olympic Academy (1966), p. 73.
11. This and following remarks are taken from the article "Do women achieve their athletic potential?" by Ann Roch, illustrating the outcome of this poll in *Sportswoman* 4 (1976): 18-20.
12. These quotations come from L. Schreiber "The Great American Tomboy", *Women-sports* (October 1975). Further viewpoints are in J.B. Rohrbaugh, "Feminity on the line", *Psychology Today* (August 1979): 30-43.
13. *Women's Sports* 2 (1980): 61.

References and Further Reading

I have not burdened the text with references and citations. Much of the information in this book came from the publications listed below. In listing them I have tried to indicate their general approach and technical sophistication in order that readers may follow up particular points which interest them. Appendix A, the American College of Sports Medicine Opinion Statement on *The Participation of the Female Athlete in Long-Distance Running* includes a detailed bibliography on that particular point.

1. JOURNALS, MAGAZINES AND STATISTICAL PUBLICATIONS

Association of Track and Field Statisticians Annual. Records and 100 best performances for all men's events each year.

The ATFS Women's Track and Field Handbook. Listings of up to the top 150 all time best performances in the regular women's events.

Athletics Weekly. Results, statistics and general articles primarily on British track and field athletics, cross country and road racing.

Australian Journal of Sports Medicine. Although this is a scientific journal it has many general review articles and book reviews of interest to the general reader.

Besford, P. *Encyclopaedia of Swimming.* 2nd ed. London: Hale, 1976, An excellent book, though it has a slight emphasis on British sport.

British Journal of Sports Medicine. See remarks concerning Australian journal.

Buchanan, I. *Encyclopaedia of British Athletics Records.* London: Stanley Paul, 1961. Although encyclopaedic for men's athletics it does not mention women's records at all.

Cycling. A British weekly covering all aspects of cycling including the competitions and records discussed in chapter ten of this book.

Exercise and Sports Sciences Review. New York: Academic Press. An annual series of authoritative rigorous academic reviews.

Hopkins, John. *The Marathon.* London: Stanley Paul, 1966. A comprehensive history except for the fact that it makes no mention of any women's attempts at the distance.

Human Biology. An academic journal which often has detailed articles on the comparative anatomy and physiology of men and women.

International Athletics Annual. A publication of the British Amateur Athletics Board now sadly defunct; the last issue being 1973. Its statistics and general articles are still valuable.

Journal of Physical Education and Recreation. An important journal. Although academic it often has very readable articles.

Journal of Sports Medicine. See comment concerning *Journal of Physical Education.*

Marathon Handbook. Mountain View Ca.: World Publications. A more or less annual publication which provides a wealth of statistics on men's and women's marathoning.

McWhirter, N. and R. *Guiness Book of Olympic Records.* London: Penguin Books, 1976. A full set of results for all sports from all Olympiads and brief descriptions of each of the Games. It is revised for each Olympiad.

Medicine and Science in Sports. A very important academic journal.

Modern Athlete and Coach. A monthly Australian journal collecting a very wide variety of articles on training and coaching and athletics in general.

Olympic Review. The monthly publication of the International Olympic Commission. As well as general articles it contains up to date records of all Olympic sports.

The Physician and Sportsmedicine. An important academic journal. Many of the articles are accessible to non-medical readers.

Pozzoli, P. R., ed. *Women's Athletics Yearbook.* London: Women's Track and Field World. An annual encyclopaedic publication covering the whole range of women's participation. The 1976 edition was unfortunately the last.

Progressive World Record Lists 1913–1970. London: IAAF. The complete progressive lists of all record holders in events officially recognized by the IAAF. There are annual supplements since 1970.

Research Quarterly. An American academic journal concentrating on physical education.

Roberts, Dave. *Distance Running Records.* London: The International Athlete, 1962.

Runner's World. A very varied, popular, not too technical magazine for all runners.

Sports Illustrated. A weekly American magazine largely concerned with American sports.

Sportswoman. A recently established monthly American non-specialist magazine covering most aspects of women's sports.

Swimming World. An American monthly covering all aspects of swimming including statistics.

Track and Field News. The principal American monthly on athletics. The December and January issues are comprehensive summaries, with a wealth of statistics, of the preceding year's women's and men's athletics respectively. The coverage is world wide although the depth and breadth of American coverage is greater.

Watman, M. *Encyclopaedia of Athletics.* 4th ed. London: Hale, 1976. An excellent book although it has a slight emphasis on British sport.

Willoughby, P. *The Super Athletes.* New York: Barnes, 1970. Included here because of its collection of unusual records, including many by women.

Womens Sports. Another non-specialist journal covering all aspects of women's sport. A similar earlier and now defunct journal was called *Womensport.*

2. GENERAL SPORT BOOKS, BIOGRAPHIES AND AUTOBIOGRAPHIES

Arlott, J. A., ed. *The Oxford Companion to Sports and Games.* Oxford: OUP, 1976. An encyclopaedic work on all sports and many of sports' major personalities.

Bannister, R. *First Four Minutes*. London: Putnam, 1955. The absorbing story of Bannister's sporting life and his attitudes to running.

Fixx, J. *The Complete Book of Running*. New York: Random House, 1977. A bestseller. A jogging enthusiast packs a lot of information and some advice in a very easy to read format.

Huey, L. *A Running Start: An Athlete a Woman*. New York: Quadrangle Books, 1976. An autobiography by an angry young woman of American sport.

Kelly, G. *Mr Controversial: The Story of Percy Wells Cerutty*. London: Stanley Paul, 1964.

Kostrubala, T. *The Joy of Running*. Philadelphia and New York: J. B. Lippincott, 1976. The benefits of running from the point of view of a psychiatrist.

Lydiard, A. and Gilmour, G. *Run to the Top*. London: Herbert Jenkins, 1962. The methods and philosophy of one of the world's most successful running coaches.

Michener, J. A. *On Sport*. London: Secker and Warburg, 1976. A comprehensive review of the state of American sport in the 1970s.

Peters, M. *Mary P: An Autobiography*. London: Stanley Paul, 1974. The disasters and triumphs and hard work of one ultimately successful woman athlete.

Quercitani, R. *A History of Track and Field Athletics*. Oxford: OUP, 1964. Although excellent and comprehensive in what it does cover, it does *not* cover women's athletics at all.

Stampfl, F. *Franz Stampfl on Running*. London: Herbert Jenkins, 1955. A valuable presentation of Stampfl's ideas on training and coaching.

Weiss, P. B. *Sport: A Philosophic Enquiry*. Carbondall: Southern Illinois University Press, 1969. A book which contains some useful insights but many unsubstantiated assumptions.

3. SEX, SEX DIFFERENCES AND WOMEN IN SPORT

de Beauvoir, S. *The Second Sex*. London: Jonathon Cape, 1953. One of the first and authoritative, if closely argued, books on women's socialization and social psychology.

Boslooper, T. D. and Hayes, M. *The Femininity Game*. New York: Stein and Day, 1973. A rather breathless review of women's behaviour and its implications for sport.

Gerber, E. W. *The American Woman in Sport*. Reading, Mass.: Addison-Wesley, 1974. An American college level book covering all aspects of women's sport: sociology, physiology and psychology.

Hoepner, B. J., ed. *Women's Athletics: Coping with Controversy*. Oakland, Calif.: DGWS Publications, 1974. Deals with the history and sociology of American women in sport.

Klafs, C. E. and Lyon, M. J. *The Female Athlete*. 2nd ed. St Louis: C. V. Mosby & Co., 1978. An enormous amount of sound information in this American college level text.

Lang, T. *The Difference Between a Man and a Woman*. London: Michael Joseph, 1971. Biological and social differences are explored in an entertaining manner.

Maccoby, E. E. *The Development of Sex Differences*. London: Tavistock Publications, 1967. Detailed, authoritative, university level review.

Maccoby, E. E. and Jacklin, C. N. *The Psychology of Sex Differences*. Stanford:

Stanford University Press, 1975. Detailed, authoritative, university level review.

Mandel, W. M. *Soviet Women.* New York: Anchor Books, 1975. A detailed survey.

Montagu, A. *The Natural Superiority of Women.* New York: Macmillan, 1968. A provocative but readable review of sex differences.

Nicholson, J. *A Question of Sex.* London: Fontana, 1979. A comprehensive summary of the differences between men and women written in an easily understood manner.

Oakley, A. *Sex, Gender and Society.* London: Temple Smith, 1972. A very readable synthesis of biological and social differences between men and women.

Oglesby, C. A. *Women and Sport: From Myth to Reality.* Philadelphia: Lea and Febiger, 1978. An up to date American college level review.

Pallett, G. *Women's Athletics.* London: Normal Press, 1955. Very valuable for its detailed early history of women's athletics.

Pozzoli, P. R. *Irish Women's Athletics.* London: Women's Track and Field World, 1977. An idiosyncratic but detailed review of one country's women's athletics.

Simri, U. *A historical analysis of the role of women in the modern Olympic Games.* Netanya: Wingate Institute for Physical Education and Sport, 1977. Covers some areas in detail but also omits some important aspects.

Ulyott, J. *Women's Running.* Mountain View, Calif.: World Publications, 1976. A readable polemic by a woman doctor and successful marathon runner.

Webster, F. A. M. *Athletics of Today for Women: History, Development and Training.* London: Warne, 1930. A comprehensive review of women's athletics as it was in 1930.

World Publications. *The Female Runner.* Mountain View, Calif.: World Publications, 1974. A collection of short, readable, non-specialist articles.

4. PHYSIOLOGY AND GENERAL BIOLOGY

Astrand, P. O. and Rodahl, K. *Textbook of Work Physiology.* 2nd ed. New York: McGraw Hill, 1978. One of the most detailed and authoritative advanced texts. It is not confined to sports physiology.

Cooper, K. H. *The New Aerobics.* New York: Bantam Books, 1970.

Cooper, K. H. & Cooper, M. *Aerobics for Women.* New York: Bantam Books, 1972. Two deservedly popular but authoritative books.

Frederick, E. C. *The Running Body.* Mountain View, Calif.: World Publications, 1973. A short accessible popularization.

de Garay, A. C., L. Levine & J. E. Lindsay Carter, *Genetic and Anthropological Studies of Olympic Athletes.* New York: Academic Press, 1974. A research monograph.

Klafs, C. E. and Arnheim, D. D. *Modern Principles of Athletic Training.* 4th ed. St Louis: C. V. Mosby, 1978. A sound text.

Knapp, B. *Skill in Sport.* London: Routledge and Kegan Paul, 1963. A full clear account, but now a little out of date.

Jokl, E. and Simon, E. *International Research in Sport and Physical Education.* Springfield, Ill.: C. C. Thomas, 1964.

Larson, L., ed. *Encyclopaedia of Sports Sciences and Medicine.* New York: Macmillan, 1971. Covers enormous areas in great detail.

Mathews, D. K. and Fox, E. L. *The Physiological Basis of Physical Education and Athletics.* 2nd ed. Philadelphia: W. B. Saunders, 1976. A clear and very comprehensive text. It contains an enormous amount of detail on most aspects of sport biology.

Pyke, F. and Watson, G. *Focus on Running.* Artarmon, NSW: Harper & Row, 1978. A mainly technical but very clear coverage of running.

Ryan, A. and Allman, F. *Sports Medicine.* An advanced level text.

Shephard, R. J. *The Fit Athlete.* Oxford: Oxford University Press, 1978. A useful popular work but a little uneven in its treatment of some aspects of sport.

Tanner, J. M. *The Physique of the Olympic Athlete.* London: George Allen and Unwin, 1964. A research monograph.

Thomas, V. *Exercise Physiology.* London: CLS, 1975. A college level review which gets away from text book style and would be very useful for athlete and coach.

5. PSYCHOLOGY AND SOCIOLOGY OF SPORT

Butt, D. S. *The Psychology of Sport.* New York: Van Nostrand Reinhold, 1976. A readable, almost racily written survey of the subject with some emphasis on women's sports psychology.

Bennett, B. L., *Comparative Physical Education and Sport.* Philadelphia: Lea and Febiger, 1975. An American college level text.

Carl Diem Institute. *The Olympic Idea.* Cologne: Carl Diem Institute, 1966. Baron Pierre de Coubertin's speeches and articles are translated into English.

Coakley, J. J. *Sport in Society: Issues and Controversies.* St Louis: C. V. Mosby, 1978. A comprehensive up to date college level treatment of the sociology of American sport.

Edwards, H. *Sociology of Sport.* Homewood, Ill.: Dorsey Press, 1973. A readable book by an angry young man of American sport.

Hart, M. M. *Sport in the Socio-Cultural Process.* Dubuque, Iowa: W. C. Brown, 1972. A review aimed at the American college student.

Jokl, E. and Jokl, P. *The Physiological Basis of Athletic Records.* Springfield, Ill.: C. C. Thomas, 1968. Despite its title this book sets sporting achievements very much into their social and cultural context.

Jokl, E. & Simon, E., eds. *International Research in Sport and Physical Education.* Springfield, Ill.: C. C. Thomas, 1964. A collection of useful papers.

Jokl, E. *Sport in the Cultural Pattern of the World.* Helsinki: Helsinki Institute of Occupational Health, 1956. A very detailed survey based largely on participation in the 1952 Olympics.

Loy, J. W. and Kenyon, G. S., eds. *Sport, Culture and Society.* New York: The Macmillan Co., 1969. A college level collection of articles.

McIntosh, P. *Sport in Society.* New York: IPS, 1963. A short readable history of sport from ancient times to the present.

Pearson, K. *Surfing Subcultures of Australia and New Zealand.* St Lucia, Qld.: University of Queensland Press, 1979. An authoritative and fascinating study of the history and sociology of surfing set in a context of sport in general.

Riordan, J. O. *Sport in Soviet Society.* Cambridge: Cambridge University Press, 1976. A very detailed history and survey of current Russian sport.

Riordan, J. O., ed. *Sport Under Communism.* London: C. Hurst & Co. 1978. A comparative survey of sport in Russia, East Germany, Czechoslovakia, China and Cuba.

Sage, G. H. *Sport and American Society*. Reading, Mass.: Addison Wesley, 1974. A readable American college level text.

Snyder, E. E. and Spreitzer, E. *Social Aspects of Sport*. Englewood Cliffs.: Prentice Hall, 1975. Another American college level text with its own particular viewpoint.

Talamini, J. T. and Page, C. H., eds. *Sport and Society*. Boston: Little Brown, 1973. A collection of articles dealing primarily with the USA.

APPENDIX A

American College of Sports Medicine Opinion Statement on *The Participation of the Female Athlete in Long-Distance Running*

A statement produced in 1979 which thoroughly and comprehensively documents their opinion that "there exists no conclusive scientific or medical evidence that long distance running is contra-indicated for the healthy trained female athlete".

It is partly the authority of this opinion which has persuaded the IAAF to recognize women's long distance track records and consider the inclusion of a women's marathon in World, European and Olympic Championships.

In the Olympic Games and other international contests, female athletes run distances ranging from 100 meters to 3,000 meters, whereas male athletes run distances ranging from 100 meters through 10,000 meters as well as the marathon (42.2 km). The limitations on distance for women's running events has been defended at times on the grounds that long-distance running may be harmful to the health of girls and women.

Opinion Statement

It is the opinion of the American College of Sports Medicine that females should not be denied the opportunity to compete in long-distance running. There exists no conclusive scientific or medical evidence that long-distance running is contraindicated for the healthy, trained female athlete. The American College of Sports Medicine recommends that females be allowed to compete at the national and international level in the same distances in which their male counterparts compete.

Supportive Information

Studies (10, 20, 32, 41, 54) have shown that females respond in much the same manner as males to systematic exercise training. Cardiorespiratory function is improved as indicated by significant increases in maximal oxygen uptake (4, 6, 13, 16, 30). At maximal exercise, stroke volume and cardiac output are increased after training (30). At standardized submaximal exercise intensities after training, cardiac output remains unchanged, heart rate decreases, and stroke volume increases (6, 30, 31). Also, resting heart rate decreases after training (30). As is the case for males, relative body fat content is reduced consequent to systematic endurance training (33, 35, 51).

Long-distance running imposes a significant thermal stress on the participant. Some differences do exist between males and females with regard to thermoregulation during prolonged exercise. However, the differences in thermal stress response are more quantitative than qualitative in nature (36, 38, 47). For example, women experience lower evaporative heat losses than do men exposed to the same thermal stress (29, 40, 53) and usually have higher skin temperatures and deep body temperatures upon onset of sweating

(3, 18, 45). This may actually be an advantage in reducing body water loss so long as thermal equilibrium can be maintained. In view of current findings (10, 11, 15, 40, 48, 49, 50), it appears that the earlier studies which indicated that women were less tolerant to exercise in the heat than men (36, 53) were misleading because they failed to consider the women's relatively low level of cardiorespiratory fitness and heat acclimatization. Apparently, cardiorespiratory fitness as measured by maximum oxygen uptake is a most important functional capacity as regards a person's ability to respond adequately to thermal stress (9, 11, 15, 47). In fact, there has been considerable interest in the seeming cross-adaptation of a life style characterized by physical activity involving regular and prolonged periods of exercise hyperthermia and response to high environmental temperatures (1, 37, 39). Women trained in long-distance running have been reported to be more tolerant of heat stress than non-athletic women matched for age and body surface area (15). Thus, it appears that trained female long-distance runners have the capacity to deal with the thermal stress of prolonged exercise as well as the moderate-to-high environmental temperatures and relative humidities that often accompany these events.

The participation of males and females in road races of various distances has increased tremendously during the last decade. This type of competition attracts the entire spectrum of runners with respect to ability — from the elite to the novice. A common feature of virtually all of these races is that a small number of participants develop medical problems (primarily heat injuries) which frequently require hospitalization. One of the first documentations of the medical problems associated with mass participation in this form of athletic competition was by Sutton and co-workers (46). Twenty-nine of 2,005 entrants in the 1971 Sydney City-to-Surf race collapsed; seven required hospitalization. All of the entrants who collapsed were males, although 4% of the race entrants were females. By 1978 the number of entrants increased approximately 10 fold with females accounting for approximately 30% of the entrants. In the 1978 race only nine entrants were treated for heat injury and again all were males (43). In a 1978 Canadian road race, in which 1,250 people participated, 15 entrants developed heat injuries — three females and 12 males, representing 1.3% and 1.2% of the total number of female and male entrants, respectively (27). Thus, females seem to tolerate the physiological stress of road race competition at least as well as males.

Because long-distance running competition sometimes occurs at moderate altitudes, the female's response to an environment where the partial pressure of oxygen is reduced (hypoxia) should be considered. Buskirk (5) noted that, although there is little information about the physiological responses of women to altitude, the proportional reduction in performances at Mexico City during the Pan American and Olympic Games was the same for males and females. Drinkwater et al. (13) found that women mountaineers exposed to hypoxia demonstrated a similar decrement in maximal oxygen uptake as that predicted for men. Hannon et al. (23, 24) have found that females tolerate the effects of altitude better than males because there appears to be both a lower frequency and shorter duration of mountain sickness in women. Furthermore, at altitude women experience less alteration in such variables as resting heart rate, body weight, blood volume, electrocardiograms, and blood chemistries than men (23, 24). Although one study has reported that women and men experience approximately the same respiratory changes with altitude exposure (44), another (22) reports that women hyperventilate more than men, thereby increasing the partial pressure of arterial oxygen and decreasing the partial pressure of arterial carbon dioxide. Thus, females tolerate the stress of altitude at least as well as men.

Long-distance running is occasionally associated with various overuse syndromes such as stress fracture, chondromalacia, shinsplints, and tendonitis. Pollock et al. (42) have shown that the incidence of these injuries for males engaged in a program of jogging was as high as 54% and was related to the frequency, duration, and intensity of the exercise training. Franklin et al. (19) recently reported the injury incidence of 42 sedentary females exposed to a 12-week jogging program. The injury rate for the females appeared to be comparable to that found for males in other studies although, as the investigators indicated, a decisive interpretation of presently available information may be premature because of the limited orthopedic injury data available for women. It has been suggested that the anatomical differences between men's and women's pelvic width and joint laxity may lead to a higher incidence of injuries for women who run (26). There are no data available, however, to support this suggestion. Whether or not the higher intensity training programs of competitive male and female long-distance runners result in a difference in injury rate between the sexes is not known at this time. It is believed, however, that the incidence of injury due to running is related more to distances run in training, the running surfaces encountered, biomechanics of the back, leg and foot, and to foot apparel (28).

Of particular concern to female competitors and to the American College of Sports Medicine is evidence which indicates that approximately one-third of the competitive female long-distance runners between the ages of 12 and 45 experience amenorrhea or oligomenorrhea for at least brief periods (7, 8). This phenomenon appears more frequently in those women with late onset of menarche, who have not experienced pregnancy, or who have taken contraceptive hormones. This same phenomenon also occurs in some competing gymnasts, swimmers, and professional ballerinas as well as sedentary individuals who have experienced some instances of undue stress or severe psychological trauma (25). Apparently, amenorrhea and oligomenorrhea may be caused by many factors characterized by loss of body weight (7, 21, 25). Running long distances may lead to decreased serum levels of pituitary gonadotrophic hormones in some women and may directly or indirectly lead to amenorrhea or oligomenorrhea. The role of running and the pathogenesis of these menstrual irregularities remains unknown (7, 8).

The long-term effects of these types of menstrual irregularities for young girls that have undergone strenuous exercise training are unknown at this time. Eriksson and co-workers (17) have reported, however, that a group of 28 young girl swimmers, who underwent strenuous swim training for 2.5 years, were normal in all respects (e.g., childbearing) 10 years after discontinuing training.

In summary, a review of the literature demonstrates that males and females adapt to exercise training in a similar manner. Female distance runners are characterized by having large maximal oxygen uptakes and low relative body fat content (52). The challenges of the heat stress of long-distance running or the lower partial pressure of oxygen at altitude seem to be well tolerated by females. The limited data available suggests that females, compared to males, have about the same incidence of orthopedic injuries consequent to endurance training. Disruption of the menstrual cycle is a common problem for female athletes. While it is important to recognize this problem and discover its etiology, no evidence exists to indicate that this is harmful to the female reproductive system.

References

1. Allan, J. R. The effects of physical training in a temperate and hot climate on the physiological response to heat stress. *Ergonomics* 8:445–453, 1965.
2. Astrand, P. O., L. Engstrom, B. Eriksson, P. Karlberg, I. Nylander, and C. Thoren. Girl swimmers. *Acta Paediat. Scand.* Suppl. 147, 1963.
3. Bittel, J. and R. Henane. Comparison of thermal exchanges in men and women under neutral and hot conditions. *J. Physiol. (Lond.)* 250:475–489, 1975.
4. Brown, C. H., J. R. Harrower, and M. F. Deeter. The effects of cross-country running on pre-adolescent girls. *Med. Sci. Sports* 4:1–5, 1972.
5. Buskirk, E. R. Work and fatigue in high altitude. In: *Physiology of work capacity and fatigue.* E. Simonson (Ed.), Springfield, Illinois: Charles C. Thomas, pp. 312–324, 1971.
6. Cunningham, D. A. and J. S. Hill. Effect of training on cardiovascular response to exercise in women. *J. Appl. Physiol.* 39:891–895, 1975.
7. Dale, E. D. H. Gerlach, D. E. Martin, and C. R. Alexander. Physical fitness profiles and reproductive physiology of the female distance runner. *Phy. and Sportsmed.* 7: 83–95, 1979 (Jan).
8. Dale, E., D. H. Gerlach, and A. L. Withite. Menstrual dysfunction in distance runners. *Obst. Gyne.* 54:47–53, 1979.
9. Dill, B. D., L. F. Soholt, D. C. McLean, T. F. Drost, Jr., and M. T. Loughran. Capacity of young males and females for running in desert heat. *Med. Sci. Sports* 9: 137–142, 1977.
10. Drinkwater, B. L. Physiological responses of women to exercise. In: *Exercise and sports sciences reviews.* J. H. Wilmore (Ed.), New York, NY: Academic Press, Vol. 1, pp. 125–153, 1973.
11. Drinkwater, B. L., J. E. Denton, I. C. Kupprat, T. S. Talag, and S. M. Horvath. Aerobic power as a factor in women's response to work in hot environments. *J. Appl. Physiol.* 41:815–821, 1976.
12. Drinkwater, B. L., J. E. Denton, P. B. Raven and S. M. Horvath. Thermoregulatory response of women to intermittent work in the heat. *J. Appl. Physiol.* 41:57–61, 1976.
13. Drinkwater, B. L., L. J. Folinsbee, J. F. Bedi, S. A. Plowman, A. B. Loucks, and S. M. Horvath. Response of women mountaineers to maximal exercise during hypoxia. *Avia. Space Environ. Med.* 50:657–662, 1979.
14. Drinkwater, B. L., I. C. Kupprat, J. E. Denton, J. L. Crist, and S. M. Horvath. Response of prepubertal girls and college women to work in the heat. *J. Appl. Physiol.: Respirat. Environ. Exercise Physiol.* 43:1046–1053, 1977.
15. Drinkwater, B. L., I. C. Kupprat, J. E. Denton, and S. M. Horvath. Heat tolerance of female distance runners. *Annals NY Acad. Sci.* 301:777–792, 1977.
16. Eddy, D. O., K. L. Sparks, and D. A. Adelizi. The effect of continuous interval training in women and men. *Europ. J. Appl. Physiol.* 37:83–92, 1977.
17. Eriksson, B. O., I. Engstrom, P. Karlberg, A. Lundin, B. Saltin, and C. Thoren. Long-term effect of previous swimtraining in girls. A 10-year follow-up on the "Girl Swimmers". *Acta Paediat. Scand.* 67:285–292, 1978.
18. Fox, R. H., B. E. Lofstedt, P. M. Woodward, E. Eriksson, and B. Werkstrom. Comparison of thermoregulatory function in men and women. *J. Appl. Physiol.* 26: 444–453, 1969.
19. Franklin, B. A., L. Lussier, and E. R. Buskirk. Injury rates in women joggers. *Phy. and Sportsmed.* 7:105–112, 1979 (Mar).
20. Fringer, M. N. and G. A. Stull. Changes in cardiorespiratory parameters during periods of training and detraining in young adult females. *Med. Sci. Sports* 6:20–25, 1974.
21. Frisch, R. E. Fatness and the onset and maintenance of menstrual cycles. *Res. In Reprod.* 6:1, 1977.
22. Hannon, J. P. Comparative altitude adaptability of young men and women. In: *Environmental stress: individual human adaptations.* L. J. Folinsbee et al. (Eds.), San Francisco: Academic Press, pp. 335–350, 1978.

23. Hannon, J. P., J. L. Shields, and C. W. Harris. A comparative review of certain responses of men and women to high altitude. In: *Proceedings symposia on arctic biology and medicine.* VI. *The physiology of work in cold and altitude.* C. Helfferich, (Ed.), Fort Wainwright, Alaska: Arctic Aeromedical Laboratory, pp. 113–245, 1966.

24. Hannon, J. P., J. L. Shields, and C. W. Harris. Effects of altitude acclimatization on blood composition of women. *J. Appl. Physiol.* 26:540–547, 1969.

25. Harris, D. V. (quoted in) Secondary amenorrhea linked to stress. *Phy. and Sportsmed.* 6:24, 1978 (Oct).

26. Haycock, C. E., and J. V. Gillette. Susceptibility of women athletes to injury: Myths vs. Reality. *JAMA* 236:163–165, 1976.

27. Hughson, R. L. and J. R. Sutton. Heat stroke in "run for fun". *Br. Med. J.* 2 (No. 6145): 1158, 1978 (Oct).

28. James, S. L., B. J. Bates, and L. R. Osternig. Injuries to runners. *Am. J. Sports Med.* 6:40–50, 1978 (Mar–Apr).

29. Kawahata, A. Sex differences in sweating. In: *Essential problems in climatic physiology.* M. Yoshimura, K. Ogata and S. Ito (Eds.), Kyoto: Nankodo, pp. 169–184, 1960.

30. Kilbom, A. Physical training in women. *Scand. J. Clin. Lab. Invest.* 28:1–34, Suppl. 119, 1971.

31. Kollis, J., H. L. Barlett, P. Oja, and C. L. Shearburn. Cardiac output of sedentary and physically conditioned women during submaximal exercise. *Aust. J. Sports Med.* 9:63–68, 1977.

32. Lamb, D. R. *Physiology of exercise: responses and adaptations.* New York: Macmillan Publishing Co., Inc., p. 252, 1978.

33. Mayhew, J. L. and P. M. Gross, Body composition changes in young women with high resistance weight training. *Res. Q. Am. Assoc. Health Phys. Ed.* 56:433–440, 1974.

34. Moody, D. L., J. Kollias, and E. R. Buskirk. The effect of a moderate exercise program on body weight and skinfold thickness in overweight college women. *Med. Sci. Sports* 1:75–80, 1969.

35. Moody, D. J., J. H. Wilmore, R. N. Girandola, and J. P. Royce. The effects of a jogging program on the body composition of normal and obese high school girls. *Med. Sci. Sports* 4:210–213, 1972.

36. Morimoto, T., Z. Slabochova, R. K. Naman, and F. Sargent, II. Sex differences in physiological reactions to thermal stress. *J. Appl. Physiol.* 22:526–532, 1967.

37. Nadel, E. R., K. B. Pandolf, M. F. Roberts, and J. A. J. Stolwijk. Mechanisms of thermal acclimation to exercise and heat. *J. Appl. Physiol.* 37:515–520, 1974.

38. Nunneley, S. A. Physiological responses of women to thermal stress: A review. *Med. Sci. Sports* 10:250–255, 1978.

39. Pandolf, K. B. Effects of physical training and cardiorespiratory physical fitness on exercise-heat tolerance: recent observations. *Med. Sci. Sports* 11:60–65, 1979.

40. Paolone, A. M., C. L. Wells, and G. T. Kelley. Sexual variations in thermoregulation during heat stress. *Aviat. Space Environ. Med.* 49:715–719, 1978.

41. Pollock, M. L. The quantification of endurance training programs. In: *Exercise and sports sciences reviews.* J. H. Wilmore (Ed.), New York, NY: Academic Press, Vol. 1, pp. 155–188, 1973.

42. Pollock, M. L., L. R. Gettman, C. A. Milesis, M. D. Bah, L. Durstine, and R. B. Johnson. Effects of frequency and duration of training on attrition and incidence of injury. *Med. Sci. Sports* 9:31–36, 1977.

43. Richards, R., D. Richards, P. Schofield, V. Ross, and J. Sutton. Reducing the hazards in Sydney's *The Sun* City-to-Surf Runs, 1971–1979, *Med. J. Aust.* 2:453–457, 1979.

44. Shields, J. L., J. P. Hannon, C. W. Harris and W. S. Platner. Effects of altitude acclimatization on pulmonary function in women. *J. Appl. Physiol.* 25:606–609, 1968.

45. Stolwijk, J. A. J., Responses to the thermal environment. *Red. Proc.* 36:1655–1658 1977.

46. Sutton, J., M. J. Coleman, A. P. Millar, L. Lararus, and P. Russo. The medical problems of mass participation in athletic competition. *Med. J. Aust.* 2:127- 133, 1972.
47. Wells, C. L. Responses of physically active and acclimatized men and women to work in a desert environment. *Med. Sci. Sports* (accepted for publication, 1980).
48. Wells, C. L. Sexual differences in heat stress response. *Phys. and Sportsmed.* 5: 79--90, 1977 (Sept).
49. Wells, C. L., and S. M. Horvath. Metabolic and thermoregulatory responses of women to exercise in two thermal environments. *Med. Sci. Sports* 6:8–13, 1974.
50. Wells, C. L., and A. M. Paolone. Metabolic responses to exercise in three thermal environments. *Aviat. Space Environ. Med.* 48:989–993, 1977.
51. Wilmore, J. H. Alterations in strength, body composition and anthropometric measurements consequent to a 10-week weight training program. *Med. Sci. Sports* 6:133–138, 1974.
52. Wilmore, J. H., and C. H. Brown. Physiological profiles of women distance runners. *Med. Sci. Sports* 6:178–181, 1974.
53. Wyndham, C. H., J. F. Morrison, and C. G. Williams. Heat reactions of male and female Caucasions. *J. Appl. Physiol.* 20:357–364, 1965.
54. Yaeger, S. A., and P. Brynteson. Effects of varying training periods on the development of cardiovascular efficiency of college women. *Res. Q. Am. Assoc. Health Phys. Educ.* 41:589–592, 1970.

APPENDIX B

Progressive List of World Records for Women's Track and Field Athletics

This appendix contains all the IAAF officially recognized world records for the standard events taken from their official lists. A number of earlier performances than these officially recognized records have been included in order to emphasize the standards reached during the 1920s and 1930s, which were the early days of women's international athletics, and the improvements which have occurred since then. These are taken from the *Women's Athletics Year-book*, edited by Peter Pozzoli. This book in fact records track and field performances as far back as 1895 for many events and is a mine of information for those who wish to pursue this topic further. Some additional records come from F. A. M. Webster's book *Athletics of Today for Women*, published in 1930. The records for the non-standard events 5000 and 10,000 metres are also given because of the potential importance of these events in the near future.

1.   100 METRES †

1921	M. Kiessling	Germany	12.8
1926	G. Wittman	Germany	12.6
1926	G. Wittman	Germany	12.4
1927	E. Edwards	GB	12.4
1927	E. Robinson	USA	12.2
1928	K. Hitomi	Japan	12.2
1928	E. Robinson	USA	12.2
1928	M. Cook	Canada	12.0
1930	T. Schuurman	Holland	12.0
1932	S. Walaciewicz	Poland	11.9
1933	S. Walaciewicz	Poland	11.8
1936	H. Stephens	USA	11.7
1936	H. Stephens	USA	11.5
1948	F. Blankers-Koen	Holland	11.5
1952	M. Jackson	Australia	11.5
1952	M. Jackson	Australia	11.4
1955	S. de la Hunty	Australia	11.3
1958	V. Krepkina	USSR	11.3
1960	W. Rudolph	USA	11.3
1961	W. Rudolph	USA	11.2
1964	W. Tyus	USA	11.2
1965	I. Kirszenstein	Poland	11.1
1965	W. Tyus	USA	11.1
1967	B. Ferrel	USA	11.1

† Official world record not recognized until 1934.

1968	L. Samotyosova	USSR	11.1
1968	I. Szewinska	Poland	11.1
1968	W. Tyus	USA	11.0
1970	Chi Cheng	Taiwan	11.0
1970	R. Meissner	GDR	11.0
1971	R. Stecher	GDR	11.0
1972	R. Stecher	GDR	11.0
1972	E. Strophahl	GDR	11.0
1973	R. Stecher	GDR	10.9
1973	R. Stecher	GDR	10.8
1977	M. Oelsner	GDR	10.88*

* Electronic timing

2. 200 METRES †

1920	M. Mejzlikova	Czechoslovakia	29.0
1922	M. Lines	GB	26.8☆
1924	E. Edwards	GB	26.2☆
1925	E. Edwards	GB	26.0
1926	E. Edwards	GB	25.8
1927	E. Edwards	GB	25.3
1929	K. Hitomi	Japan	24.7
1932	S. Walaciewicz	Poland	24.1
1934	S. Walaciewicz	Poland	23.8
1935	S. Walaciewicz	Poland	23.6
1952	M. Jackson	Australia	23.6
1952	M. Jackson	Australia	23.4
1956	B. Cuthbert	Australia	23.2
1960	B. Cuthbert	Australia	23.2
1960	W. Rudolph	USA	22.9
1964	M. Burvill	Australia	22.9
1965	I. Kirszenstein	Poland	22.7
1968	I. Szewinska	Poland	22.5
1970	Chi Cheng	Taiwan	22.4
1972	R. Stecher	GDR	22.4
1973	R. Stecher	GDR	22.1
1974	I. Szewinska	Poland	22.21*
1978	M. Koch	GDR	22.06*
1979	M. Koch	GDR	22.03*
1979	M. Koch	GDR	21.71*

* Electronic timing.
† Official world record not recognized until 1935
☆ 220 yards

3.   400 METRES [†]

1913	A. Miller	Canada	71.6 ☆
1917	A. Bierbrauer	Austria	70.0
1921	L. Charushnikova	USSR	65.0
1923	M. Lines	GB	62.4 ☆
1923	V. Palmer	GB	60.8 ☆
1924	E. Edwards	GB	60.8 ☆
1928	F. L. Haynes	GB	60.8 ☆
1929	M. E. King	GB	60.6 ☆
1929	M. E. King	GB	59.2 ☆
1930	N. Halstead	GB	58.8 ☆
1932	N. Halstead	GB	56.8 ☆
1950	Z. Petrova	USSR	56.7
1951	Z. Petrova	USSR	56.0
1951	V. Pomogayeva	USSR	56.0
1953	U. Donath	GDR	55.7
1954	N. Otolenko-Pletnyeva	USSR	55.5
1954	U. Donath	GDR	55.0
1955	Z. Safronova	USSR	54.8
1957	M. Itkina	USSR	54.0
1957	M. Itkina	USSR	53.6
1957	M. Itkina	USSR	53.4
1962	M. Itkina	USSR	53.4
1962	Sin Kim Dan	N. Korea	51.9
1969	N. Duclos	France	51.7
1969	C. Besson	France	51.7
1970	M. Neufville	Jamaica	51.0
1972	M. Zehrt	GDR	51.0
1974	I. Szewinska	Poland	49.9
1976	C. Brehmer	GDR	49.77*
1976	I. Szewinska	Poland	49.29*
1978	M. Koch	GDR	49.19*
1978	M. Koch	GDR	48.94*
1979	M. Koch	GDR	48.59*
1979	M. Koch	GDR	48.60*

[†] Official world record not recognized until 1957
☆   440 yards
*   Electronic timing

4.   800 METRES [†]

1914	B. Hjullhammer	Sweden	2:50.8
1921	L. Breard	France	2:30.2
1922	M. Lines	GB	2:26.6
1925	E. Trickey	GB	2:26.6
1925	E. Trickey	GB	2:24.0
1927	L. Batschauer	Germany	2:23.7

[†] Official world record not recognized until 1928

1928	L. Radke	Germany	2:16.8
1931	M. Dollinger	Germany	2:16.8
1944	A. Larsson	Sweden	2:15.9
1945	A. Larsson	Sweden	2:14.8
1945	A. Larsson	Sweden	2:13.8
1950	Y. Vasiljeva	USSR	2:13.0
1951	V. Pomogayeva	USSR	2:12.2
1951	N. G. Pletnyeva	USSR	2:12.0
1952	P. Sopolova	USSR	2:11.7
1952	N. G. Pletnyeva	USSR	2:08.5
1952	N. G. Pletnyeva	USSR	2:08.2
1953	N. Otkolenko-Pletnyeva	USSR	2:07.3
1953	N. Otkolenko-Pletnyeva	USSR	2:06.6
1953	N. Otkolenko-Pletnyeva	USSR	2:05.0
1960	L. Shevstova	USSR	2:04.3
1960	L. Shevstova	USSR	2:04.3
1962	D. Willis	Australia	2:01.2
1964	A. Packer	GB	2:01.1
1967	J. Pollock	Australia	2:01.0
1968	V. Nikolic	Yugoslavia	2.00.5
1971	H. Falck	FDR	1:58.5
1973	S. Zlateva	Bulgaria	1:57.5
1976	T. Kazankina	USSR	1:54.9
1980	N. Olizarenko	USSR	1:54.9
1980	N. Olizarenko	USSR	1:53.5

5. 1000 METRES [†]

1918	M. Cadies	France	3:30.6
1921	L. Breard	France	3:27.8
1922	L. Breard	France	3:12.0
1924	E. Trickey	GB	3:08.2
1931	G. Lunn	GB	3:04.2
1934	G. Lunn	GB	3:00.6
1954	Y. Vasiljeva	USSR	2:52.6
1969	W. Pohland	GDR	2:42.1
1971	G. Hoffmeister	GDR	2:41.2
1972	M. Politz	GDR	2:39.1
1972	G. Hoffmeister	GDR	2:35.9
1978	U. Bruns	GDR	2:32.0
1978	T. Providokhina	USSR	2:30.6

[†] There is no official world record for this event for women but it was run very frequently in the 1920s.

6. 1500 METRES †

1913	L. Aaltonen	Finland	5:44.0
1927	A. Mushkina	USSR	5:18.2
1934	A. Mushkina	USSR	5:07.0
1936	Y. Vasilieva	USSR	4:47.2
1937	Y. Vasieleva	USSR	4:45.2
1940	A. Zaitseva	USSR	4:41.8
1944	Y. Vasilieva	USSR	4:38.0
1946	O. Ovsiannikova	USSR	4:37.8
1952	N. Pletnyeva	USSR	4:37.0
1956	P. Perkins	GB	4:35.4
1956	D. Leather	GB	4:30.0
1957	D. Leather	GB	4:29.7
1958	D. Leather	GB	4:22.2
1962	M. Chamberlain	NZ	4:19.0
1967	A. Smith	GB	4:17.3
1967	M. Gommers	Netherlands	4:15.6
1969	P. Pigni	Italy	4:12.4
1969	J. Jehlickova	Czechoslovakia	4:10.7
1971	K. Burneleit	GDR	4:09.6
1972	L. Bragina	USSR	4:06.9
1972	L. Bragina	USSR	4:06.5
1972	L. Bragina	USSR	4:05.1
1972	L. Bragina	USSR	4:01.4
1976	T. Kazankina	USSR	3:56.0
1980	T. Kazankina	USSR	3:55.0
1980	T. Kazankina	USSR	3:52.47

7. MILE

1936	G. A. Lunn	GB	5:23.0
1937	G. A. Lunn	GB	5:17.0
1939	E. Forster	GB	5:15.3
1952	I. E. A. Oliver	GB	5:11.0
1953	A. Harding	GB	5:09.6
1953	A. Oliver	GB	5:08.0
1953	D. Leather	GB	5:02.6
1953	E. Treybal	Romania	5:00.3
1954	D. Leather	GB	5:00.2
1954	D. Leather	GB	4:59.6
1955	D. Leather	GB	4:50.8
1962	M. Chamberlain	NZ	4:41.4
1967	A. Smith	GB	4:37.0
1969	M. Gommers	Netherlands	4:36.8
1971	E. Tittel	FDR	4:35.3
1973	P. Pigni	Italy	4:29.5

†   Official world record not recognized until 1967

1977	N. Maracescu	Romania	4:23.8
1979	N. Maracescu	Romania	4:22.1
1980	M. Decker	USA	4:21.7

8. 3000 METRES †

1966	R. Picco-Angeloni	Canada	9:44.0
1969	P. Pigni	Italy	9:22.0
1971	A. Smith	GB	9:13.4
1972	L. Bragina	USSR	8:53.0
1974	L. Bragina	USSR	8:52.8
1975	I. Knutsson	Sweden	8:51.0
1976	S. Ulmasova	USSR	8:48.4
1976	L. Bragina	USSR	8:27.1

† Official world record not recognized until 1971

9. 5000 METRES †

1966	E. Pasquali	Italy	16:45.0
1969	P. Pigni	Italy	15:53.6
1972	A. Beames	Australia	15:48.6
1977	N. Maracescu	Romania	15:41.5
1977	J. Merril	USA	15:37.0
1978	K. Mills	USA	15:35.5
1978	L. Olaffson	Denmark	15:08.8

† Official world record not recognized until 1980

10. 10000 METRES †

1967	A. O'Brien	Ireland	38:06.4
1969	C. Cook	USA	34:49.0
1972	A. Beames	Australia	34:08.0
1975	C. Vahlensieck	FDR	34:01.4
1977	L. Olaffson	Denmark	33:34.2
1977	P. Neppel	USA	33:15.1
1978	G. Waitz	Norway	32:43.2
1978	L. Olaffson	Denmark	31:45.4

† Official world record not recognized until 1980

11.   4 x 100 METRES RELAY †

1921	Turn-und Sportverein Munich	52.1
1926	England	49.8
1928	Canada	49.4
1928	Canada	48.4
1932	USA	47.0
1936	Germany	46.4
1952	Australia	46.1
1952	USA	45.9
1952	Germany	45.9
1953	USSR	45.6
1955	USSR	45.6
1956	USSR	45.2
1956	Germany	45.1
1956	Australia	44.9
1956	Germany	44.9
1956	Australia	44.5
1960	USA	44.4
1961	USA	44.3
1964	USA	43.9
1968	USSR	43.9
1968	USSR	43.9
1968	USSR	43.9
1968	USA	43.4
1968	Netherlands	43.4
1968	USA	42.8
1972	FDR	42.8
1973	GDR	42.6
1974	GDR	42.6
1974	GDR	42.50*
1978	GDR	42.27*
1979	GDR	42.09*
1980	GDR	41.85*
1980	GDR	41.60*

† Official world record not recognized until 1936
* Electronic timing

12.   4 x 200 METRES RELAY †

1921	En Avant, France	2:00.8
1923	England	1:52.6
1928	GB	1:51.6
1928	Linnets, France	1:50.4
1929	Linnets, France	1:47.6
1929	France	1:47.6
1932	Germany	1:45.8
1938	Germany	1:45.3

† Official world record not recognized until 1932

1944	Netherlands	1:41.0
1950	Dynamo, USSR	1:40.6
1951	USSR	1:39.7
1952	Southern Counties, GB	1:39.7
1953	GDR	1:39.5
1953	USSR	1:39.0
1953	USSR	1:36.4
1956	GDR	1:36.4
1956	Australia	1:36.3
1958	GDR	1:36.0
1963	USSR	1:35.1
1967	USSR	1:34.4
1968	UK	1:33.8
1977	UK	1:31.6
1979	USSR	1:30.8
1980	GDR	1:28.2

13.   4 x 400 METRES RELAY [†]

1954	Spartan Ladies, GB	4:09.6
1958	GB	3:49.9+
1967	Goteborgs KIK, Sweden	3:49.4
1969	Moscow	3:47.4
1969	Latvia	3:43.2
1969	GB	3:37.6
1969	France	3:34.2
1969	FDR	3:33.9
1969	GB	3:30.8
1969	France	3:30.8
1971	GDR	3:29.3
1972	GDR	3:28.8
1972	GDR	3:28.5
1972	GDR	3:23.0
1976	GDR	3:19.2

[†]   Official world record not recognized until 1969
+   yards

14.   3 x 800 METRES RELAY[†] and 4 x 800 METRES RELAY

1928	S.C. Charlottenburg, Germany	8:04.0
1933	fB Breslaw, Germany	7:37.4
1937	G.S. Veni-Unica, Italy	7:32.0
1943	France	7:15.8
1949	Southern Counties, GB	7:07.8
1950	USSR	6:49.6
1951	USSR	6:44.8
1952	USSR	6:38.4

[†]   Official world record not recognized until 1933
Changed to 4 x 800 in 1969

1953	USSR	6:35.6
1953	USSR	6:33.2
1955	USSR	6:27.6
1958	Ukraine	6:27.4
1966	USSR	6:21.2
1967	Germany	6:21.0
1967	GB	6:20.0
1968	Netherlands	6:15.5
1969	GDR	8:33.0
1970	GB	8:27.0
1971	FDR	8:16.8
1973	Bulgaria	8:08.6
1975	USSR	8:05.2
1976	USSR	7:52.3

15. 100 METRES HURDLES [†]

1921	M. Rilhac	France	15.6
1961	P. Ryan	Australia	13.4
1964	P. Nutting-Price	GB	13.4
1965	G. Kuznetsova	USSR	13.2
1966	V. Bolshova	USSR	13.0
1967	G. Kuznetsova	USSR	13.0
1969	P. Ryan	Australia	12.8
1971	K. Balzer	GDR	12.6
1972	A. Ehrhardt	GDR	12.59*
1978	G. Rabsztyn	Poland	12.48*
1980	G. Rabsztyn	Poland	12.36*

† Official world record not recognized until 1969
* Electronic timing

16. 400 METRES HURDLES [†]

1971	L. Macounova	Czechoslovakia	60.7
1972	L. Macounova	Czechoslovakia	60.7
1973	D. Piecyk	Poland	56.7
1977	T. Storoshova	USSR	55.74*
1977	K. Rossley	GDR	55.63*
1978	K. Kacperczyk	Poland	55.44*
1978	T. Zelensova	USSR	54.89*
1979	M. Makeeva	USSR	54.78*
1980	K. Rossley	GDR	54.28*

† Official world record not recognized until 1973
* Electronic timing

17.   LONG JUMP†

1921	M. Kiessling	Germany	5.54
1927	M. A. Gunn	GB	5.57
1928	M. A. Gunn	GB	5.67
1928	K. Hitomi	Japan	5.98
1939	C. Schulz	Germany	6.12
1943	F. Blankers-Koen	Netherlands	6.25
1954	Y. Williams	NZ	6.28
1955	G. Vinogradova	USSR	6.28
1955	G. Vinogradova	USSR	6.31
1956	E. Krzesinska	Poland	6.35
1956	E. Krzesinska	Poland	6.35
1960	H. Claus	FDR	6.40
1961	H. Claus	FDR	6.42
1961	T. Schelkanova	USSR	6.48
1962	T. Schelkanova	USSR	6.53
1964	T. Schelkanova	USSR	6.70
1964	M. Rand	GB	6.76
1968	V. Viscopoleanu	Romania	6.82
1970	H. Rosendahl	FDR	6.84
1976	A. Voigt	GDR	6.92
1976	S. Siegl	GDR	6.99
1978	V. Bardauskiene	USSR	7.07
1978	V. Bardauskiene	USSR	7.09

† Official world record not recognized until 1928

18.   HIGH JUMP †

1921	A. Finn	Germany	1.45
1922	S. Holt	GB	1.45
1922	M. Voorhees	USA	1.45
1923	E. Seine	USA	1.48
1924	S. C. Eliott-Lynn	GB	1.49
1924	U. Troyen	Belgium	1.50
1925	P. Green	GB	1.52
1926	P. Green	GB	1.57
1927	P. Green	GB	1.59
1928	E. Catherwood	Canada	1.60
1928	C. Gisolf	Netherlands	1.61
1932	J. Shirley	USA	1.65
1939	P. Odum	GB	1.66
1941	I. Pfenning-Fisher	Switz.	1.66
1943	F. Blankers-Koen	Netherlands	1.71
1951	S. Lerwill	GB	1.72
1954	A. Chudina	USSR	1.73
1956	T. Hopkins	GB	1.74
1956	I. Balas	Romania	1.75
1956	M. McDaniel	USA	1.76

† Official world record not recognized until 1932

1957	I. Balas	Romania	1.77
1957	Cheng Feng-jung	China	1.77
1958	I. Balas	Romania	1.78
1958	I. Balas	Romania	1.80
1958	I. Balas	Romania	1.81
1958	I. Balas	Romania	1.82
1958	I. Balas	Romania	1.83
1959	I. Balas	Romania	1.84
1960	I. Balas	Romania	1.85
1960	I. Balas	Romania	1.86
1961	I. Balas	Romania	1.87
1961	I. Balas	Romania	1.88
1961	I. Balas	Romania	1.90
1961	I. Balas	Romania	1.91
1971	I. Gusenbauer	Austria	1.92
1972	U. Meyfarth	FDR	1.92
1972	J. Blagoyeva	Bulgaria	1.94
1974	R. Witschas	GDR	1.94
1974	R. Witschas	GDR	1.95
1977	R. Ackerman	GDR	1.96
1977	R. Ackerman	GDR	1.97
1977	R. Ackerman	GDR	2.00
1978	S. Simeoni	Italy	2.01

19. PUTTING THE SHOT [†]

1923	V. Morris	France	9.41
1927	L. Lange	Germany	11.32
1927	G. Heublin	Germany	11.86
1928	G. Heublin	Germany	11.96
1929	G. Heublin	Germany	12.85
1931	G. Heublin	Germany	13.70
1932	G. Mauermayer	Germany	14.33
1934	G. Mauermayer	Germany	14.38
1945	A. Andreyeva	USSR	14.39
1948	T. N. Sevrukova	USSR	14.59
1949	K. A. Tochenova	USSR	14.86
1950	A. Andreyeva	USSR	15.02
1952	G. Zybina	USSR	15.28
1952	G. Zybina	USSR	15.37
1952	G. Zybina	USSR	15.42
1953	G. Zybina	USSR	16.18
1953	G. Zybina	USSR	16.20
1954	G. Zybina	USSR	16.28
1955	G. Zybina	USSR	16.29
1955	G. Zybina	USSR	16.67
1956	G. Zybina	USSR	16.76
1959	T. Press	USSR	17.25
1960	T. Press	USSR	17.42

[†] Official world record not recognized until 1926

1960	T. Press	USSR	17.78
1962	T. Press	USSR	18.55
1965	T. Press	USSR	18.59
1968	N. Chizhova	USSR	18.67
1968	M. Gummel	GDR	18.87
1968	M. Gummel	GDR	19.07
1968	M. Gummel	GDR	19.61
1969	N. Chizhova	USSR	19.72
1969	N. Chizhova	USSR	20.09
1969	M. Gummel	GDR	20.10
1969	N. Chizhova	USSR	20.10
1969	N. Chizhova	USSR	20.43
1971	N. Chizhova	USSR	20.43
1972	N. Chizhova	USSR	20.63
1972	N. Chizhova	USSR	21.03
1973	N. Chizhova	USSR	21.20
1973	N. Chizhova	USSR	21.45
1976	M. Adam	GDR	21.67
1976	I. Khristova	Bulgaria	21.89
1977	H. Fibingerova	Czechoslovakia	22.32
1980	L. Slupianek	GDR	22.36
1980	L. Slupianek	GDR	22.45

20. THROWING THE DISCUS [†]

1923	Y. Tembouret	Belgium	27.39
1924	V. Morris	France	30.10
1926	F. Birchenough	GB	31.49
1926	H. Konopacka	Poland	37.69
1928	H. Konopacka	Poland	39.62
1932	R. Osburn	USA	40.13
1932	L. Copeland	USA	40.61
1932	M. Didrikson	USA	40.81
1932	J. Wajsowna	Poland	42.43
1933	J. Wajsowna	Poland	43.08
1934	J. Wajsowna	Poland	44.20
1936	G. Mauermeyer	Germany	48.31
1947	N. Dumbadze	USSR	52.83
1948	N. Dumbadze	USSR	53.25
1951	N. Dumbadze	USSR	53.37
1952	N. Romashkova	USSR	53.61
1952	N. Dumbadze	USSR	57.04
1960	T. Press	USSR	57.15
1961	T. Press	USSR	57.43
1961	T. Press	USSR	58.06
1961	T. Press	USSR	58.98
1963	T. Press	USSR	59.29
1965	T. Press	USSR	59.70
1967	L. Westermann	FDR	61.26

[†] Official world record not recognized until 1936

1968	C. Spielberg	GDR	61.64
1968	L. Westermann	FDR	62.54
1969	L. Westermann	FDR	62.70
1969	F. Melnik	USSR	63.96
1971	F. Melnik	USSR	64.22
1971	F. Melnik	USSR	64.88
1972	F. Melnik	USSR	65.42
1972	F. Melnik	USSR	65.48
1972	F. Melnik	USSR	66.76
1972	A. Menis	Romania	67.32
1973	A. Menis	Romania	67.44
1973	A. Menis	Romania	67.58
1973	A. Menis	Romania	69.48
1974	A. Menis	Romania	69.90
1975	A. Menis	Romania	70.20
1976	A. Menis	Romania	70.50
1978	E. Jahl	GDR	70.72
1980	E. Jahl	GDR	71.50
1980	M. Vegova-Petkova	Bulgaria	71.80

21. THROWING THE JAVELIN [†]

1916	M. Votila	Finland	30.45
1928	H. Hargus	Germany	38.39
1929	E. Braumuller	Germany	40.27
1930	E. Braumuller	Germany	42.28
1932	N. Gindele	USA	46.74
1942	A. Steineuer	Germany	47.24
1947	H. Bauma	Austria	48.21
1948	H. Bauma	Austria	48.63
1949	N. Smirnitskaya	USSR	49.59
1949	N. Smirnitskaya	USSR	53.41
1954	N. Konayeva	USSR	53.56
1954	N. Konayeva	USSR	55.11
1954	N. Konayeva	USSR	55.48
1958	D. Zatopkova	Czechoslovakia	55.73
1958	A. Pazera	Australia	57.40
1958	B. Zalogaitite	USSR	57.49
1960	E. Ozolina	USSR	57.92
1960	E. Ozolina	USSR	59.55
1963	E. Ozolina	USSR	59.78
1964	Y. Gorchakova	USSR	62.40
1972	E. Gryzieckava	Poland	62.70
1972	R. Fuchs	GDR	65.06
1973	R. Fuchs	GDR	66.10
1974	R. Fuchs	GDR	67.22
1976	R. Fuchs	GDR	69.12
1977	K. Schmidt	USA	69.32
1979	R. Fuchs	GDR	69.52
1980	R. Fuchs	GDR	69.96
1980	T. Biryulina	USSR	70.08

† Official world record not recognized until 1932

APPENDIX C

Progressive List of World Records for Women's Track and Field Athletics since 1972

World swimming records have been broken much more frequently than track and field records, so it is impracticable to include them all. Furthermore the events and the conditions under which they are held have changed a good deal over the years. In the first fifty years of FINA there were 1,059 world records approved — 581 for men and 478 for women. Since 1958 the frequency of record breaking has become, if anything, even greater. 1972 has been chosen since this is when timing to 1/100th of a second became mandatory. A comprehensive list of all earlier records can be found in Pat Besford's *Encyclopaedia of Swimming*.

1. 100 METRES

January 1972	S. Gould	Australia	58.5
July 1973	K. Ender	GDR	58.25
August 1973	K. Ender	GDR	58.12
September 1973	K. Ender	GDR	57.61
September 1973	K. Ender	GDR	57.54
July 1974	K. Ender	GDR	57.51
August 1974	K. Ender	GDR	56.96
March 1975	K. Ender	GDR	56.38
July 1975	K. Ender	GDR	56.22
1976	K. Ender	GDR	55.73
July 1976	K. Ender	GDR	55.65
1978	B. Krause	GDR	55.41
July 1980	B. Krause	GDR	54.98
July 1980	B. Krause	GDR	54.79

2. 200 METRES

August 1972	S. Babashoff	USA	2:05.21
September 1972	S. Gould	Australia	2:03.56
August 1974	K. Ender	GDR	2:03.22
August 1974	S. Babashoff	USA	2:02.94
March 1975	K. Ender	GDR	2:02.27
	B. Krause	GDR	2:00.25
July 1976	K. Ender	GDR	1:59.20
August 1978	C. Woodhead	USA	1:58.53
July 1979	C. Woodhead	USA	1:58.43
August 1979	C. Woodhead	USA	1:58.23

3.   400 METRES

August 1972	S. Gould	Australia	4:19.04
August 1973	K. Rothhammer	USA	4:18.07
June 1974	H. Greenwood	USA	4:17.33
August 1974	S. Babashoff	USA	4:15.77
June 1975	S. Babashoff	USA	4:14.76
July 1976	P. Thumer	GDR	4:09.89
January 1978	T. Wickham	Australia	4:08.45
August 1978	K. Lineham	USA	4:07.66
August 1978	T. Wickham	Australia	4:06.28

4.   800 METRES

August 1972	J. Harshbarger	USA	8:53.83
September 1972	K. Rothhammer	USA	8:53.68
September 1973	N. Calligaris	Italy	8:52.97
January 1974	J. Turral	Australia	8:50.1
August 1974	J. Harshbarger	USA	8:47.66
August 1974	J. Harshbarger	USA	8:47.59
March 1974	J. Turral	Australia	8:43.48
July 1976	P. Thumer	GDR	8:37.14
January 1978	M. Ford	Australia	8:34.86
February 1978	M. Ford	Australia	8:31.30
March 1978	T. Wickham	Australia	8:30.53
August 1978	T. Wickham	Australia	8:24.62
February 1980	C. Woodhead	USA	8:18.77

5.   1500 METRES

February 1973	S. Gould	Australia	16:56.9
August 1973	J. Harshbarger	USA	16:54.14
December 1973	J. Turral	Australia	16:49.9
January 1974	J. Turral	Australia	16:48.2
July 1974	J. Turral	Australia	16:43.4
August 1974	J. Turral	Australia	16:39.28
August 1974	J. Turral	Australia	16:33.94
August 1977	A. Brown	USA	16:24.60
January 1978	T. Wickham	Australia	16:14.93
February 1979	T. Wickham	Australia	16:06.63
August 1979	K. Lineham	USA	16:04.49

APPENDIX D

Female Olympic Medal Winners by Nation

Table 44. Female Olympic medal winners by nation in Summer Games up to and including 1976.

		Gold	Silver	Bronze	Total
1	USA	91	63	56	210
2	USSR	68	52	60	180
3	GDR	34	31	18	83
4	Germany	22	31	28	81
5	Great Britain	17	35	25	77
6	Australia	21	22	23	66
7	Hungary	17	16	22	55
8	Holland	12	15	8	35
9	Romania	8	8	14	30
10	Czechoslovakia	13	8	5	26
11	Poland	6	8	9	23
12	Canada	2	7	14	23
13	France	6	7	5	18
14	Denmark	5	5	8	18
15	Sweden	2	5	11	18
16	Italy	3	5	6	14
17	Bulgaria	3	4	5	12
18	Austria	2	2	7	11
19	Japan	4	4	2	10
20	South Africa	2	1	4	7
21	New Zealand	1	0	2	3
22	Cuba	0	1	2	3
23 =	Finland	1	1	0	2
23 =	Yugoslavia	1	1	0	2
25	Argentine	0	2	0	2
26	Mexico	0	1	1	2
27 =	Chile	0	1	0	1
27 =	Switzerland	0	1	0	1
29	Norway	0	0	1	1
	P.R. Korea	0	0	1	1
	South Korea	0	0	1	1
	Taiwan	0	0	1	1

Notes:

a. The table includes: discontinued Olympic events; mixed doubles, archery competitions of 1904, 1908 and 1920.

b. The table does not include: open Olympic events; arts competitions; the 1906 interim Games.

c. Medals gained by East Germans up to 1968 are listed under "Germany".

d. Czechoslovakian listing includes pre-World War I Bohemia.

Table 45. Female Olympic medal winners by nation in Winter Games up to and including 1980.

		Gold	Silver	Bronze	Total
1	USSR	29	14	17	60
2	USA	11	18	15	44
3	Austria	8	14	10	32
4	Germany	10	11	7	28
5	Finland	5	11	7	23
6	GDR	6	7	7	20
7 =	France	5	5	5	15
7 =	Holland	5	6	4	15
9	Canada	5	4	4	13
10	Norway	5	2	4	11
11 =	Switzerland	6	2	2	10
11 =	Sweden	4	3	3	10
13	Great Britain	2	2	5	9
14	Hungary	0	1	4	5
15 =	Lichtenstein	2	1	1	4
15 =	Italy	1	1	2	4
17 =	Czechoslovakia	0	0	3	3
18	Poland	0	1	1	2
19	Belgium	1	0	0	1
20	P.R. Korea	0	1	0	1

Index

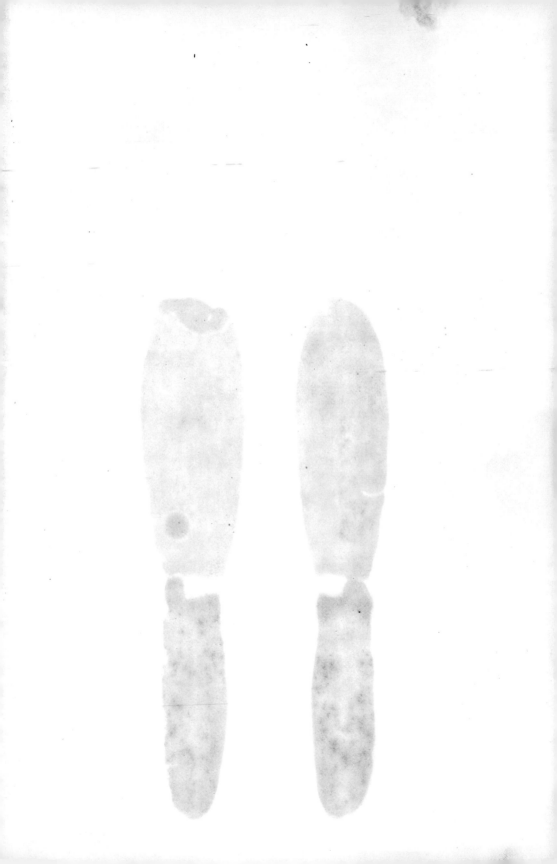

DATE DUE

FEB 26 1994	
MAY 03 1994	
APR 18 1995	
NOV 18 1995	
DEC 19 1996	
MAY 09 1997	
APR 22 2001	
DEC 06 2004	
NOV 28 2005	
APR 26 2007	

GAYLORD   PRINTED IN U.S.A.